INSTANTLY
Mediterranean

INSTANTLY
Mediterranean

Vibrant, Satisfying Recipes *for Your*
Instant Pot®, Electric Pressure Cooker & Air Fryer

EMILY PASTER
PHOTOGRAPHY BY LEIGH OLSON

TILLER PRESS

New York   London   Toronto   Sydney   New Delhi

TILLER PRESS

An Imprint of Simon & Schuster, Inc.
1230 Avenue of the Americas
New York, NY 10020

First Tiller Press trade paperback edition September 2021

TILLER PRESS and colophon are registered trademarks of Simon & Schuster, Inc.

For information about special discounts for bulk purchases, please contact Simon & Schuster Special Sales at 1-866-506-1949 or business@simonandschuster.com.

The Simon & Schuster Speakers Bureau can bring authors to your live event. For more information or to book an event, contact the Simon & Schuster Speakers Bureau at 1-866-248-3049 or visit our website at www.simonspeakers.com.

Cover and interior design by Matt Ryan
Photography by Leigh Olson
Author photo on page 224 by Doug McGoldrick

Manufactured in China

10 9 8 7 6 5 4 3 2 1

Library of Congress Cataloging-in-Publication Data
Names: Paster, Emily, author. | Olson, Leigh, photographer.
Title: Instantly Mediterranean : vibrant, satisfying recipes for your Instant Pot, electric pressure cooker, and air fryer / by Emily Paster ; photography by Leigh Olson.
Description: New York : Tiller Press, [2021] | Includes index. | Summary: "Discover how to make delicious, mouthwatering Mediterranean recipes right in your electric pressure cooker and air fryer"— Provided by publisher.
Identifiers: LCCN 2021005810 (print) | LCCN 2021005811 (ebook) | ISBN 9781982173074 (paperback) | ISBN 9781982173081 (ebook)
Subjects: LCSH: Cooking, Mediterranean. | Smart cookers. | Hot air frying. | LCGFT: Cookbooks.
Classification: LCC TX725.M35 P37 2021 (print) | LCC TX725.M35 (ebook) | DDC 641.59/1822--dc23
LC record available at https://lccn.loc.gov/2021005810
LC ebook record available at https://lccn.loc.gov/2021005811

ISBN 978-1-9821-7307-4
ISBN 978-1-9821-7308-1 (ebook)

To my daughter, Zoë Regenstein,
a Jewish girl with a Greek name.
You first saw the Mediterranean only a few
months before I started writing this book,
but you have always understood the
importance of a coastline, sparkling water,
and, above all, good food.

CONTENTS

Introduction

Like many of you, I love my Instant Pot®.

For the past several years, I have used it nearly every day, whether I am steaming a dozen hard-boiled eggs to satisfy a ravenous teenage boy; turning chicken bones into rich, golden stock; or making a one-pot dinner for my family. I have been amazed by all the different ways the Instant Pot makes my life easier. Not only does it allow me to cook certain dishes—and foods—that previously seemed too time-consuming, but the hands-off nature of today's electric pressure cookers also makes it easy to prepare meals in advance to accommodate my kids' crazy schedules. In short, these appliances are a godsend for a busy working parent like me.

More recently, another appliance has come into my life: the air fryer. Like many people, at first I thought the air fryer was a one-trick pony, designed to make fried foods without all the fat of deep-frying. I quickly learned that air fryers can do so much more. They deliver crispy chicken, caramelized vegetables, and seared-on-the-outside, tender-on-the-inside meat and fish—all in a fraction of the time it would take in the oven. The air fryer has quickly become my family's go-to appliance for reheating leftovers, roasting vegetables, and, of course, creating healthier versions of deep-fried favorites. In short, my electric pressure cooker and my air fryer have become important allies in the ongoing fight to make mealtime easier, more convenient, and less stressful.

One of the main reasons I have embraced the electric pressure cooker and the air fryer so enthusiastically in both my personal and professional lives is that these appliances not only make it easier to cook in general, but have made it easier for me to cook my very favorite types of food. Pressure cooking, in particular, allows me, in my everyday working-mom life, to cook the kinds of foods I used to cook before I had children and the kinds of dishes I make when I am developing recipes for work—healthy foods like beans, legumes, and whole grains; elegant soups and hearty stews; and succulent braised meats.

I began to realize that by using these beloved kitchen appliances, it was easier than ever for me to cook the Mediterranean, Middle Eastern, and North African foods that are my passion. It also occurred to me that many home cooks are likewise drawn to Mediterranean cuisine, with its reputation for rich flavors and healthfulness, and that these appliances could make it more accessible and realistic for them as well. It was then that the idea for this book was born.

TASTING MEDITERRANEAN

I first dipped my toes in the azure waters of the Mediterranean Sea on a family trip to Provence and the South of France when I was fourteen years old. My most recent visit to the Mediterranean was in late 2019, when my husband and I took our teenage children to Israel and Jordan. Between 1988 and 2019, I was lucky enough to travel to many parts of Spain and Italy, as well as return to France many times. In college—where I majored in French—I spent a year living in Paris with the Zémors, a Sephardic Jewish family who hailed from Algeria but had moved to France when Algeria gained its independence in the 1950s. During that year with my generous and warm hosts, I ate extraordinary French and North African food and celebrated a year's worth of Jewish holidays in the Sephardic tradition—experiences that altered me forever.

My travels around the Mediterranean, my formative experience living with a North African Jewish family in France, and my own Jewish identity have all contributed to my abiding passion for and interest in the food of the Mediterranean. As a food writer and recipe developer, I have spent years learning about and cooking the food of this region—with a focus on the cuisines of the Sephardic Jews and Israel in particular. I have come to the conclusion that Mediterranean food (about which I will say much more in the pages that follow) is among the healthiest, most sustainable, and tastiest food in the world. And now it is easier than ever to prepare this food at home in a way that fits our hectic contemporary lifestyle. I am thrilled to show you how to use your electric pressure cooker and air fryer to make Mediterranean cuisine if not quite in an instant, then at least in less time than ever before.

There is nothing more Mediterranean than taking delight in preparing delicious, nourishing food and serving it to friends, family, and cherished guests. It is my sincere hope that whether you are cooking dinner on a busy weeknight or preparing a holiday feast for a crowd, these recipes will help you channel that Mediterranean spirit in your own kitchen.

WHAT IS MEDITERRANEAN CUISINE?

On the surface, the answer to this question is quite simple: it is the cuisine of the region surrounding the Mediterranean Sea. But the real answer is much more complicated, in part because the land surrounding the Mediterranean Sea is not monolithic. The part of the globe that we try to encapsulate in the phrase "the Mediterranean" is, in truth, incredibly rich, diverse, and varied—in topography, culture, religion, and history.

The Mediterranean is made up of several distinct regions, including southern Europe; Greece and Turkey,

which is known as the eastern Mediterranean; the part of the Middle East that is often called the Levant; and North Africa. Over twenty countries border the Mediterranean, from Spain and Morocco on one end to Syria, Lebanon, Israel, and Egypt on the other. These countries are Catholic, Eastern Orthodox, Muslim, and Jewish; their lands include high mountains and rocky shores, sandy beaches and coastal wetlands, semi-arid steppes and thick scrub.

All these different regions have their own cuisines and culinary traditions. Indeed, the concept of a distinctive pan-Mediterranean cuisine is actually quite recent; some attribute it to Elizabeth David's classic 1950 tome *A Book of Mediterranean Food*. And yet these widely varied regions and countries do share some common traits that link them together—geographically, culturally, and, yes, culinarily—so that we may, in fairness, talk about "the Mediterranean" as a region with a distinct cuisine. First, there is the Mediterranean Sea (once known simply as "the Great Sea"), which lends its name to, and connects, the entire region. Naturally, seafood is an important part of all Mediterranean cuisines, although how that seafood is prepared—and indeed which seafood the people will eat—varies from country to country.

There is also a distinct climate to the Mediterranean region: hot and dry summers and mild but wet winters through which occasionally blows a fierce wind—be it the mistral in Provence or the sirocco, which travels from North Africa to Italy and Malta. A common climate naturally leads to some common crops. Olives grow all over the region and have been cultivated since ancient times. Thus, olive oil is the preferred fat of the Mediterranean, which is not to say that butter and animal fats, such as lard, are never used. But you simply cannot have Mediterranean food without olive oil.

Wheat was one of the first grains to be domesticated by humans, and that practice began in the eastern Mediterranean. Since those early days—before recorded history, even—wheat, particularly durum wheat, has occupied a significant portion of the Mediterranean's arable land. So it is not surprising that bread is another ingredient found all around the Mediterranean Sea, be it Provençal fougasse, Italian focaccia, Turkish pide, or Middle Eastern pita.

There are, of course, other foods that are common to all—or nearly all—cuisines of the Mediterranean: legumes, beans, and pulses; cheese and yogurt; members of the allium family, including leeks, onions, and garlic; fresh green herbs, like dill, oregano, thyme, parsley, and mint; grapes; citrus fruits; and certain vegetables, some of which are native to the region, like fennel, and some of which did not even arrive in the Mediterranean until as late as the 1500s—that is, New World vegetables like tomatoes and peppers.

The fact that the different parts of the Mediterranean share so many common ingredients—some of which are not even native to the area—highlights another important characteristic of the region: its interconnectedness. The people of the Mediterranean have always interacted with one another, even though they came from different tribes, empires, cultures, and religions. Through the ages, they traded with one another, fought with one another, conquered one another, tolerated one another, and colonized one another. And all the while, the various peoples of the Mediterranean were simultaneously interacting with other civilizations and cultures *outside* the region. The famed Silk Road that ran through Central Asia on its way to China passed through the eastern Mediterranean. The Roman Empire, at one time, stretched all the way to England. The Arabs of the Middle East traded extensively with the Persians. A few centuries later, the Spanish established trade routes with the Americas. And so, once a spice, vegetable, or cooking technique arrived in one part of the Mediterranean, it could easily spread to the whole region. The best example of this is, once again, the tomato—that New World vegetable (or fruit, technically) without which we can hardly imagine Mediterranean food.

SEASONAL EATING

Beyond ingredients, there are certain ways of thinking about, preparing, and even consuming food that are common to the different parts of the Mediterranean. With its distinctive climate that permits agriculture nearly all year round, the Mediterranean region has always allowed for eating with the seasons in a way that was not possible in other, harsher climes, where preserving summer foods to last through the winter was the only way to survive. (Which is not to say that Mediterranean cooks did not seek to preserve their seasonal crops; they certainly did, and still do today.) Perhaps because of the wide variety of flavorful ingredients available to them, the people of the Mediterranean have long made preparing, serving, and enjoying food central to their lives. Mealtimes are leisurely, guests are welcome, and good cooks—be they a grandmother, a neighbor, or a local restaurant owner— are celebrated.

Nowhere is this passion for eating, drinking, and sharing food with family and friends more evident than the tradition—nearly universal around the Mediterranean—of a spread of small plates to be enjoyed before, or in between, meals, and usually over a glass of the local spirit. In Spain, these plates are called tapas; in Greece, *mezedes*; in Venice, *cichetti*; and in the Middle East and North Africa, mezze. The name may differ, but the concept remains the same. Sitting with friends over a glass and a spread of small plates—which may be hot or cold, raw or cooked, but are invariably delicious—is a way of life around the Mediterranean.

MEDITERRANEAN CUISINE VS. THE MEDITERRANEAN DIET

Because of the fertility of the land and the long tradition of agriculture in the Mediterranean, the diet of the region's people grew, over centuries, to emphasize cereal grains, vegetables and fruit, and seafood, with little meat. This type of diet is naturally quite healthy, particularly for the cardiovascular system. The health benefits of

Mediterranean cuisine became widely known in the 1970s with the emergence of scientific research—some of which has since been debunked—showing that the people of the Mediterranean had lower incidences of heart disease than their counterparts in northern Europe. Since then, many people have adopted the so-called Mediterranean diet, which is *not* the same thing as Mediterranean cuisine. The Mediterranean diet, for example, focuses on how people eat in Italy and Greece in particular, which, as we know, is only a fraction of the Mediterranean region. The Mediterranean diet also incorporates ingredients that are heart-healthy, but not actually native to the region—salmon, for example.

It is important to note that this book is inspired by Mediterranean cuisine, not the Mediterranean diet. I have drawn upon the traditions and foodways of the entire region—not just southern Europe—for these recipes. Indeed, alongside familiar French, Spanish, and Italian dishes, you will find plenty of recipes from Turkey, Israel, Egypt, and North Africa. And I have tried to focus, if not exclusively, then at least heavily on truly Mediterranean ingredients—to the extent that they are readily available in North America. While many of the recipes in this book are extremely healthy—with lots of whole grains, vegetables, and plant-based protein—this is not a diet book; the recipes are healthy because the food of the Mediterranean is naturally so. In addition to the (many) light, fresh, plant-based recipes, there are also plenty of recipes that are hearty and designed to fortify you on a chilly night. You will likewise find some indulgent desserts that could hardly be considered health food but are worthy of a special occasion. And in truth, balancing freshness, vibrancy, and healthfulness on the one hand with comfort, pleasure, and celebration on the other is very much the ethos of the Mediterranean.

CREATING YOUR OWN MEZZE SPREAD

Whether it is Spain's tapas or the Middle East's mezze, sharing a spread of small plates among friends, family, or guests is a Mediterranean tradition. While Spanish tapas are usually enjoyed at a restaurant, people in the Middle East often serve mezze at home—not surprising, perhaps, in a part of the world where hospitality is a cardinal virtue. But offering mezze to your guests is not supposed to be difficult or a burden; it is supposed to be as pleasurable to serve mezze as it is to eat them. To that end, the food is typically prepared in advance or can be cooked or assembled quickly to allow the host to relax and partake as well. And everyone simply helps themselves, without fuss or formality.

With the help of your electric pressure cooker, air fryer, and the recipes in this book, you can create a Mediterranean mezze spread of your own that will allow you to stay cool and relaxed while entertaining. To plan your menu, start with some easy, store-bought items, such as marinated olives, nuts, or vegetable crudités. Then select two or three different dips to prepare in the days before the party. Aim for one creamy, starchy dip like Smooth and Creamy Hummus (page 41) or Skordalia (page 50); a yogurt-based one like Quick Labneh (page 191) or Tzatziki (page 56); and a seasonal vegetable spread, such as Matbucha (page 45), Pumpkin Chershi (page 48), or Muhammara (page 183). Feel free to buy bread to save time, but if you are feeling ambitious, make your own Whole Wheat Pita (page 58) or Laffa Bread (page 142) to go with the dips.

To round out the spread, include a cold salad or two, such as Classic Tabbouleh (page 92), Jeweled Barley Salad (page 95), Lebanese Potato Salad (page 110), or Circassian Chicken (page 138)—all of which can be prepared hours before the party. Finally, add one or two hot dishes that can either be prepared in advance and kept warm, such as Albóndigas (page 126), or formed in advance and cooked in the air fryer at the last minute, such as Arancini di Riso (page 194), Fried Potatoes with Smoked Paprika Aioli (page 186), or Herby Green Falafel (page 196). Be sure to keep the menu well balanced; for example, if you include a potato salad, do not serve fried potatoes as well. Or embrace a theme: create a Greek-inspired spread with skordalia, tzatziki, Gigantes Plaki (page 119), and Lamb and Bulgur Kofta (page 204). Above all, do as much as you can in advance so you can embrace the mezze spirit and have a wonderful time at your own party.

The Mediterranean Pantry

Many of the Mediterranean's best-loved ingredients are now familiar to Americans as well. Twenty-first-century Americans think nothing of cooking with olive oil, yogurt, whole grains, garlic, and fresh herbs. Given the rise in popularity of Middle Eastern cuisine, we are even starting to be blasé about chickpeas and tahini. Nearly all American supermarkets today carry an impressive variety of Mediterranean ingredients; combine that with the ability to order almost anything online, and there are very few regional Mediterranean foods that are truly impossible to source with a little advance notice.

In this book, I have made every effort to call for ingredients that are readily available at a typical grocery store, with some here and there that might require a trip to Whole Foods or Trader Joe's. There are a handful of ingredients, at most, that you might have to source online or at a Middle Eastern market, but they are well worth the extra effort to achieve authentic Mediterranean flavor. The following list notes a few ingredients that are part of a well-stocked Mediterranean pantry but are less common in North America.

ALEPPO PEPPER: A spice made from ground dried Halaby peppers, a variety of red chile. Named after the Syrian city of Aleppo, this spice is known for its mild heat and fruity, earthy flavor and is commonly used in Middle Eastern cuisine.

BAHARAT: A warm, earthy Middle Eastern spice blend that typically contains paprika, coriander, cumin, cardamom, allspice, cloves, nutmeg, cinnamon, and black pepper.

BULGUR: Cracked whole-grain durum wheat groats that come in different grinds, from coarse to extra-fine. Bulgur is used frequently in Middle Eastern and Turkish cuisine.

DUKKAH: An Egyptian nut-and-seed mixture typically consisting of hazelnuts and sesame, cumin, fennel, and coriander seeds. Find a recipe on page 81.

HARISSA: A spicy, fruity chile paste popular in North Africa and the Middle East, made with sweet and hot peppers, garlic, olive oil, and warm, earthy spices.

LENTILS: A kind of pulse (the edible seed of a plant in the legume family), like chickpeas and fava beans. There are many varieties, including red, brown, black, beluga, and green Le Puy lentils from France. Lentils are an important source of vegetable-based protein, high in fiber and vitamins such as iron, potassium, and folate.

PINE NUTS: Also known as pignoli or piñons, pine nuts are the edible seeds of pine trees, not true nuts. They are common in many Mediterranean cuisines, especially Italian.

POMEGRANATE MOLASSES: Pomegranate juice that has been reduced, with or without added sugar, to a thick, sweet-tart syrup. Used in Middle Eastern and Persian cooking.

PRESERVED LEMONS: Lemons that have been pickled in salt and their own juices. Commonly used in North African cuisine.

RAS EL HANOUT: A pricey and luxurious Moroccan spice blend that typically includes, among other ingredients, black pepper, cinnamon, nutmeg, allspice, cumin, cardamom pods, rose petals, and grains of paradise, which are the seeds of a West African plant known for their pungency.

ROSE WATER: Water infused with the essence of roses. Used as a flavoring agent, rose water is an important ingredient in Middle Eastern, Indian, and Persian cuisines.

SMOKED PAPRIKA: A spice ground from dried smoked pimiento peppers. Sometimes called pimentón or Spanish paprika, smoked paprika is characterized by its bright red color and smoky aroma and flavor.

SUMAC: A tart, citrusy spice made from ground sumac berries. Sumac is an essential component in the Middle Eastern spice blend za'atar.

TAHINI: A paste made from ground sesame seeds. Widely used in Middle Eastern cooking.

ZA'ATAR: The name for both a variety of wild thyme that grows in the Middle East and a popular seasoning made by combining the dried herb with sumac and sesame seeds.

How to Use an Electric Pressure Cooker

In the past decade, there has been a revolution in home cooking. In the never-ending quest to make cooking and preparing meals more convenient and accessible, busy cooks have given in to the pressure—pressure *cooking*, that is. Electric pressure cookers, led by the ubiquitous Instant Pot, burst onto the scene in 2010 and grow more popular every year. Nearly every established kitchen brand has created its own programmable electric pressure cooker or multicooker. New, more elaborate models—and new accessories for these appliances—come out every year.

With enhanced safety features and multiple, easy-to-use settings, this generation of electric pressure cookers is empowering home cooks of all types to create succulent soups, stews, and braises in a fraction of the time these dishes would take to cook on the stove. Healthy, plant-based meals made with beans, legumes, and whole grains no longer require long soaks and hours of simmering to emerge tender and perfectly cooked. Electric pressure cookers even take the uncertainty out of cooking delicate ingredients like eggs, custards, and seafood.

The Instant Pot and its raft of competitors offer many advantages over traditional stovetop cooking and oven roasting. The most obvious advantage is speed. By combining heat and pressure, electric pressure cookers are able to cook certain types of foods—namely tough cuts of meat, dried legumes, and firm vegetables—in a fraction of the time it would take on the stove. But there are other advantages as well, such as how little monitoring these appliances require. Once you place your food in your Instant Pot or other pressure cooker, you can simply walk away. The machine will cook the food to perfection and then, if need be, hold it at a safe temperature until you are ready to eat. In other instances, the moist steam heat in a pressure cooker creates the perfect environment to prevent certain delicate foods from drying out or overcooking, making these appliances far superior to the oven for this type of baking.

But electric pressure cookers do have their limitations, and if you do not understand what these appliances do well—and what they do less well—you could end up frustrated and wondering what all the fuss is about. To that end, let's briefly review how electric pressure cookers work, how they can make your life in the kitchen easier, and what you need to get the most out of your appliance. This introduction is *not* a substitute for reading the manual that came with your appliance and familiarizing yourself with how your particular model works, however, so please do that if you have not already.

HOW ELECTRIC PRESSURE COOKERS WORK

There are certain foods, such as dried beans, grains, and tough cuts of meat, that simply must be cooked in liquid; cooking them by any other method will not work, or results in tough, inedible food. When cooking food in liquid on the stove or in the oven, the maximum temperature that food can reach is the boiling point of water, 212°F at sea level. For that reason, it can sometimes take a long time—hours, even—to cook these foods to the point of being tender and succulent.

A pressure cooker, be it electric or the older stovetop kind, works differently than other types of cooking. The pressure cooker is a sealed environment from which steam cannot escape. Thus, when the liquid inside a pressure cooker evaporates and creates steam, that steam builds up and creates pressure. This pressure causes the temperature in the pot to rise over 212°F, up to around 240°F in most cases. Thus, foods inside the pressure cooker can get hotter and cook faster—sometimes up to 60 percent faster—than they would on the stove. And because the food is still surrounded by liquid, it stays moist and does not dry out.

If the idea of steam and pressure building up inside your pressure cooker with no way to escape sounds a bit scary, do not be concerned. Today's pressure cookers have multiple safety features that prevent them from building up *too much* pressure. For one, the new generation of electric pressure cookers operate at a lower pressure than the stovetop appliances of the past. In addition, they automatically regulate the heat and pressure to keep it within a safe range by releasing some of the steam as needed through a valve—even when that valve is closed or set to "Sealing." This is why it is safe to use your Instant Pot or other electric pressure cooker while tending to other tasks.

One thing you may have noticed in this explanation of pressure cooking is that for it to work, you must have steam. Thus, you must start the cooking process with enough liquid to evaporate and create this steam. As a result, nearly all the recipes in this book call for at least a cup of liquid, such as water or broth. (Some ingredients release liquid as they cook, which can contribute to the total amount, so on occasion, you may see a recipe that calls for less than a cup of added liquid.) If you do not have sufficient liquid in the pressure cooker, it will not build up enough pressure to cook the food. On the flip side, because the liquid cannot escape once it has evaporated—as it does when you're cooking on the stovetop—most recipes meant for the pressure cooker call for less liquid than stovetop recipes. If you add *too much* liquid to a pressure cooker recipe, it will end up thin, watery, and not as flavorful. In short, you need liquid to cook foods under pressure, but only as much liquid as you want in your final dish.

Another important note: You may remember from high school chemistry class that material expands when heated. So, too, will ingredients expand when heated in your pressure cooker. Thus, you do not want to overfill the inner pot. Aim to fill the pot no more than halfway for ingredients that expand during cooking, like grains and beans, and two-thirds full for other foods, including soups and stews.

MASTERING YOUR ELECTRIC PRESSURE COOKER

While the Instant Pot may be the best known of them, there are many brands of electric pressure cookers and multicookers on the market today. It can be a little tricky to generalize across different brands, but, in truth, most of these appliances share the same basic features and work in a similar way. Certainly, the recipes in this book will work with any electric pressure cooker or multicooker on the market. To that end, let's review the parts of a typical electric pressure cooker and the important functions to know.

First, all electric pressure cookers are countertop appliances that plug into an outlet. The appliance consists of an outer body that houses its electrical hardware and a removable interior cooking vessel or pot. These machines come with a lid that has a steam or pressure release valve and a float valve. The pressure release valve can be set to a closed (or "Sealing") position to allow the machine to build up pressure or to an open (or "Venting") position to release the steam within the pot. The float valve, which is hidden from view in some models, floats up when the machine reaches pressure and sinks down when that pressure is released. The underside of the lid has a silicone sealing ring, which is necessary to create a tight seal. Most appliances also come with some sort of trivet or rack that fits in the inner pot.

Today's electric pressure cookers and multicookers are programmable, which means you can select different functions and pressure levels, as well as set cooking times. The appliances have buttons, dials, or knobs with which you select these functions or make adjustments and a display panel so you can see what you have selected. For our purposes, the most important functions are the **SAUTÉ** function, the **PRESSURE COOK** function, and the **KEEP WARM** function. Your machine may have buttons for specific functions (like "Steam") or specific foods (like "Beans" or "Poultry"). While you may find these buttons useful and convenient for some recipes, I rarely use them here. To make this book as versatile and straightforward as possible, I developed these recipes using the Pressure Cook (or Manual) function. (A handful of recipes in this book call for the Yogurt function, which many machines have, but these recipes contain very detailed instructions on how to use this functionality.)

As I mentioned, most electric pressure cookers, including the Instant Pot, have a **SAUTÉ** function. This function works by heating the inner pot from underneath like a burner on your stove and does not require liquid. The Sauté function allows you to brown meat or sauté aromatics at the start of a recipe, just as you would if you were making the recipe on the stove. Of course, you could do this in a saucepan or skillet on the stovetop and then transfer the ingredients to the pressure cooker, but that is less convenient and dirties more dishes. (That being said, the small size of the pressure cooker's inner pot forces you to work in batches, so there are times when it is quicker to sauté ingredients in a large skillet on the stovetop.) Depending on your pressure cooker, you can usually adjust the heat of the Sauté function to low, medium, or high settings, but do not expect the precise control of stovetop cooking. When using the Sauté function, leave the pressure cooker lid off or open; if you need to cover the inner pot while sautéing, use a regular pot lid that fits the diameter of the pot or a tempered glass lid designed for this purpose. Do not leave your appliance unattended when using the Sauté function.

For our purposes, the most important function of your electric pressure cooker is, in fact, the **PRESSURE COOK** function. The button for this function may be labeled "Pressure Cook" or "Manual." It is also likely that you can direct your machine to cook at high or low pressure. Once you have selected the Pressure Cook function and adjusted the pressure level, the next step is to set the cooking time. It is important to note that this time is the number of minutes that the machine will cook your food *once it reaches pressure*. Regardless of the model, the machine will take some amount of time to come up to pressure, and that time is not included in the cooking time. When using the Pressure Cook function, make sure the pressure release valve is closed or set to the "Sealing" position; if it is in the open ("Venting") position, the steam will escape and the machine will not be able to build up pressure. Once the machine has reached the appropriate pressure level, the float valve will rise and the timer should begin to count down. At this point, the lid will be locked and you will not be able to open the appliance until the cooking cycle is complete.

Once the cooking cycle is complete and the timer has counted all the way down to 0, the machine switches automatically to Keep Warm mode. If you do nothing, the accumulated pressure will eventually dissipate naturally, but this can take 10 to 20 minutes or even longer, depending on the recipe. This process is typically referred to in pressure cooker recipes as a **"natural"** pressure release. Alternatively, you can open the pressure release valve and release the pressure manually. The steam will shoot out from the valve—more on this in the Safety and Care section—and in a few minutes, you will be able to open the lid. Opening the pressure release valve is often called a **"manual"** or **"quick"** pressure release. In addition to specifying high or low pressure and the cooking time, most electric pressure cooker recipes, including the ones in this book, specify which kind of release you should use. Some recipes turn out better if the pressure releases naturally for a certain amount of time—say, 10 minutes— or entirely. On the other hand, some foods will overcook, dry out, or become rubbery if left in the machine while the pressure releases naturally, in which case the recipe will call for a manual pressure release. And in still other cases, it does not make a difference; you can release the pressure manually if you are in a rush, or let it dissipate naturally if you are otherwise occupied when the timer goes off.

The **KEEP WARM** function is an especially handy

feature of the new generation of electric pressure cookers. When the appliance completes the cooking cycle, it will automatically switch to Keep Warm, holding the food at a temperature high enough to prevent the growth of harmful bacteria—but low enough to prevent overcooking—for several hours, until you are ready to serve or store it. (Note that while the Instant Pot and other electric pressure cookers will hold the food at a safe temperature without overcooking many foods, some foods, like rice, can scorch after several hours.) This functionality is akin to, but better than, the slow cookers of old. You can put the ingredients in your pressure cooker, set it to cook for a certain amount of time, and walk away, then return when it is convenient to do so.

Some of the recipes in this book instruct you to use an additional piece of cookware—such as a steamer basket, soufflé dish, cake pan, or ramekins—which you then set on the rack or trivet that came with your pressure cooker. In these instances, you will add liquid, usually water, to the inner pot while the cookware is elevated above the bottom of the inner pot on the rack. The water turns to steam under pressure and essentially steams the food. This is a very gentle and moist method of cooking, perfect for delicate dishes like custards. It also prevents dairy foods from curdling, which they would if cooked directly in the inner pot. And it allows you to pressure cook certain foods that otherwise do not contain enough liquid, like cakes. See page 18 for a list of the accessories that will allow you to get the most out of your electric pressure cooker.

SAFETY & CARE

As I explained on page 14, the Instant Pot and its many competitors have multiple safety features that make them less intimidating than the stovetop pressure cookers of old. Indeed, this generation of electric pressure cookers is very safe and easy to use. But they are electrical appliances that get very hot and generate a lot of steam, so it is important to take some commonsense safety precautions.

First (and this may seem obvious), only cook in the removable inner pot of your appliance. Do not allow any liquid to get into the electrical housing that surrounds the inner pot. When your electric pressure cooker or multicooker is in use, especially in Pressure Cook mode, the top and sides can become extremely hot. Avoid touching any metal parts in particular. In addition, take great care when opening the steam valve to release the pressure manually. A forceful geyser of hot steam will shoot up from the valve and can cause burns or damage cabinetry. (Some newer machines have a button you can press to release the steam so your hands do not need to be close to the valve.) I like to cover the steam valve with a dish towel prior to opening it, which reduces the noise and absorbs some of the moisture. Once you remove the lid of the appliance, remember that the inner pot is also hot and use caution when handling it.

Caring for your Instant Pot or electric pressure cooker is quite easy. To clean it, first allow the machine to cool down. Do not wash the base or electrical housing with water or submerge it because this can damage the machine. If necessary, simply wipe the exterior with a damp cloth. The removable inner pot can be washed by hand or in the dishwasher. Soaking it in hot water can help to remove caked-on or scorched foods. Likewise, the rack or trivet is dishwasher safe. The various parts of the lid can be washed by hand as needed.

On the lid, the silicone sealing ring, in particular, deserves some attention. This piece is critical to the continued functioning of your electric pressure cooker. If it appears worn or has cracks, replace it right away. Many manufacturers sell just this piece, and may even offer them in packs of two. Some people also find that the ring retains odors when used to cook strongly flavored foods. To prevent this, wash it after each use, either by hand or in the dishwasher. Some people go as far as to have two rings—one for savory foods and one for sweet foods— so cheesecake does not end up tasting like bouillabaisse, for example.

Accessories

Your electric pressure cooker or multicooker is ready to use right out of the box. But there are a few accessories that can help maximize the appliance's potential and allow you to cook a wider variety of dishes. You will find that some of the recipes in this book, especially the desserts, require additional accessories.

STEAMER BASKET: A wire-mesh or expandable metal steamer basket (or small metal colander) keeps vegetables out of the water when steaming them in your electric pressure cooker. Look for a small size that fits in the inner pot of your appliance.

CAKE PANS, RAMEKINS, AND BAKING DISHES: For making cakes, cheesecakes, bread puddings, and egg dishes, invest in a few small pieces of cookware that fit inside your pressure cooker when elevated on a rack or trivet. Some especially useful items include a 7-inch springform pan; a 7-inch cheesecake pan with a removable bottom; a 1½-quart round ceramic soufflé dish; and a set of 4- or 6-ounce round porcelain ramekins.

SILICONE BAKEWARE SLING: Lifting hot cookware or bakeware out of the deep inner pot of your electric pressure cooker can be awkward. A silicone bakeware sling with long handles makes this task much easier. Both Instant Pot and OXO make good versions. Another option is to make a sling out of a long piece of aluminum foil folded over on itself. Place the foil sling under the cookware, then fold the ends of the strip into the pot so they don't interfere with sealing the lid. To remove the cookware, simply lift it out using the ends of the aluminum foil as handles.

TEMPERED GLASS LID: As mentioned earlier, you never want to use the pressure cooker lid when sautéing in your electric pressure cooker. If you need to cover the inner pot while using the Sauté function, use a regular metal pot lid that fits the appliance or invest in an inexpensive tempered glass lid that is designed for this purpose.

IMMERSION BLENDER: An immersion blender allows you to purée sauces or soups directly in the inner pot of an electric pressure cooker instead of having to transfer them to a food processor or blender. This tool comes in handy for stovetop cooking as well.

FAT SEPARATOR: Large cuts of meat, such as brisket, pot roast, or lamb shanks, render a significant amount of fat when braised, which can make the broth or sauce in which they are cooked greasy. A fat separator is a measuring cup that allows you to separate the fat from the flavorful sauce or cooking liquid. I prefer ones that allow you to pour the liquid from the bottom, leaving behind the fat that has risen to the top.

EXTRA INNER POT: If you think you may want to cook two dishes in your electric pressure cooker for the same meal, such as Italian Sausage Ragù (page 137) and Polenta with Butter and Cheese (page 100), an extra inner pot can save you from having to stop and do dishes in the middle of cooking.

THE MEDITERRANEAN PRESSURE COOKER

In many ways, Mediterranean cuisine is especially well suited to pressure cooking. As discussed earlier, Mediterranean cuisine relies heavily on whole grains, plant-based proteins like beans and legumes, and seasonal vegetables. Many of these exceptionally nutritious and healthy foods cook in liquid and, in the past, required hours of soaking and cooking to soften and become palatable. When traditional Mediterranean cooks did have access to meat, they used all of the animal, including tough, inexpensive cuts, such as legs and joints, that also required long, slow cooking in liquid to become tender and succulent. In an era when one or more members of the household were at home during the day and food preparation was a large part of daily life, soaking, stewing, and braising foods in this leisurely manner made perfect sense.

Today, many of us are attracted to the vibrancy and healthfulness of Mediterranean cuisine. We want to shift to more of a plant-based diet, to eat more seasonally and sustainably, and to incorporate healthy and flavorful foods like fish, whole grains, and legumes into our everyday diets. We have sampled Israeli, Moroccan, Greek, and Spanish foods in our favorite restaurants and aspire to bring these intriguing flavors and dishes into our own kitchens. But it can be challenging to integrate the traditional foods and methods of Mediterranean cooking—such as long simmering, stewing, and braising—into a busy, contemporary life, especially when most people work outside the home.

The Instant Pot and other electric pressure cookers and multicookers put the best aspects of Mediterranean cuisine within reach for today's busy cook. These appliances allow us to cook the signature ingredients of Mediterranean cuisine—beans and legumes, whole grains, and vegetables—in a fraction of the time it would take on the stove. Moreover, electric pressure cookers are ideal for transforming tough cuts of meat into tender, succulent stews and braises, again without the hours of cooking they would usually require. These appliances even take the fear out of cooking delicate ingredients like fish and shrimp, which abound in Mediterranean cuisine and which many of us are anxious about cooking at home.

Throughout this book, you will see the very best of Mediterranean cuisine—the Middle East's many dips and spreads, Spanish paella, Provençal bouillabaisse, Moroccan tagines, and Italian risotto—adapted and updated for today's pressure cookers. By harnessing the ability of these appliances to cook ingredients quickly, reliably, and without a lot of babysitting, it is easier than ever to bring the flavors and goodness of the Mediterranean into your home.

How to Use an Air Fryer

Whether you own a stand-alone air fryer, a combination pressure cooker and air fryer, or a special lid that transforms your pressure cooker into an air fryer, you likely have come to love the speed and convenience of air-frying. Air fryers cook food quickly and deliver delicious results: crispy chicken, caramelized vegetables, and seared-on-the-outside, tender-on-the-inside meat and fish—all in a fraction of the time it would take in the oven.

In a way, the air fryer is the perfect complement to your pressure cooker. As discussed earlier, the great advantage of an electric pressure cooker is its ability to cook certain kinds of foods—namely braises, stews, dried beans, and grains—far more quickly than if they were cooked on the stovetop. But pressure cookers have their limitations. They do an outstanding job with the foods I just mentioned—anything that steams or cooks in liquid. But if you are craving something crispy, crunchy, seared, or caramelized, a pressure cooker is not going to be able to help you. In that case, turn to your air fryer.

In short, both a pressure cooker and an air fryer have an important place in your kitchen. Both will help you, albeit in different ways, in the seemingly never-ending struggle to prepare healthy, delicious, and satisfying meals that actually fit into your busy schedule. Put together, they can cook almost anything, as you will see from the wide variety of recipes in this book.

HOW AIR FRYERS WORK

An air fryer is essentially a powerful countertop convection oven. Like convection ovens, air fryers are equipped with fans that forcefully circulate hot air around the cooking chamber so that food cooks quickly and evenly. Your air fryer also has an exhaust system that whisks away moisture, which helps to brown and caramelize foods. And its small size enables the air fryer to heat up quickly. All these factors put together mean that the air fryer does an excellent job of making the exterior of your food brown and crispy while keeping the interior moist and juicy—in far less time than it would take in a conventional oven.

You may be wondering, at this point, *Why is this countertop oven called an air fryer?* In truth, it is a bit of a misnomer. The name comes from the fact that when you brush or spray food with oil and cook it in the air fryer, the powerful fan circulates microdroplets of the oil around the food. This, in some ways, mimics the effects of deep-frying. It is this ability—to produce crispy, crunchy foods without the mess and calories of deep-frying—that initially made this appliance so popular with home cooks. But many people who bought an air fryer to produce healthier versions of their favorite deep-fried treats have been pleasantly surprised by how versatile and useful this appliance is for making everything from fun party appetizers to quick and nutritious family dinners to scrumptious desserts.

MASTERING YOUR AIR FRYER

Now that we understand how an air fryer works, let's review what you can do with your air fryer. First, you can mimic—not replicate exactly, but mimic—the taste and texture of deep-fried foods using just spoonfuls of oil as opposed to cups. You can also bake and roast meat, fish, and vegetables—again, with very little added fat—in less time and sometimes with better results than in the oven. You can even use your air fryer to reheat foods without making them limp and soggy like reheating in the microwave does. (Try this with pizza especially!) And you can do all this without heating up the whole house, in a portable appliance that can be moved around as needed.

As mentioned, to cook deliciously browned and crispy foods in the air fryer, you will need a small amount of fat. For foods coated with flour, bread crumbs, or another dry coating—which is ideal for the air fryer—spray them with oil or cooking spray just prior to cooking. For foods like potatoes, vegetables, and lean meats, such as skinless pieces of chicken, brush or toss them with a little bit of oil right before cooking. One to two teaspoons of oil is perfect, but not more than a tablespoon, because excess oil can drip through the basket to the bottom of the drawer and scorch. For foods that are naturally fatty, such as red meat or skin-on chicken, there is no need to add oil at all.

When air-frying, it is important not to crowd the air fryer basket—even if that means cooking food in two or three batches. (For many, this is the biggest drawback of the air fryer. Yet cooking in batches in the air fryer is often still quicker than using the oven.) Overfilling the basket prevents the hot air from circulating, so the food will steam instead of baking or roasting. On a related note, be sure to flip or turn the food during cooking to make sure all sides are exposed to the hot air. As you will see, most of the recipes in this book include instructions for working in batches and for turning food during cooking.

Air fryers heat up and cook quickly, which is convenient, but also requires that you pay attention to prevent overcooking. Preheating the air fryer ensures that the basket is nice and hot when you add the food, but 2 to 3 minutes of preheating is sufficient, versus the much longer preheating time your oven requires. And if you forget to preheat, do not worry—preheating matters much less for the air fryer than it does for your oven. Not only does the air fryer cook food quickly, the fan dries food out, so watch carefully to prevent burning and overcooking, which could make your food dry and tough. Open the drawer to check on food while it cooks, especially if you are new to using your air fryer and learning how it works.

SAFETY & CARE

Air fryers are safe and user-friendly, but they are electrical appliances that get very hot, very quickly, so it is important to observe some commonsense safety precautions. First, never rinse the housing or electrical components of your air fryer or submerge them in water. Wash the removable basket or tray only. If any other parts need cleaning, first unplug the appliance and let it cool down completely, then use a damp cloth or sponge to wipe it clean. Because of its exhaust system, your air fryer needs at least 5 inches of clearance on all sides to allow the air to vent. In other words, do not place your air fryer right up against a wall, backsplash, or another object. Keep your hands and face away from the vents, which may release hot air or steam during cooking, and never place anything on top of your air fryer. Set your air fryer on a stable, heatproof surface, and consider investing in a heat-resistant mat to place under the air fryer to protect your countertops. When you remove the drawer containing the basket, use caution and always set the basket down on a heat-resistant surface.

Unlike your oven, your air fryer should be cleaned after each use. Leftover food particles and residue in your machine can cause odors or impart an unpleasant taste to food. Take extra care with the nonstick coating lining the air fryer basket. If it starts to chip or wear off, food will stick to the basket and the whole appliance will not work as well. Use only nonstick-safe utensils, such as those made of or tipped with silicone, to remove food from the basket. Spray food with cooking spray *before* placing it in the basket, because these sprays can contain propellants that harm the basket's nonstick coating.

AIR FRYER ACCESSORIES

Like your electric pressure cooker, your air fryer is ready to use right out of the box. But there are a few accessories that can help you maximize the air fryer's potential and cook a wider variety of dishes. Most of these items are sold in multipiece accessory kits, which may be less expensive than buying the pieces individually.

CAKE OR PIZZA PAN: A round pan that fits inside your air fryer will allow you to bake quick breads, cakes, tarts, and egg dishes such as quiches and frittatas.

SKEWERS: Because regular skewers are too long to fit most air fryers, you may want to invest in a set of reusable metal skewers specially designed for your machine. (Bamboo skewers cut to size and soaked in water for 30 minutes before use to prevent scorching will also work.)

OIL MISTER AND SILICONE BASTING BRUSH: One of the most important accessories you can buy is a refillable oil sprayer or mister, which will allow you to spray breaded food with the oil of your choice. Look for one specifically designed to spray oil, because oil can clog the nozzle of a regular spray bottle. Use a basting brush to lightly brush oil on foods, such as fish or skinless chicken.

DOUBLE-TIERED RACK: These racks allow you to cook twice as much food at once by doubling the available cooking surfaces while still allowing air to circulate. A tiered rack is also useful for cooking two different foods at once—say, a protein and a vegetable. (If you do not have a rack, however, do not be tempted to stack foods directly on top of each other the way that you might in a pressure cooker.)

SILICONE-TIPPED TONGS AND SILICONE SPATULA: These enable you to turn or remove food without damaging the nonstick surface of the air fryer basket.

THE MEDITERRANEAN AIR FRYER

Within the broad umbrella of Mediterranean cuisine, there are many dishes that are well suited to cooking in the air fryer. First, although Mediterranean cuisine has a well-deserved reputation for healthfulness, let us not forget that people around the Mediterranean love fried foods, too—from Italy's fritto misto to the Middle East's falafel. In this book, you will find air-fried—and therefore lighter—versions of some of the Mediterranean's most cherished fried dishes, including falafel, arancini, and even Spain's iconic churros. But these fried foods are only a small fraction of the Mediterranean-inspired recipes that I have adapted to the air fryer. I use the powerful dry heat and fast-moving air of the air fryer to char, roast, and caramelize some of the Mediterranean's signature vegetables, including eggplant, peppers, and cauliflower. Some of these vegetables turn into dips and spreads, while others become quick side dishes and plant-based main courses. Finally, I even use the air fryer to stand in for a flaming-hot grill—one of the Mediterranean's favorite methods of cooking meat.

While throughout this book, I call for extra-virgin olive oil—the signature fat of Mediterranean cooking—it is not always the best choice for the air fryer. Extra-virgin olive oil has a low smoke point and the air fryer cooks food at high temperatures. Instead, for air-frying, I recommend using a neutral-tasting oil with a high smoke point, such as vegetable, canola, or grapeseed oil.

1

TOMATO & PEPPER SHAKSHUKA **PG 26**

GREEN SHAKSHUKA WITH LABNEH & DUKKAH **PG 27**

CORN, TOMATO & ZUCCHINI PASHTIDA
(ISRAELI CRUSTLESS QUICHE) **PG 31**

POLENTA WITH BAKED EGGS & MUSHROOMS **PG 32**

BREAKFAST

VEGETABLE & CHEESE STRATA **PG 33**

ASHURA WITH PISTACHIOS & DRIED FRUIT
(TURKISH GRAIN PORRIDGE) **PG 34**

VANILLA YOGURT PARFAITS WITH
PISTACHIO-HONEY GRANOLA **PG 35**

Tomato & Pepper Shakshuka

SERVES 2

3 tablespoons extra-
  virgin olive oil

1 yellow onion, halved
  and sliced

1 red bell pepper, sliced

2 garlic cloves, minced

2 tablespoons harissa

1 teaspoon ground
  cumin

1 teaspoon kosher salt

1 (28-ounce) can whole
  tomatoes, with their
  juices

2 teaspoons sugar

4 large eggs

1 tablespoon chopped
  fresh cilantro
  (optional)

2 scallions, white and
  light green parts
  only, sliced

Labneh (page 52),
  Quick Labneh
  (page 191), or plain
  Greek yogurt, for
  serving (optional)

Shakshuka is the delightful name for a Tunisian dish of eggs poached in a piquant tomato-and-pepper sauce. Although originally from North Africa, shakshuka is an iconic Israeli breakfast food, and recently it has become quite trendy as brunch fare in the United States as well. Although I have put this recipe in the breakfast chapter, do not hesitate to serve shakshuka for a quick meatless dinner if the mood strikes. An electric pressure cooker is the perfect tool for poaching eggs so that the whites are set but the yolks are still runny. With a loaf of crusty bread or some warm pitas to soak up the sauce, shakshuka is welcome any time of day.

Cooking the eggs for 0 minutes may sound odd, but it takes several minutes for the electric pressure cooker to come up to pressure and the eggs are actually being cooked during that time. *Photo on page 29.*

1. Pour the olive oil into the inner pot of your electric pressure cooker. Select the Sauté function and set the heat level to "Less." When the oil is shimmering, after about 2 minutes, add the onion and sauté until softened, about 3 minutes. Add the bell pepper and sauté until soft, about 5 minutes.

2. Add the garlic, harissa, cumin, and salt and stir to combine. Sauté for a few minutes more, until fragrant. Press Cancel to turn off the Sauté function.

3. Add the tomatoes (with their juices) to the pot, crushing them with your hands or using a wooden spoon to break them up. Add the sugar and stir to combine.

4. Close the lid and make sure the pressure release valve is closed. Select the Pressure Cook function and set the cooking time to 5 minutes at high pressure.

5. When the cooking program is complete, release the pressure manually. Remove the lid and stir the tomato sauce. Taste and adjust the seasoning.

6. Carefully crack the eggs into the sauce, taking care not to break the yolks. Close the lid and make sure the pressure release valve is closed. Select the Pressure Cook function and set the cooking time to 0 minutes at low pressure.

7. When the cooking program is complete, release the pressure manually. The whites of the eggs should be set but the yolks should still be runny.

8. Divide the sauce and eggs between two bowls. Top with the cilantro (if using) and scallions. Add a dollop of labneh or yogurt (if using) and serve.

NOTE: Harissa is a spicy (but not too spicy), fruity chile paste popular throughout North Africa and the Middle East. It's an important ingredient in Mediterranean dishes that have a hint of heat, like shakshuka, but is also used frequently as a condiment. It typically includes sweet and hot peppers, garlic, olive oil, and a variety of warm, earthy spices like cumin, coriander, and caraway. You should be able to find jarred harissa in grocery stores that stock a good variety of international products, or look for it online.

Green Shakshuka with Labneh & Dukkah

SERVES 2 OR 4

4 tablespoons (½ stick)
unsalted butter

1 leek, white and light
green parts only,
halved and thinly
sliced

3 garlic cloves, minced

1 teaspoon kosher salt

¼ teaspoon red pepper
flakes

15 ounces trimmed dark
leafy greens, such
as baby spinach,
chard, lacinato
(Tuscan) kale, or a
combination, cut into
ribbons

4 large eggs

1 to 2 teaspoons Dukkah
(page 81)

Labneh (page 52),
Quick Labneh
(page 191), or crème
fraîche, for serving

Crusty bread, for
serving

If you ever tire of the classic tomato-and-pepper shakshuka, try this version, where the eggs are poached on a bed of sautéed greens, such as spinach or chard. A generous dollop of labneh or crème fraîche offsets the bitterness of the greens, and a sprinkle of dukkah provides welcome crunch. One egg with greens is a nice portion if you're serving this green shakshuka as part of a larger breakfast or brunch spread. If the shakshuka is the main attraction, such as at lunch or even dinner, then give each person two eggs and half the greens, and don't forget the bread.

Cooking the eggs for 0 minutes may sound odd, but it takes several minutes for the electric pressure cooker to come up to pressure and the eggs are actually being cooked during that time. Zero minutes is the perfect amount of time to ensure set whites and still-runny yolks. *Photo on page 28.*

1. Put the butter in the inner pot of your electric pressure cooker. Select the Sauté function and set the heat level to "Normal." When the butter has melted, after about 2 minutes, add the leek and sauté until softened and beginning to break down, about 4 minutes. Add the garlic, salt, and red pepper flakes and sauté for an additional minute, until the garlic is fragrant.

2. Add between one-fifth and one-quarter of the greens and ½ cup water and stir to combine. Let the first batch of greens wilt and cook down before adding the next batch. Continue adding the greens in batches and sautéing until you have added all the greens and they are wilted and soft, about 8 minutes total. Press Cancel to turn off the Sauté function.

3. Make four small depressions in the greens with a back of a spoon and crack an egg into each depression. Close the lid and make sure the pressure release valve is closed.

4. Select the Pressure Cook function and set the cooking time to 0 minutes at low pressure. When the cooking program is complete, release the pressure manually.

5. Divide the eggs and greens evenly among two or four bowls, depending on how many you are serving. Top each bowl with ½ teaspoon of the dukkah and a generous dollop of labneh or crème fraîche. Serve immediately, with crusty bread.

Corn, Tomato & Zucchini Pashtida (Israeli Crustless Quiche)

SERVES 4 TO 6

2 tablespoons extra-virgin olive oil

1 medium zucchini, diced

6 large eggs

½ cup heavy cream, half-and-half, or whole milk

1 cup cooked corn kernels

1 pint cherry or grape tomatoes, quartered

3 scallions, white and light green parts only, sliced

4 ounces fresh goat cheese

Kosher salt and freshly ground black pepper

1 tablespoon unsalted butter

A staple in Israeli kitchens, *pashtida* is a baked egg dish similar to a quiche but without a pastry crust, which makes it lighter and easier to prepare. (This recipe is also suitable for anyone avoiding gluten.) In Israel, pashtidas are usually filled with seasonal vegetables and one of many local fresh cheeses. This version combines all the best vegetables of summer—corn, tomatoes, and zucchini—with fresh goat cheese. When cooked in the steamy environment of an electric pressure cooker, your pashtida will emerge light, fluffy, and perfectly custardy. This dish takes over 30 minutes to cook, but nearly all that time is hands-off, allowing you to tend to other tasks, such as preparing a green salad to serve alongside. Pashtida is a perfect dish to serve at brunch.

1. Pour the olive oil into the inner pot of your electric pressure cooker. Select the Sauté function and set the heat level to "Less." When the oil is shimmering, after about 2 minutes, add the zucchini and sauté until softened, about 3 minutes. Press Cancel to turn off the Sauté function and transfer the zucchini to a small bowl.

2. Whisk the eggs and the cream in a large bowl until combined. Add the sautéed zucchini, corn, tomatoes, and scallions and stir. Crumble the goat cheese and add it to the egg mixture. Season well with salt and pepper.

3. Butter the bottom and sides of a 1½-quart soufflé dish small enough to fit in the pressure cooker. Pour the egg mixture into the soufflé dish and cover the dish with foil. (This will protect the pashtida from condensation dripping from the lid.)

4. Pour 1½ cups water into the inner pot of the pressure cooker. Place the trivet in the pot and set the soufflé dish on the trivet.

5. Close the lid and make sure the pressure release valve is closed. Select the Pressure Cook function and set the cooking time to 25 minutes at high pressure.

6. When the cooking program is complete, allow the pressure to release naturally for 10 minutes, then manually release the remaining pressure and remove the lid.

7. Remove the soufflé dish from the pressure cooker and carefully remove the foil, making sure not to drip any water onto the pashtida.

8. Let the pashtida rest for about 10 minutes to firm up.

9. Run a knife along the outer edge of the pashtida to separate it from the soufflé dish. Cut into wedges and serve warm or at room temperature.

Polenta with Baked Eggs & Mushrooms

SERVES 4

4 tablespoons (½ stick) unsalted butter

1 cup polenta, yellow corn grits (not instant), or coarse stone-ground cornmeal

1 teaspoon kosher salt, plus more for seasoning

2 tablespoons extra-virgin olive oil

8 ounces button mushrooms, wiped clean and sliced

Freshly ground black pepper

½ cup grated Parmigiano-Reggiano or pecorino cheese, plus more for serving

4 large eggs

¼ cup fresh basil leaves, cut into ribbons

Heavy cream, for serving (optional)

Imagine starting the day with a bowl of creamy, cheesy polenta topped with a barely set egg so that you can swirl the still-runny yolk into the porridge. Add some sautéed mushrooms and a sprinkle of fresh basil, and you have a warm, comforting, Tuscan-inspired breakfast that puts a bowl of oatmeal to shame. The mushrooms and basil are just the tip of the iceberg when it comes to topping this deceptively simple bowl of polenta and eggs. For a brunch party, put out an array of possible add-ins—such as sun-dried tomatoes, sautéed spinach, crispy bacon, or diced ham—and let each guest customize their own bowl.

1. Place 2 tablespoons of the butter in the inner pot of your electric pressure cooker. Select the Sauté function and set the heat level to "Less." When the butter has melted, after about 2 minutes, add the polenta and stir to coat the grains with the butter. Toast the polenta for 1 minute.

2. Press Cancel to turn off the Sauté function. Add 4 cups water and 1 teaspoon salt to the polenta and stir to combine.

3. Close the lid and make sure the pressure release valve is closed. Select the Pressure Cook function and set the cooking time to 8 minutes at high pressure.

4. While the polenta is cooking, combine the remaining 2 tablespoons butter and the olive oil in a large, heavy skillet and heat over medium-high heat until the butter has melted. Add half the mushrooms, making sure not to crowd the skillet. Sauté the mushrooms, without stirring, for 2 to 3 minutes, until browned. Turn and cook for a few minutes more, until browned on the second side. Transfer to a paper towel–lined plate and repeat with the remaining mushrooms. Season the mushrooms with salt and pepper and set aside.

5. When the cooking program is complete, allow the pressure to release naturally for at least 10 minutes, then manually release the remaining pressure and remove the lid. Stir the polenta thoroughly with a spatula, scraping up anything stuck to the bottom of the pot. (Typically, the top layer of the polenta will be thin with more liquid, while the bottom layer will be thick and might be sticking to the pot. Continue to stir until the polenta is an even consistency throughout.) Stir in the cheese.

6. Make four wells in the polenta with a spoon. Carefully crack one egg into each well, taking care not to break the yolks. Close the lid and make sure the pressure release valve is closed. Select the Pressure Cook function and set the cooking time to 0 minutes at low pressure. (The eggs will cook in the time it takes for the machine to come to pressure.)

7. When the cooking program is complete, release the pressure manually. The whites of the eggs should be set but the yolks should still be runny.

8. Divide the polenta and eggs evenly among four bowls. Top each bowl with the sautéed mushrooms and basil. If desired, add a splash of cream to each bowl and season with salt and pepper. Serve immediately, and pass additional cheese at the table.

Vegetable & Cheese Strata

SERVES 4 TO 6

2 tablespoons extra-virgin olive oil

2 tablespoons unsalted butter, plus more for greasing

½ yellow onion, diced

3 scallions, white and light green parts only, sliced

4 ounces mushrooms, wiped clean and sliced

1 red bell pepper, sliced

1 green bell pepper, sliced

1 teaspoon kosher salt

Freshly ground black pepper

4 cups bread cubes, preferably from a day-old loaf of Italian or country bread, cut into 1-inch cubes

1 cup grated fontina, Gruyère, or Emmental cheese

½ cup grated Parmigiano-Reggiano cheese

4 large eggs

2 cups milk, preferably whole

1 tablespoon Dijon mustard

Dash of hot sauce (optional)

I wanted to include a savory bread pudding in this book—like the wonderful vegetable and cheese strata my mother used to make for holiday brunches. Because of the name, I had always assumed that strata was an Italian dish. So imagine my surprise when my research revealed that strata is actually an American invention and the name is not even really Italian. In Italy, a baked dish like this is called a *sformato*. While strata may not be authentically Mediterranean, this dish still has much to recommend it. Bread puddings are among the dishes that come out exceptionally well when cooked in a pressure cooker. And because the strata must be made in advance—so the bread can absorb the custard—this remains a perfect dish to serve when entertaining at breakfast or brunch.

1. Combine the olive oil and butter in a large heavy skillet and heat over medium heat until the butter has melted and the oil is shimmering. Add the onion, scallions, and mushrooms and sauté until the onion has softened, about 5 minutes. Add the bell peppers and season the vegetables with the salt and black pepper to taste. Sauté until the peppers are softened, about 5 minutes more. Remove from the heat and set aside.

2. Butter a 1½-quart soufflé dish. Arrange half the bread cubes in the dish and spread half the vegetables over the bread. Sprinkle half the cheeses over the vegetables. Repeat these layers one more time.

3. Whisk together the eggs, milk, mustard, and hot sauce (if using) in a medium bowl with a spout or large measuring cup. Pour the egg mixture over the bread and vegetables in the soufflé dish and press down to submerge the bread cubes. Cover with foil and refrigerate for at least 4 hours and preferably overnight.

4. Pour 1½ cups water into the inner pot of the pressure cooker. Place the trivet in the pot. If using a bakeware sling, place the covered soufflé dish in the sling and lower it onto the trivet; otherwise, carefully place the dish on top of the trivet. Close the lid and make sure the pressure release valve is closed. Select the Pressure Cook function and set the cooking time to 30 minutes at low pressure.

5. When the cooking program is complete, allow the pressure to release naturally for at least 10 minutes, then manually release the remaining pressure and remove the lid. Remove the soufflé dish from the pressure cooker and carefully remove the foil, making sure not to drip any water on the strata.

6. Serve immediately.

NOTE: You can certainly sauté the vegetables in the electric pressure cooker using the Sauté function rather than on the stovetop, if that is more convenient.

Ashura with Pistachios & Dried Fruit (Turkish Grain Porridge)

SERVES 4 TO 6

1 cup pearl barley

½ cup wheat berries

2 cups whole milk

½ cup brown sugar

½ cup shelled pistachios, preferably unsalted

½ teaspoon ground cinnamon

½ teaspoon rose water or pure vanilla extract

½ to ¾ cup dried fruits, such as raisins, cranberries, cherries, and apricots, chopped if large

Honey, for drizzling

Seeds of 1 pomegranate (optional)

Porridges are popular breakfast fare all over the world—whether the grain used is oats, rice, or, in this case, barley. *Ashura* (also spelled *ashure* or *asure*) is a lightly sweetened grain porridge, popular in Turkey as a pudding eaten for dessert or, when made with milk, as breakfast. Some call ashura the world's oldest dessert, because legend has it that Noah prepared a similar porridge on the ark by throwing all his remaining foodstuffs into one pot and serving the resulting mixture to his weary family. In Turkey, ashura usually contains beans as well as grains, but I have opted to stick with grains for ease of preparation. With whole grains, nuts, and dried fruits, this warm, comforting barley porridge will keep everyone satisfied until lunch. This recipe makes a large batch to feed the whole family or even a houseful of guests. Alternatively, make this recipe over the weekend and reheat an individual portion every morning, adding more liquid as needed to thin the porridge.

1. Place the pearl barley and the wheat berries in the inner pot of your electric pressure cooker and cover with 2¼ cups water. Close the lid and make sure the pressure release valve is closed. Select the Pressure Cook function and set the cooking time to 12 minutes at high pressure.

2. Meanwhile, combine the milk and brown sugar in a small saucepan and bring to a simmer over medium-low heat, stirring to dissolve the sugar. Remove from the heat and set aside.

3. When the cooking program is complete, allow the pressure to release naturally for 10 minutes, then manually release the remaining pressure and remove the lid.

4. Press Cancel to turn off the Keep Warm function. The grains should have absorbed most, if not all, of the water but will still be quite al dente.

5. Select the Sauté function and set the heat level to "Less." Add the pistachios to the grain mixture and stir to combine. While stirring, gradually add the warm milk mixture to the grains, then cook, stirring continuously, until the grains have absorbed all the milk and reached a porridge-like consistency, about 10 minutes. Press Cancel to turn off the Sauté function. Stir in the cinnamon and rose water.

6. Divide the porridge among individual bowls. Add about 2 tablespoons of the dried fruit to each bowl, drizzle with honey, and top with pomegranate seeds, if desired. Serve warm.

NOTE: Wheat berries are whole kernels of wheat with only the inedible outer husk removed. Wheat flour is made from ground, milled wheat berries. (Indeed, you can grind your own flour at home using wheat berries, if that is of interest.) As you might imagine, wheat berries are a whole grain, packed with nutrients, that normally take a long time to cook; the electric pressure cooker speeds up the cooking process tremendously.

Vanilla Yogurt Parfaits with Pistachio-Honey Granola

**MAKES ABOUT
4 CUPS YOGURT
AND 4 CUPS
GRANOLA, ENOUGH
FOR 8 PARFAITS**

YOGURT

½ gallon whole milk (not ultra-pasteurized; see Note, page 51)

½ cup heavy cream (not ultra-pasteurized; see Note, page 51)

2 tablespoons plain yogurt with live and active cultures

¼ cup sweetened condensed milk

2 teaspoons pure vanilla extract

You can use your electric pressure cooker not only to make tangy plain yogurt—perfect for folding into dips and spreads—but also to make lightly sweetened, vanilla-scented yogurt to serve with jam, fruit, or granola. This yogurt is especially popular with children and has significantly less sugar than store-bought commercial varieties. Pair your homemade vanilla yogurt with a Mediterranean-inspired homemade granola and seasonal fresh fruit for a beautiful yogurt parfait that is far superior to anything you will find at the fast-food drive-through. This recipe makes plenty of yogurt and granola—both of which will keep for up to a week—so you can enjoy parfaits all week long. You might even be inspired to make them for a group at your next brunch party.

1. Make the yogurt: Pour the milk and cream into the inner pot of your electric pressure cooker. Close the lid and make sure the pressure release valve is set to "Venting." Select the Yogurt function and press the Adjust button until "More" is illuminated. The word "Boil" will appear on the display. The pressure cooker will heat the yogurt to 180°F to pasteurize it; this can take as long as 30 minutes.

2. When the milk reaches 180°F, the machine will beep and the display will read "Yogt." Remove the lid.

3. Press Yogurt and then Adjust until the display once again reads "Boil." Set a timer for 5 minutes. The pressure cooker will hold the milk at 180°F, which will help thicken the yogurt.

4. When the timer goes off, turn off the pressure cooker and remove the inner pot. Cool the milk to 115°F—if you don't have a thermometer, it should feel hot to the touch but not painfully hot. You can place the pot on a rack and allow it to cool naturally, which can take about 30 minutes. Alternatively, to speed up this process considerably, place the pot in an ice bath and stir the milk until it cools to the target temperature.

5. When the milk has cooled, transfer ½ cup of the milk to a small bowl and whisk in the plain yogurt to inoculate the milk with a starter culture.

6. Return the milk-yogurt mixture to the pot, add the sweetened condensed milk and vanilla, and whisk gently to combine. Place the inner pot back in the pressure cooker (if the pot was in an ice bath, be sure to dry the bottom before returning it to the pressure cooker).

7. Select the Yogurt function and press the Adjust button until "Normal" is illuminated. Set the timer for 10 hours.

8. At the completion of the Yogurt cycle, turn off the pressure cooker and remove the inner pot. You will have a large amount of runny, tangy yogurt. The next step is to strain the liquid whey out of the yogurt, which will reduce its volume by more than half. Place a large fine-mesh strainer over a deep bowl and line the strainer with a paper towel, coffee filter, or several layers of cheesecloth. (Depending on the size of your strainer, you may need to use two strainers and two bowls.)

9. Ladle the yogurt into the strainer and set aside to drain for 4 to 8 hours, until it has reached your desired consistency. Transfer the yogurt into an airtight plastic or glass container for storage. Save the clear, yellowish whey left in the bowl for another use (see Note, page 53).

Ingredients & recipe continue

GRANOLA

2½ cups rolled oats

1 cup shelled roasted pistachios, preferably unsalted

½ cup chopped dried apricots

1 teaspoon vanilla extract

½ teaspoon ground cinnamon

½ teaspoon ground cardamom

Pinch of fine sea salt (optional if using salted pistachios)

⅓ cup honey plus more for drizzling (optional)

¼ cup extra-virgin olive oil

¼ cup brown sugar

1 pound fresh fruit, such as sliced banana, sliced pitted peaches or nectarines, strawberries, blueberries, raspberries, blackberries, or a combination, for serving

10. At any point while the yogurt is cooking or straining, prepare the granola: Preheat the oven to 325°F. Line a rimmed baking sheet with parchment paper.

11. Combine the oats, pistachios, apricots, vanilla, cinnamon, cardamom, and salt in a large bowl and toss to combine.

12. In a small saucepan, combine the honey, olive oil, and brown sugar and heat over medium heat, stirring to dissolve the sugar. Pour the wet ingredients over the oat mixture and stir with a spatula to coat the oat mixture evenly. Spread the granola over the prepared baking sheet and flatten it into an even layer.

13. Bake the granola until brown and fragrant, 20 to 25 minutes, stirring three or four times to ensure even browning.

14. Remove the granola from the oven and push it toward the center of the baking sheet and press down on it with a spatula. (This will help the granola form clusters.) Allow the granola to cool completely, then break it up with your hands. Store the granola in a clean glass jar or other airtight container at room temperature until needed for the parfaits.

15. To assemble a parfait, layer about ¼ cup of the yogurt in the bottom of a drinking glass, parfait dish, or 8-ounce glass jar. Top with 2 tablespoons of the granola and sliced seasonal fresh fruit or berries. Repeat these three layers one more time and drizzle the top with honey, if desired. Serve immediately or cover and refrigerate for up to several hours until needed.

2

DIPS, SPREADS & BREADS

Masabacha (Whole Chickpeas in Lemon Tahini Sauce)

**SERVES 4 TO 6
AS AN APPETIZER**

8 ounces dried
    chickpeas (about
    1¼ cups)

2 teaspoons kosher salt

4 garlic cloves, peeled

½ cup tahini

Juice of 2 lemons

3 tablespoons ice water

Chopped fresh flat-leaf
    parsley, for garnish

Extra-virgin olive oil, for
    garnish

Masabacha is often called "deconstructed hummus." Instead of puréeing chickpeas and tahini together, as one does to make hummus, you cover whole cooked chickpeas in a lemony tahini sauce. Thus, while hummus has just one texture—smooth and creamy—masabacha adds another element, with soft, whole chickpeas giving your teeth something to bite into. Enjoy masabacha just as you would hummus—with warm pitas or crunchy vegetables. Top with lots of chopped parsley and a drizzle of your best olive oil for a striking presentation.

1. Place the chickpeas and 1 teaspoon of the salt in the inner pot of your electric pressure cooker and cover with 4 cups cold water. Close the lid and make sure the pressure release valve is closed. Select the Pressure Cook function and set the cooking time to 50 minutes at high pressure.

2. While the chickpeas are cooking, prepare the tahini sauce. In a small bowl, or using a mortar and pestle, mash the garlic and remaining 1 teaspoon salt until it forms a paste.

3. Combine 1 teaspoon of the garlic paste, the tahini, and the lemon juice in a food processor and process until smooth. With the motor running, slowly add the ice water. Leave the tahini sauce in the food processor while the chickpeas finish cooking.

4. When the cooking program is complete, allow the pressure to release naturally for at least 15 minutes, then manually release the remaining pressure and remove the lid. (You can also leave the pressure cooker on Keep Warm with the lid on for up to 10 hours.)

5. Drain the chickpeas, reserving 1 cup of the cooking water, and set aside.

6. Add ¾ cup of the cooked chickpeas to the tahini sauce in the food processor and process until smooth. If the mixture is too thick, add a little of the reserved cooking water, 1 tablespoon at a time (you are trying to achieve the consistency of a thin hummus). Taste and adjust the seasoning, adding more of the garlic paste, if desired.

7. Combine the sauce with the remaining cooked chickpeas and spread the masabacha in a shallow bowl or dish. Top with parsley and drizzle with olive oil. Serve warm or at room temperature.

Smooth & Creamy Hummus

**SERVES 6 TO 8
AS AN APPETIZER**

8 ounces dried
chickpeas (about
1¼ cups)

1 teaspoon baking soda

⅓ cup tahini

Juice of 2 lemons

4 to 6 garlic cloves,
peeled

2 tablespoons extra-
virgin olive oil, plus
more for drizzling

1 teaspoon kosher salt

½ teaspoon ground
cumin

Freshly ground black
pepper

¼ cup ice water

Smoked paprika, for
garnish (optional)

Chopped fresh flat-leaf
parsley, for garnish
(optional)

Whole Wheat Pita
(page 58) or
vegetables crudités,
for serving

Hummus has officially taken over America. This creamy spread of chickpeas and tahini has moved from Middle Eastern restaurants and hors d'oeuvre platters to supermarkets and elementary school lunch boxes. But while all of us are familiar with hummus, few bother to make this naturally vegan, high-protein staple from scratch. Perhaps we are dissuaded by the prospect of soaking dried chickpeas for hours. Or perhaps we have been disappointed by subpar results when using canned chickpeas. The electric pressure cooker allows us to start with dried chickpeas—which are far superior to canned for achieving the smooth, creamy hummus of our dreams—but skips all the soaking and waiting. No need to plan ahead: with a pressure cooker, you can make hummus from scratch on the same day you want to eat it!

1. Place the chickpeas and baking soda in the inner pot of your electric pressure cooker and cover with 4 cups cold water. Close the lid and make sure the pressure release valve is closed. Select the Pressure Cook function and set the cooking time to 50 minutes at high pressure.

2. When the cooking program is complete, allow the pressure to release naturally for at least 15 minutes, then manually release the remaining pressure and remove the lid. (You can also leave the chickpeas in the pressure cooker on Keep Warm for up to 10 hours.)

3. Drain the chickpeas and, while they are still warm, if possible, transfer them to a food processor.

4. Add the tahini, lemon juice, garlic, olive oil, salt, and cumin and pulse several times, until the ingredients begin to form a paste. Season with pepper, then turn the food processor on and, with the motor running, pour in 2 tablespoons of the ice water. Process until the hummus is quite smooth.

5. Taste and adjust the seasoning, adding more lemon juice, garlic, salt, and/or cumin if needed. If the mixture seems too thick, add the remaining ice water, 1 tablespoon at a time.

6. Spoon the hummus into a wide, shallow bowl and drizzle with olive oil. If desired, sprinkle with paprika and parsley. Serve with pita or crudités. Leftover hummus will keep in an airtight container in the refrigerator for up to 5 days.

NOTE: With a dish as simple as hummus, the quality of your ingredients makes all the difference. Seek out small dried chickpeas that don't look like they have been sitting on a shelf for years. Be sure to use a good-quality tahini. Soom brand tahini, which is available online, is a favorite of restaurant chefs and is worth seeking out.

Hummus im Bassar (Hummus with Spiced Meat)

**SERVES 4 AS A
MAIN COURSE, OR
6 AS AN APPETIZER**

2 tablespoons extra-
virgin olive oil

1 yellow onion, diced

2 garlic cloves, minced

1½ teaspoons kosher
salt, plus more if
needed

1½ teaspoons ground
cumin

1 teaspoon ground
cinnamon

1 teaspoon ground
coriander

1 teaspoon paprika

½ teaspoon ground
allspice

1 pound ground beef

Juice of 1 lemon

1 recipe Smooth and
Creamy Hummus
(page 41)

½ cup pine nuts, lightly
toasted, for garnish

Chopped fresh flat-leaf
parsley, for garnish

Whole Wheat Pita
(page 58), warmed,
for serving

Dying to turn hummus into dinner? Top it with a mixture of sautéed onions and ground beef seasoned with warm spices like cumin, cinnamon, and allspice. This meaty dish is popular in Israeli restaurants as a festive way to feed a crowd. While this recipe calls for beef, you can also try it with ground lamb, which is common in the Middle East.

1. Pour the olive oil into the inner pot of your electric pressure cooker. Select the Sauté function and set the heat level to "Normal." When the oil is shimmering, after about 2 minutes, add the onion and garlic. Sauté until softened, about 5 minutes.

2. Add the salt, cumin, cinnamon, coriander, paprika, and allspice and sauté for a few minutes more, until fragrant. Add the ground beef and cook, breaking up the meat with a wooden spoon, until the meat is no longer pink, 6 to 8 minutes. Press Cancel to turn off the Sauté function.

3. Add half the lemon juice to the meat mixture and stir to combine. Taste and adjust the seasoning, adding more lemon juice or salt as needed.

4. While the meat is still warm, spread the hummus on a large platter and make a small crater down the middle, then spoon the meat mixture into the crater. Garnish with the pine nuts and some parsley and serve immediately. Pass a basket of warm pitas and encourage everyone to dig in.

Beet Tahini Dip

MAKES 4 CUPS

6 medium beets (1¼ to 1½ pounds), trimmed

½ cup plain Greek yogurt or homemade plain yogurt (page 56)

½ cup tahini

3 garlic cloves, peeled

¼ cup freshly squeezed lemon juice

1 teaspoon ground sumac

Kosher salt and freshly ground black pepper

Whole Wheat Pita (page 58) or vegetable crudités, for serving

The startling magenta color of this beet-based dip immediately catches the eye and makes everyone ask, "What is that?" But this dip—sometimes known as beet hummus—has more than just good looks going for it. For one thing, it is full of nutrition, and the taste is downright irresistible. The beets bring sweetness and earthiness, the yogurt and tahini add creaminess, and the lemon and sumac contribute brightness and acidity. This dip will win over even professed beet haters. It can take as long as an hour and a half to roast beets to tender perfection in the oven, but an electric pressure cooker does the job in half the time. No need to worry about peeling the beets; the skins will slip right off once the beets are cooked. If possible, make this dip the day before you intend to serve it to allow the flavors to develop fully. *Photo on page 46.*

1. Pour 1½ cups water into the inner pot of your electric pressure cooker. Place the trivet in the pot and arrange the beets on the trivet. Close the lid and make sure the pressure release valve is closed. Select the Pressure Cook function and set the cooking time to 30 minutes at high pressure.

2. When the cooking program is complete, release the pressure manually and remove the lid. Remove the beets, which should be tender when pierced with a knife, and drain.

3. As soon as the beets are cool enough to handle, slip off their skins. Coarsely chop the beets and transfer to a food processor.

4. Add the yogurt, tahini, garlic, lemon juice, and sumac to the food processor and purée until smooth. Season well with salt and pepper.

5. Serve with pita or crudités. The dip will keep in an airtight container in the refrigerator for several weeks.

Matbucha

MAKES 2 CUPS

2 red bell peppers, cut into thirds or quarters

3 tablespoons extra-virgin olive oil

2 jalapeños, minced

2 garlic cloves, minced

1 (28-ounce) can whole tomatoes, with their juices

2 teaspoons sugar

1 teaspoon ground cumin

1 teaspoon kosher salt

½ teaspoon paprika

While we might think of *matbucha* as a sauce or dip, in North Africa it is known as a salad, or, to put a finer point on it, *salade cuite*, French for "cooked salad." (*Matbucha* actually means "cooked" in Arabic.) In truth, this spicy tomato-and-pepper concoction has a variety of uses. Serve it as a dip with crusty bread or pita, use it as the base for a fiery shakshuka (see page 26), or include as a part of a larger mezze spread. Traditionally, matbucha is gently simmered on the stovetop for hours, until it reduces and becomes quite thick. This electric pressure cooker version still takes over an hour, but much of that time is hands-off, and you won't end up with tomato sauce splattered all over your stovetop. Matbucha is best prepared a few hours or even a day in advance of serving to allow the flavors to develop. *Photo on page 47.*

1. Place the trivet in your electric pressure cooker and pour in 1 cup water. Arrange the bell peppers on the trivet. Close the lid and make sure the pressure release valve is closed. Select the Pressure Cook function and set the cooking time to 5 minutes at high pressure.

2. When the cooking program is complete, release the pressure manually and remove the lid. Cover the inner pot with a clean towel and allow the peppers to steam for 10 minutes.

3. When the peppers are cool enough to handle, transfer them to a cutting board. Remove the skins from the peppers—they should slip off easily at this point. Slice the peppers.

4. Dump the water out of the inner pot, then return it to the pressure cooker and add the olive oil. Select the Sauté function and set the heat level to "Less."

5. When the oil is shimmering, after about 2 minutes, add the jalapeños and sauté until softened, about 3 minutes. Add the garlic and sauté for an additional minute, until fragrant. Press Cancel to turn off the Sauté function.

6. Add the sliced peppers, tomatoes with their juices, sugar, cumin, salt, and paprika to the pot, breaking up the tomatoes with a wooden spoon. Stir to combine.

7. Close the lid and make sure the pressure release valve is closed. Select the Pressure Cook function and set the cooking time to 20 minutes at high pressure.

8. When the cooking program is complete, release the pressure manually and remove the lid. Press Cancel to turn off the Keep Warm function.

9. Select the Sauté function and set the heat level to "Less." Reduce the sauce until it is thick enough that when you pull a spoon through the middle, it leaves a clear channel, 30 to 35 minutes. Stir occasionally at the beginning and more frequently toward the end as the sauce thickens to prevent scorching. You should end up with about 2 cups of matbucha.

10. Let the matbucha cool to room temperature, then transfer to an airtight container. Refrigerate for up to 5 days. Serve cold or at room temperature.

Pumpkin Chershi

**MAKES ABOUT
2 CUPS**

1 (4-pound) sugar or pie
    pumpkin

2 tablespoons extra-
    virgin olive oil

5 garlic cloves, minced

1 teaspoon ground
    cumin

1 teaspoon smoked
    paprika

Pinch of red pepper
    flakes

1 teaspoon kosher salt

3 tablespoons harissa

1 tablespoon honey

Juice of 1 lemon

Greek yogurt,
    for serving

Whole Wheat Pita
    (page 58), for serving

Chershi (sometimes spelled *chirshi* or *tershi*) are spicy, highly flavored condiments or dips that are typically served as mezze, the spread of hot and cold dishes that precede the main meal in the Middle East and North Africa. Pumpkin chershi comes from the cuisine of Libya and is among the most famous. It is easy to make homemade pumpkin purée by using an electric pressure cooker to cook a whole sugar, or pie, pumpkin. Once made, this purée is suitable for all kinds of fall cooking and baking projects, from pumpkin pie to pumpkin soup to this piquant and unusual pumpkin spread, which is delicious with couscous. Of course, if you are pressed for time, you can substitute 2 cups of canned pure pumpkin purée.

1. Cut a large circle around the stem of the pumpkin as you would for carving a jack-o'-lantern. Remove the stem to reveal the inside of the pumpkin. Scoop out the stringy pulp and seeds. Discard the stem, pulp, and seeds.

2. Pour 1½ cups water into the inner pot of your electric pressure cooker. Place the trivet in the pot and place the pumpkin on the trivet, cut-side up. (If your pumpkin is too big to fit, cut it in half and stack the halves cut-side up on the trivet.)

3. Close the lid and make sure the pressure release valve is closed. Select the Pressure Cook function and set the cooking time to 20 minutes at high pressure.

4. When the cooking program is complete, allow the pressure to release naturally for at least 10 minutes, then manually release the remaining pressure and remove the lid. The pumpkin flesh should be tender and easily pierced with a knife. (If not, cook it at high pressure for 5 minutes more, then check again.) Remove the pumpkin and allow it to cool. Press Cancel to turn off the Keep Warm function.

5. When the pumpkin is cool enough to handle, scrape the flesh away from the skin and transfer it to a bowl. Discard the skin and mash the flesh with a fork (or, for a smoother texture, purée it in a food processor).

6. Set a colander over a bowl and scrape the purée into the colander. Place a plate on top of the purée and place something heavy, like a can, on top of the plate. Allow the purée to drain for at least an hour to remove excess liquid. Set aside 2 cups of the purée. (Transfer the remaining purée to a clean jar or airtight container and refrigerate for up to 1 week or freeze for up to 3 months.)

7. Pour the olive oil into the inner pot of your pressure cooker. Select the Sauté function and set the heat level to "Less." When the oil is shimmering, after about 1 minute, add the garlic, cumin, paprika, and red pepper flakes. Season with salt and stir to combine. Cook just until the garlic begins to turn golden. Add the 2 cups pumpkin purée, the harissa, and the honey and stir to combine. Cook gently, just until the pumpkin is warmed through.

8. Remove from the heat and stir in the lemon juice. Taste and adjust the seasoning, adding more salt, harissa, and/or lemon juice as needed. The dip should be tangy and spicy.

9. Serve with yogurt and pita. Chershi will keep in an airtight container in the refrigerator for up to 1 week.

NOTE: Be sure to buy a pie or sugar pumpkin from a farmers' market or good grocery store. Too small for carving, pumpkins intended for eating have a thicker rind and denser, sweeter flesh. Larger pumpkins intended for carving have less flesh to make them easier to carve, and are stringy and otherwise not good to eat.

Skordalia (Greek Mashed Potato Dip)

**SERVES 6 TO 8
AS AN APPETIZER**

1½ pounds russet or other starchy baking potatoes, peeled and cut into 1-inch cubes

¾ cup slivered almonds

4 to 6 garlic cloves, peeled

6 tablespoons freshly squeezed lemon juice

1 teaspoon kosher salt, plus more for seasoning

½ cup extra-virgin olive oil, plus more for drizzling

Freshly ground black pepper

2 scallions, white and light green parts only, sliced

Minced fresh flat-leaf parsley, for garnish

Skordalia is typically served as a dip with vegetable crudités or pita. (Yes, I am suggesting you eat a mashed potato dip with bread.) But Greek cooks also serve skordalia as an accompaniment to fish, shellfish, and grilled vegetables. It's lovely—and a bit unexpected—as part of a mezze platter with other dips and spreads, such as Muhammara (page 183), Baba Ghanoush (page 182), and Cucumber Tzatziki (page 56). Steaming the potatoes in an electric pressure cooker is particularly quick, and results in potatoes that are the perfect texture for making this fluffy, creamy dip. Starchy baking potatoes, such as russets, are preferable to waxy varieties here.

1. Pour 1 cup water into the inner pot of your electric pressure cooker. Place the potatoes in a steamer basket or small colander and place the basket in the pot. Close the lid and make sure the pressure release valve is closed. Select the Pressure Cook function and set the cooking time to 8 minutes at high pressure.

2. While the potatoes are cooking, toast the almonds in a dry skillet over medium heat just until fragrant and lightly toasted, 3 to 4 minutes. (Watch the almonds so that they do not burn.)

3. Transfer the toasted almonds to a food processor. Add the garlic, lemon juice, and salt. Process until the mixture forms a paste. With the motor running, slowly pour in the olive oil and process until the mixture is very smooth. Set aside.

4. When the cooking program is complete, release the pressure manually and remove the lid. Press Cancel to turn off the Keep Warm function. Remove the steamer basket and drain the potatoes.

5. Return the potatoes to the inner pot of the pressure cooker. Select the Sauté function and set the heat level to Normal. Cook the potatoes, tossing them gently, for 1 to 2 minutes to dry them out.

6. Transfer the potatoes to a bowl and mash with a potato masher until completely smooth, or pass them through a potato ricer or food mill into a bowl.

7. Fold the almond mixture into the mashed potatoes until completely incorporated. Taste and adjust the seasoning, adding more salt or lemon juice as necessary. Season with pepper. If not serving the skordalia right away, cover and refrigerate until needed.

8. To serve, spread the skordalia in a wide, shallow bowl. Drizzle the top with olive oil. Garnish with the scallions and parsley. Serve warm or at room temperature.

Fresh Ricotta

**MAKES ABOUT
2 CUPS**

2 quarts whole milk
(not ultra-pasteurized;
see Note)

1 cup heavy cream
(not ultra-pasteurized;
see Note)

⅓ cup freshly squeezed
lemon juice (from 2 to
3 lemons)

¼ teaspoon fine sea
salt

Making homemade ricotta is almost more science experiment than cooking. An acidic ingredient—lemon juice, in this case—is used to curdle warm milk so that it separates into curds and whey. The whey is then drained, and you are left with creamy curds of fresh cheese. The Yogurt function on an electric pressure cooker gently heats the milk to the perfect temperature, making this process completely foolproof. Ricotta, obviously, is Italian, but a very similar fresh cheese is enjoyed in other parts of the Mediterranean, including Spain, Tunisia, and Greece. Use your homemade ricotta just as you would store-bought—in lasagna, to fill stuffed shells, or as the base for a white pizza. You can also use ricotta in Italian desserts, such as cannoli or Orange Ricotta Cheesecake with Raspberries (page 165). But then again, who could blame you if you simply drizzle your homemade ricotta with some fruity olive oil and enjoy it with a crusty loaf?

1. Pour the milk and cream into the inner pot of your electric pressure cooker. Close the lid and make sure the pressure release valve is set to "Venting." Select the Yogurt function and press the Adjust button until "More" is illuminated. The word "Boil" will appear on the display. The pressure cooker will heat the milk and cream to 180°F to pasteurize it; this can take as long as 30 minutes.

2. When the milk reaches 180°F, the machine will beep and the display will read "Yogt." Remove the lid and transfer the inner pot to a wire rack.

3. Add the lemon juice and salt to the milk and stir gently, just a few times, until you see the milk start to curdle and separate into curds and whey. (Don't

stir too much or the ricotta will become grainy.) Allow the milk to sit for 5 to 7 minutes, until the curds have risen to the top and are clearly separated from the liquid whey.

4. Place a large fine-mesh strainer over a deep bowl and line the strainer with a paper towel, coffee filter, or several layers of cheesecloth.

5. Gently ladle—do not pour—the curds into the lined strainer and allow the whey to drain off until the ricotta has reached your desired consistency, 15 to 30 minutes.

6. Transfer the ricotta into a storage container and refrigerate for up to 5 days.

NOTE: Avoid using ultra-pasteurized milk and cream for making ricotta. The process of ultra-pasteurization heats milk to very high temperatures, which alters the structure of the milk proteins so they will no longer coagulate into curds, as is needed for ricotta. Many organic milk brands are, in fact, ultra-pasteurized.

Labneh

MAKES 2 CUPS

2 quarts whole milk
(not ultra-pasteurized;
see Note, page 51)

½ cup heavy cream
(not ultra-pasteurized;
see Note, page 51)

2 tablespoons plain
yogurt, preferably
full-fat, with live and
active cultures

1 teaspoon kosher salt

Juice of 1 lemon

Extra-virgin olive oil,
za'atar, and fresh
herbs, for serving

Labneh is also known as yogurt cheese because it is as thick and creamy as soft cheese. This pillowy texture is achieved by straining the liquid whey out of conventional yogurt. Labneh is a staple ingredient throughout the Levant, but especially in Israel, where it is served as a sandwich spread, as the base for different mezze, and as part of lavish breakfast buffets. Labneh can also be used in cooking because it does not curdle at high temperatures.

Most labneh recipes begin with store-bought Greek yogurt and instruct you to strain it until thickened, which is a good shortcut. But with the ability to make homemade yogurt easily in an electric pressure cooker, you can start with milk and end up with tangy, creamy, made-from scratch labneh for just a few dollars. Drizzled with olive oil and sprinkled with za'atar or dried mint, labneh makes a delicious dip or a garnish for soups and stews, or simply spread it on crusty bread and enjoy.

1. Pour the milk and cream into the inner pot of your electric pressure cooker. Close the lid and make sure the pressure release valve is set to "Venting." Select the Yogurt function and press the Adjust button until "More" is illuminated. The word "Boil" will appear on the display. The pressure cooker will heat the milk and cream to 180°F to pasteurize it; this can take as long as 30 minutes.

2. When the milk reaches 180°F, the machine will beep and the display will read "Yogt." Remove the lid.

3. Press Yogurt and then Adjust until the display once again reads "Boil." Set a timer for 5 minutes. The pressure cooker will hold the milk at 180°F, which will help to thicken the yogurt.

4. When the timer goes off, turn off the pressure cooker and remove the inner pot. Cool the milk to 115°F—if you don't have a thermometer, it should feel hot to the touch but not painfully so. You can place the pot on a rack and allow it to cool naturally, which can take about 30 minutes. Alternatively, to speed up this process considerably, place the pot in an ice bath and stir the milk until it cools to the target temperature.

5. When the milk has cooled, transfer ½ cup of the milk to a small bowl and whisk in the plain yogurt to inoculate the milk with a starter culture.

6. Return the milk-yogurt mixture to the pot and place the pot back in the pressure cooker (if the pot was in an ice bath, be sure to dry the bottom before returning it to the pressure cooker). Select the Yogurt function and press the Adjust button until "Normal" is illuminated. Set the timer for 10 hours.

7. At the completion of the yogurt cycle, turn off the pressure cooker and remove the inner pot. You will have a large amount of runny, tangy yogurt. The next step is to strain the liquid whey out of the yogurt, which will reduce its volume by more than half. Place a large fine-mesh strainer over a deep bowl and line the strainer with a paper towel, coffee filter, or several layers of cheesecloth. (You may need to use two strainers and two bowls.) Ladle the yogurt into the strainer and set aside to drain for 4 to 8 hours, until it has reached your desired consistency. At this point, you will have about a quart of much thicker yogurt—similar to Greek yogurt—and a substantial amount of clear, yellowish whey in the bowl.

8. Transfer the yogurt to a small bowl, leaving the whey behind, and mix in the salt and lemon juice. Return the yogurt to the strainer. (If you were using cheesecloth to line the strainer, you can reuse it; if you used a coffee filter or paper towel, place a fresh one in the strainer. Also, if you had to use two strainers before, you should now be able to combine the yogurt into one.) Save the whey left in the bowl for another use (see Note).

9. Place the bowl in the refrigerator and allow the yogurt to drain until it is thick, spreadable, and similar in texture to cream cheese; this can take 24 to 48 hours.

10. When the labneh has achieved the desired consistency, use it as you like, serving with olive oil, za'atar, and fresh herbs, or transfer it to an airtight container and refrigerate for up to 3 weeks.

NOTE: Do not discard the whey that drains from the yogurt! Whey is extremely nutritious and can be used in place of water or milk in baked goods, as well as in soups and stews. You can also add it to smoothies for extra protein, cook pasta in it, or use it to soak steel-cut oats. This type of whey is highly acidic and can be harmful to the environment if poured down the drain.

Marinated Labneh Balls

MAKES 8 OR 9 LABNEH BALLS

---

2 cups Labneh (page 52)

3 cups extra-virgin olive oil, plus more as needed

2 or 3 dried red chiles

Zest of 1 lemon, cut into strips

2 or 3 sprigs thyme

1 teaspoon whole black peppercorns

Za'atar or dried mint, for serving (optional)

If you allow labneh to drain even further, you can form it into firm balls that will hold their shape. Covered with olive oil, these labneh balls will keep, refrigerated, for at least a month. (The olive oil will solidify in the refrigerator, so remove the jar at least 30 minutes prior to serving to allow the oil to return to room temperature and liquefy.) Serve labneh balls as an appetizer with pita, crostini, or sliced cucumber or tomato, or place a few balls on top of a large salad.

1. Prepare the labneh as instructed on page 52. Allow the yogurt to drain for at least 48 hours until it is very dry and firm. (Let the labneh drain even longer if it is still giving off liquid.)

2. Lightly coat your hands with oil. Roll the labneh into 2-inch balls and place the balls in a large glass jar with a tight-fitting lid.

3. Pour the olive oil into the jar, making sure the labneh balls are completely covered. Use additional olive oil if necessary.

4. Add the red chiles, lemon zest, thyme, and peppercorns to the jar. Cover and store in the refrigerator until needed.

5. To serve, spoon two or three balls onto a plate and drizzle with some of the oil. You can sprinkle the balls with za'atar or dried mint, if desired. Labneh balls will keep in the refrigerator for up to 1 month as long as they are covered with oil.

Cucumber Tzatziki

**MAKES 2 CUPS
TZATZIKI AND
2 CUPS PLAIN
YOGURT**

YOGURT

2 quarts whole milk
(not ultra-pasteurized;
see Note, page 51)

½ cup heavy cream
(not ultra-pasteurized;
see Note, page 51)

2 tablespoons plain
yogurt, preferably
full-fat, with live and
active cultures

TZATZIKI

1 English (hothouse)
cucumber

1 teaspoon kosher salt,
plus more if needed

2 tablespoons freshly
squeezed lemon juice

1 tablespoon extra-
virgin olive oil

2 tablespoons chopped
fresh dill

2 tablespoons sliced
fresh mint leaves

2 garlic cloves, minced

½ teaspoon freshly
ground black pepper

Made with tangy yogurt, cucumber, garlic, and fresh herbs, tzatziki is used as both a sauce and a dip throughout the Mediterranean, but especially in Greece, where it originated. You too will find so many ways to enjoy this versatile condiment. Serve it as a dip with Whole Wheat Pita (page 58) or use it as an accompaniment to Greek-, Turkish-, and Middle Eastern–inspired dishes, such as Lamb & Bulgur Kofta (page 204) and Herby Green Falafel (page 196). This recipe for tzatziki starts with making yogurt in your electric pressure cooker, a time-consuming but very hands-off project. You will need approximately half the yogurt to make the tzatziki, leaving you the rest to enjoy on its own or use in another recipe.

1. Make the yogurt: Pour the milk and cream into the inner pot of your electric pressure cooker. Close the lid and make sure the pressure release valve is set to "Venting." Select the Yogurt function and press the Adjust button until "More" is illuminated. The word "Boil" will appear on the display. The pressure cooker will heat the milk and cream to 180°F to pasteurize it; this can take as long as 30 minutes.

2. When the milk reaches 180°F, the machine will beep and the display will read "Yogt." Remove the lid.

3. Press Yogurt and then Adjust until the display once again reads "Boil." Set a timer for 5 minutes. The pressure cooker will hold the milk at 180°F, which will help thicken the yogurt.

4. When the timer goes off, turn off the pressure cooker and remove the inner pot. Cool the milk to 115°F—if you don't have a thermometer, it should feel hot to the touch but not painfully so. You can place the pot on a rack and allow it to cool naturally, which can take about 30 minutes. Alternatively, to speed up this process considerably, place the pot in an ice bath and stir the milk until it cools to the target temperature.

5. When the milk has cooled, transfer ½ cup of the milk to a small bowl and whisk in the plain yogurt to inoculate the milk with a starter culture.

6. Return the milk-yogurt mixture to the pot and place the pot back in the pressure cooker (if the pot was in an ice bath, be sure to dry the bottom before returning it to the pressure cooker). Select the Yogurt function and press the Adjust button until "Normal" is illuminated. Set the timer for 10 hours.

7. At the completion of the yogurt cycle, turn off the pressure cooker and remove the inner pot. You will have a large amount of runny, tangy yogurt. The next step is to strain the liquid whey out of the yogurt, which will reduce its volume by more than half. Place a large fine-mesh strainer over a deep bowl and line the strainer with a paper towel, coffee filter, or several layers of cheesecloth. (You may need to use two strainers and two bowls.) Ladle the yogurt into the strainer and set aside to drain for 4 to 8 hours, until it has reached your desired consistency. At this point, you will have about a quart of much thicker yogurt—similar to Greek yogurt—and a substantial amount of clear, yellowish whey in the bowl.

8. Transfer 2 cups of the yogurt to a medium bowl to make the tzatziki and refrigerate the rest in an airtight container for up to 3 weeks, reserving it for another use. (See Note on page 53 for what to do with the accumulated whey.)

9. Make the tzatziki: Grate the cucumber on the coarse side of a box grater. Place the shreds in a colander and toss with the salt. Set the colander in the sink and allow the cucumber to drain for at least 15 minutes.

Pick up handfuls of the cucumber shreds and squeeze out the excess liquid. Place the drained cucumber in the bowl with the yogurt.

10. Add the lemon juice, olive oil, dill, mint, garlic, and pepper. Stir to combine. Taste and add more salt if needed. Cover and chill for at least 1 hour prior to serving to allow the flavors to develop. Tzatziki will keep in an airtight container in the refrigerator for up to 5 days.

Whole Wheat Pita

MAKES 8 PITAS

2 teaspoons instant or active dry yeast

1 cup warm water

2 cups bread flour, plus more for dusting

½ cup whole wheat flour

2 teaspoons kosher or sea salt

Pinch of sugar

2 tablespoons olive oil, plus more for greasing

When I visit Israel, I cannot get enough of the fresh, fluffy pita bread that is served everywhere alongside creamy hummus, spicy *matbucha*, and tangy labneh. I am equally obsessed with the football-size hearth-baked pitas at Chicago's outstanding Israeli restaurant Galit. Homemade pita are not quite as good as those examples, but they are far superior to anything you will find at the grocery store. By using an electric pressure cooker's Yogurt function to proof the dough, you can cut nearly in half the time it takes for the dough to rise, which is a godsend on a busy weeknight. Not having a giant wood-fired hearth in my kitchen, I cook my pita breads on the stove. By cooking them in a dry skillet over very high heat, I am able to get the pitas nicely browned and even a little charred on the outside—as if they were baked in a super-hot wood-fired oven—but still soft and fluffy on the inside. In summer, we also love to grill the pitas on our gas grill.

1. If using active dry yeast, whisk together the yeast and warm water in a small bowl and let it sit until foamy, about 10 minutes.

2. Combine the bread flour, whole wheat flour, salt, sugar, and olive oil in a large bowl and stir to combine. If using instant yeast, add it to the flour mixture.

3. Gradually add the water-yeast mixture (or just the warm water, if using instant yeast) to the flour and stir with a fork until a dry, shaggy dough comes together. (You may not need all the water, depending on the humidity in the air and the age of your flour.)

4. Turn the dough out onto a lightly floured surface and knead with your hands until smooth and elastic, 8 to 10 minutes.

5. Place the trivet in the inner pot of your electric pressure cooker. Lightly oil a bowl small enough to fit inside the pot. Place the dough in the bowl and place the bowl on top of the trivet.

6. Close the lid and make sure the pressure release valve is set to "Venting." Select the Yogurt function and press the Adjust button until "More" is illuminated. (The 8-hour timer will begin, but you will not need it.) Let the dough rise until it has doubled in size, about 30 minutes.

7. Punch down the risen dough and turn it out onto a lightly floured surface. Divide the dough into 8 equal pieces and roll each piece into a ball. (If not baking right away, you can place the balls on a baking sheet, cover, and refrigerate them until you're ready to bake, up to overnight.)

8. Heat a large heavy skillet over high heat until water sprinkled on the skillet sizzles on contact.

9. Working with one ball at a time and keeping the others covered with a clean tea towel, use a lightly floured rolling pin to roll the dough out to ¼-inch thickness. It should be very elastic. Place the rolled-out dough in the hot skillet and cook until it begins to puff up and the underside is browned and charred in spots, about 1 minute. (To really encourage the dough to puff, cover the skillet briefly.) Flip with tongs or a spatula and cook until the second side is browned and charred in spots, 30 to 60 seconds. Transfer the cooked pita to a cooling rack and repeat with the next ball of dough. If the pitas begin to char too much or too quickly, turn the heat down to medium-high or medium as needed.

10. Serve warm or at room temperature. Leftover pitas can be stored, covered, on the counter for several days or used to make Fatteh (page 117).

NOTE: These pitas are also wonderful grilled. Get your grill smoking hot and oil the grill grates well. Place as many pitas as will fit directly on the grates. Grill for a minute or so, until they start to puff up and the underside is nicely browned with a little char, then flip and cook on the second side for 30 to 60 seconds.

Man'oushe (Lebanese Flatbread with Za'atar)

**MAKES 4
FLATBREADS**

DOUGH

1 teaspoon instant or active dry yeast

1 cup warm water

2½ cups all-purpose flour

1 tablespoon honey

1 tablespoon extra-virgin olive oil

1½ teaspoons kosher salt

TOPPING

¼ cup za'atar

¼ cup extra-virgin olive oil

Man'oushe is everywhere in Lebanon. In the morning, busy students and workers grab a paper-wrapped man'oushe from a street vendor to eat on their way to work and school. Housewives bring their homemade man'oushe dough to the local bakery to bake in the hot ovens. Throughout the eastern Mediterranean, this za'atar-smeared flatbread is universally beloved for its crispy golden brown edges and tender, chewy middle. Once again, an electric pressure cooker provides the perfect environment to proof the dough for your own homemade man'oushe—the perfect flatbread to pair with Mediterranean meals. When not eaten on the go, man'oushe is served with mint, tomatoes, olives, cucumber, and pink pickled turnips, known as *torshi left*. It would also be an outstanding accompaniment to any of the dips, spreads, or soups in this book. *Photo on page 62.*

1. Make the dough: If using active dry yeast, whisk together the yeast and warm water in a small bowl and let sit until foamy, about 10 minutes.

2. Combine the flour, honey, olive oil, and salt in a large bowl or in the bowl of a stand mixer and stir to combine. If using instant yeast, add it to the flour mixture. Gradually add the water-yeast mixture (or the warm water, if using instant yeast) to the flour and stir with a fork until a dry, shaggy dough comes together. (You may not need all the water, depending on the humidity in the air and the age of your flour.)

3. If using a stand mixer, knead the dough using the dough hook until smooth, about 5 minutes. Alternatively, turn the dough out onto a lightly floured surface and knead with your hands until smooth and elastic, 8 to 10 minutes. The dough should be sticky; add as little flour as possible to the work surface.

4. Place the trivet in the inner pot of your electric pressure cooker. Lightly oil a bowl small enough to fit inside the pot. Place the kneaded dough in the bowl and place the bowl on top of the trivet.

5. Close the lid and make sure the pressure release valve is set to "Venting." Select the Yogurt function and press the Adjust button until "More" is illuminated. (The 8-hour timer will begin, but you will not need it.) Let the dough rise until it has doubled in size, 45 to 60 minutes.

6. Preheat the oven to 450°F. Place a baking stone or an upside-down rimmed baking sheet directly on the floor of the oven, adjusting the oven racks or moving them out of the way as necessary. (You want to create an at-home version of a saj, the domed griddle pan on which man'oushe is cooked in Lebanon.) Line a second upside-down rimmed baking sheet (or a rimless cookie sheet) with parchment paper. You will use this baking sheet to transfer the dough to the oven.

7. Make the topping: Combine the za'atar and olive oil in a small bowl and set aside.

8. Punch down the risen dough and turn it out onto a lightly floured surface. Divide the dough into 4 equal pieces and roll each piece into a ball.

9. Preshape the dough by rolling each ball into a narrow oval. The dough will spring back; let it rest for 5 to 10 minutes to allow the gluten to relax.

10. For the final shaping, roll each oval out on a lightly floured surface until thin and approximately 12 inches long by 4 to 5 inches wide. Brush 1 tablespoon of the topping on each flatbread, leaving a bare edge.

11. Carefully transfer two of the flatbreads to the parchment-lined baking sheet. Open the oven and slide the parchment paper onto the baking sheet on the bottom of the oven.

12. Bake the flatbreads, rotating once halfway through, until the edges are golden brown, 8 to 10 minutes. Transfer to a cooling rack and repeat with the remaining flatbreads. These flatbreads are best enjoyed the day they are made.

NOTE: If you cannot source za'atar, you can make your own: Combine ¼ cup dried thyme leaves (not ground thyme), 2 teaspoons ground sumac, and 1 teaspoon kosher salt in a mortar and grind using the pestle, then stir in 1 tablespoon toasted sesame seeds.

Pissaladière

TOPPING

4 tablespoons (½ stick) unsalted butter

4 to 5 large yellow onions (2 to 2½ pounds), halved and sliced

2 teaspoons kosher salt

1 garlic clove, minced or grated on a Microplane

20 anchovy fillets

12 Niçoise olives, pitted

DOUGH

2¼ teaspoons instant or active dry yeast

1 cup warm water

2½ cups all-purpose flour

2 tablespoons extra-virgin olive oil

1 tablespoon sugar

1 teaspoon kosher salt

A traditional specialty of the French Riviera, pissaladière is the perfect flatbread for those who can never have enough salt. The yeasted dough that makes up the base of the pissaladière is quite similar to a pizza dough—and indeed, you can use this recipe to make excellent homemade pizza. But instead of tomato sauce and cheese, this dough is topped with a base of meltingly tender caramelized onions, briny anchovies, and tiny Niçoise olives. (If you do not care for anchovies, or prefer to keep this recipe vegetarian, simply omit the anchovies.) My version of pissaladière relies on the electric pressure cooker first to caramelize the onions and then to provide the perfect environment for the dough to rise. This is a delightful first course for a French-themed dinner party—especially when served with a chilled rosé—or pair the pissaladière with a green salad for a light lunch. *Photo on page 63.*

1. Make the topping: Begin by caramelizing the onions. Put the butter in the inner pot of your electric pressure cooker. Select the Sauté function and set the heat level to "More." When the butter is melted, after about 2 minutes, add the onions and salt and stir to coat with the butter.

2. Cover the inner pot with a tempered glass lid designed for the Instant Pot or another lid that fits. (Do not use the regular lid.) Cook the onions, covered, for 10 minutes to soften them. Remove the lid and continue to cook the onions until they are very soft, light brown, and beginning to melt, about 20 additional minutes. Stir occasionally at first, then more frequently, as the onions cook down. Make sure to scrape up any onions on the bottom that are sticking. (If the Sauté cycle shuts off automatically before the onions are caramelized, turn it back on and continue cooking.)

3. When the onions are done, press Cancel to turn off the Sauté function. Remove the onions to a bowl and let cool. (This may be done up to 4 days in advance. Refrigerate the onions until needed or freeze for up to 3 months.) If proceeding to make the dough, wash or wipe out the inner pot of the pressure cooker.

4. Make the dough: If using active dry yeast, whisk together the yeast and water in a small bowl and let stand until foamy, about 10 minutes.

5. Combine the flour, olive oil, sugar, and salt in a large bowl or the bowl of a stand mixer and stir to combine. If using instant yeast, add it directly to the flour mixture. Gradually add the water (or the water-yeast mixture, if using active dry yeast) and stir with a fork until a dry, shaggy dough comes together. (You may not need all the water depending on the humidity in the air or the age of your flour.)

6. If using a stand mixer, knead the dough using the dough hook until smooth, about 5 minutes. Alternatively, turn the dough out onto a lightly floured surface and knead with your hands until smooth and elastic, 5 to 7 minutes.

7. Place the trivet in the inner pot of the pressure cooker. Lightly oil a bowl that is small enough to fit inside. Place the kneaded dough in the bowl and place the bowl on top of the trivet.

8. Close the lid and make sure the pressure release valve is set to "Venting." Select the Yogurt function and press the Adjust button until "More" is illuminated. (The 8-hour timer will begin, but you will not need it.) Let the dough rise until it has doubled in size, about 30 minutes.

9. Preheat the oven to 450°F. Lightly oil a rimmed 13 x 18-inch baking sheet.

10. Remove the dough and place it on the prepared baking sheet. Using your fingers, press and stretch the dough, without tearing it, to cover the baking sheet in an even layer. (If the dough is springing back, let the dough relax for 5 to 10 minutes, then resume.) Cover and let the dough proof for 30 minutes.

11. When the dough has proofed, spread the caramelized onions and garlic in an even layer on top, leaving a small border on all sides. Arrange the anchovies and olives in a decorative pattern on top of the onions—a diamond pattern is traditional.

12. Bake until the edges and bottom are golden brown, 20 to 25 minutes. Serve warm or at room temperature, cut into squares.

Focaccia with Roasted Garlic

**MAKES 1 LARGE
FOCACCIA TO
SERVE 4 TO 6**

2¼ teaspoons instant
or active dry yeast

Pinch of sugar

2¾ to 3 cups warm
water

6¼ cups bread flour

1 tablespoon kosher
salt, plus more for
seasoning

½ cup extra-virgin olive
oil

2 heads garlic, top
third cut off to reveal
the cloves

Freshly ground black
pepper

Flaky sea salt

You are likely familiar with focaccia, the dimpled, pizza-like flatbread that hails originally from the Liguria region of Italy. Crispy-on-the-outside, chewy-on-the-inside focaccia is the perfect accompaniment to many of the soups and stews in this book, or any other dish with a fragrant sauce that begs to be soaked up with bread. But you can also serve sliced focaccia as a snack or hors d'oeuvre for company. In Italy, focaccia is often topped with fresh herbs (like rosemary), cheese, or tomato. My version is studded with cloves of sweet roasted garlic. An electric pressure cooker performs double duty here: First we use the warmth of the Yogurt function to proof the bread dough. Then we use the Steam function to soften the garlic, which greatly shortens the time it takes to roast in the oven.

1. If using active dry yeast, whisk together the yeast, a pinch of sugar and 1 cup of warm water in a small bowl and let sit until foamy, about 10 minutes.

2. Combine the flour and salt in a large bowl or the bowl of a stand mixer and stir to combine. If using instant yeast, add it and the sugar directly to the flour mixture. Gradually add 2½ cups of warm water to the flour and stir with a fork until a dry, shaggy dough comes together. For active dry yeast, add the water-yeast mixture to the flour and gradually add another 1½ cups water.

3. If using a stand mixer, knead the dough using the dough hook on low speed, gradually adding 6 to 8 tablespoons more water, 1 tablespoon at a time. The dough should be loose and sticking to the sides of the bowl, but not wet or sticky. Knead until smooth and very elastic, about 5 minutes. (Alternatively, knead the dough by hand in a bowl, gradually adding the additional water, then turn the dough out onto a lightly floured surface and knead until smooth and elastic, 5 to 7 minutes.) The dough should be tacky, but not too sticky to work with.

4. Place the trivet in the inner pot of the electric pressure cooker. Add 3 tablespoons of olive oil to a bowl that is small enough to fit inside. Place the kneaded dough in the bowl and turn to coat with the oil. Place the bowl on top of the trivet. (You may also want to oil the sides of the inner pot, as the dough will likely rise over the bowl and touch the sides of the inner pot.)

5. Close the lid and make sure the pressure release valve is set to "Venting." Select the Yogurt function and press the Adjust button until "More" is illuminated. (The 8-hour timer will begin, but you will not need it.) Let the dough rise until it has doubled in size, about 1 hour.

6. Pour 2 tablespoons of olive oil on a rimmed 13 x 18-inch baking sheet and brush it all over the bottom of the baking sheet. Add the risen dough to the baking sheet and fold it in half. Turn the dough 90 degrees and fold it in half again. Cover the dough and let it rest for 10 minutes.

7. Uncover the dough and gently stretch it, without tearing, to cover the baking sheet in an even layer. (If the dough is springing back, let the dough relax for 5 to 10 minutes, then resume.) Cover tightly and chill the dough for at least 8 hours and up to 24 hours. (A longer chilling time equals more flavor.)

8. Approximately an hour before you plan to bake the focaccia, remove it from the refrigerator and let it rise, still covered, in a warm spot.

9. Meanwhile, roast the garlic. Preheat the oven to 425°F. Line a small baking sheet or dish with foil. Add 1 cup water to the inner pot of the pressure cooker. Place the trivet in the pot and arrange the heads of garlic on the trivet, cut-side up. Close the lid and make sure the pressure release valve is closed. Select the Steam function and set the cooking time to 10 minutes at high pressure.

10. When the cooking program is complete, release the pressure manually and remove the lid. Remove the heads of garlic and place them on the lined baking sheet. Drizzle the tops of the heads with 1 tablespoon of olive oil and season with the kosher salt and pepper. Roast in the oven until browned, about 20 minutes.

11. Remove the garlic and raise the oven temperature to 450°F.

12. When the garlic is cool enough to touch, squeeze the cloves from the garlic heads and set aside. Cut any large cloves in half.

13. Using your fingers, make small indentations or dimples all over the surface of the bread dough. Place the garlic cloves in the indentations.

14. Brush the remaining 2 tablespoons of olive oil over the surface of the dough and sprinkle with flaky sea salt. Bake until the focaccia is golden brown, 20 to 25 minutes.

15. Focaccia is best the day it is made, but can be wrapped up and stored on the counter for up to 2 days.

3

SOUPS & STEWS

Potager Vegetable Broth

**MAKES ABOUT
2 QUARTS**

2 tablespoons extra-
virgin olive oil

2 yellow onions, sliced
(or use 1 leek and
1 onion)

8 ounces mushrooms,
halved

4 celery stalks, chopped

2 carrots, peeled and
chopped

1 parsnip, peeled and
chopped

4 garlic cloves, peeled

1 tomato, cut into
wedges

Several sprigs flat-leaf
parsley

1 bay leaf

1 teaspoon whole black
peppercorns

1 teaspoon kosher salt

A *potager* is a traditional French vegetable garden, and this broth is made from the vegetables you might find in such a garden. Carrot, tomato, and parsnip add sweetness, while the mushrooms contribute umami. Browning the vegetables at the beginning creates a broth with richer flavor. Use this broth in any soup, risotto, or grain recipes calling for vegetable broth, including those in this book. Knowing how to create a flavorful vegetable broth is especially helpful when cooking vegetarian and vegan dishes. I like to make this broth when I find some vegetables that are a bit past their prime in my refrigerator. Rather than toss them out, which is wasteful, I use the vegetables to make broth, which I then freeze so I have it on hand whenever I need it.

1. Pour the olive oil into the inner pot of your electric pressure cooker. Select the Sauté function and set the heat level to "More." When the oil is shimmering, after about 2 minutes, add the onions and sauté until softened, about 5 minutes.

2. Add the mushrooms, celery, carrots, parsnip, garlic, and tomato and stir to coat the vegetables with oil. Sauté the vegetables until they soften and begin to give off liquid, 7 to 8 minutes. Press Cancel to turn off the Sauté function.

3. Bundle the parsley, bay leaf, and peppercorns in a square of muslin or cheesecloth and tie it closed. Add the bundle to the pressure cooker along with the salt. Cover the vegetables with 9 cups of cold water.

4. Close the lid and make sure the pressure release valve is closed. Select the Pressure Cook function and set the cooking time to 30 minutes at high pressure.

5. When the cooking program is complete, allow the pressure to release naturally for at least 20 minutes, then manually release the remaining pressure and remove the lid. (You can also leave it on the Keep Warm setting for up to 10 hours.)

6. Remove the inner pot. Use a large strainer to scoop the vegetables and muslin bundle out of the broth. Discard. Taste and adjust the seasoning, adding salt if necessary, keeping in mind that you may wish to add salt when using the broth in a dish.

7. Line a fine-mesh strainer with cheesecloth or muslin and place it over a large bowl. Strain the broth into the bowl to catch and remove any small pieces or solids.

8. If not using right away, store the broth in a large airtight glass or plastic container in the refrigerator for up to 1 week or freeze for up to 3 months for longer-term storage.

Chicken Broth

**MAKES ABOUT
2¹/₂ QUARTS**

3 pounds bony chicken parts or chicken bones

1 yellow onion, coarsely chopped

2 carrots, peeled and quartered

3 celery stalks, halved

1 parsnip, peeled and quartered

3 garlic cloves, peeled

1 teaspoon kosher salt

1 teaspoon whole black peppercorns

1 bay leaf

2 sprigs thyme

In Mediterranean cuisine, chicken broth is the base for many soups and stews, as well as being a critical ingredient in risotto and other grain-based dishes. Store-bought chicken broth is convenient, but nothing matches the taste of homemade. Before the Instant Pot, it took hours of simmering on the stove to make rich, golden chicken broth. An electric pressure cooker, however, cuts that time in half by combining heat and pressure to extract as much flavor as possible from the humble ingredients. My secret to flavorful chicken broth with a hint of sweetness is adding a parsnip to the usual aromatics—a trick I learned from my grandmother.

You can use inexpensive, bony chicken parts, such as wings, backs, or necks, to make stock. However, you can save even more money by using cooked chicken bones left over from previous meals, such as the carcass of a whole roast chicken. You can even store leftover chicken bones in the freezer to use for making broth at a later date.

1. Place all the ingredients in the electric pressure cooker and cover with 2½ quarts of cold water. Do not fill the pot more than two-thirds full.

2. Close the lid and make sure the pressure release valve is closed. Select the Pressure Cook function and set the cooking time to 60 minutes at high pressure.

3. When the cooking program is complete, allow the pressure to release naturally for at least 20 minutes, then manually release the remaining pressure and remove the lid. (You can also leave it on Keep Warm for up to 10 hours.)

4. Remove the inner pot. Use a large strainer to scoop the bones and vegetables out of the broth and discard the solids.

5. Line a fine-mesh strainer with cheesecloth or muslin and place it over a large bowl. Strain the broth into the bowl to remove the remaining solids and any impurities.

6. If using the broth right away, working in batches if necessary, pour the broth into a fat separator to remove the fat, which could make your soup or stew greasy. Otherwise, allow the broth to cool to room temperature and store in a large airtight glass or plastic container in the refrigerator for up to 1 week. The rendered fat—also known as schmaltz—will naturally rise to the top and solidify. Scoop out the layer of schmaltz and store it separately to use in cooking (it will keep in the refrigerator for up to 1 week) or discard it. The broth can also be frozen for up to 3 months for longer-term storage.

Parmesan Brodo

MAKES 2 QUARTS

2 tablespoons extra-virgin olive oil

1 yellow onion, quartered

1 head garlic, top third cut off to reveal the cloves

12 ounces Parmigiano-Reggiano cheese rinds

3 or 4 sprigs flat-leaf parsley

1 bay leaf

1 teaspoon whole black peppercorns

One of my culinary splurges is imported Parmigiano-Reggiano cheese, which is far superior to domestic Parmesan in complexity and depth of flavor. When I am spending this much on an ingredient, however, I do not want to waste any of it, which is why when I come to the end of a hunk of Parmigiano-Reggiano, I stash the rind in the freezer. I often add a rind to soups, such as Soupe au Pistou (page 84), and risottos to boost their flavor. When I have saved enough rinds, however, I use them to make this luxurious Parmesan broth in my electric pressure cooker. Parmesan broth makes an outstanding base for minestrone or tortellini in brodo, and can be used instead of stock for making risotto. (If you do not already have a stash of Parmesan rinds, you can usually buy just the rinds for a reasonable price at a grocery store that has a good cheese counter or at a cheese shop.)

1. Pour the olive oil into the inner pot of your electric pressure cooker. Select the Sauté function and set the heat level to "Less." When the oil is shimmering, after about 2 minutes, add the onion and garlic head, both cut-side down. Cook, turning the onion once, until the onion and garlic are lightly browned, 3 to 5 minutes. Press Cancel to turn off the Sauté function.

2. Add the cheese rinds, parsley, bay leaf, and peppercorns and cover with 8 cups cold water. Close the lid and make sure the pressure release valve is closed. Select the Pressure Cook function and set the cooking time to 30 minutes at high pressure.

3. When the cooking program is complete, allow the pressure to release naturally for at least 20 minutes, then manually release the remaining pressure and remove the lid. (You can also leave it on Keep Warm for up to 10 hours.)

4. Remove the inner pot. Line a fine-mesh strainer with cheesecloth or muslin and place it over a large bowl. Strain the broth into the bowl and discard the solids.

5. If not using right away, allow the broth to cool and store in a large airtight glass or plastic container in the refrigerator for up to 1 week or freeze for up to 3 months for longer-term storage.

NOTE: As you might imagine, a broth made from cheese rinds has a lot of fat. When the broth is refrigerated, that fat will rise to the top and congeal. You can remove most of the fat before using, but save some to swirl into the warm broth.

Ribollita

SERVES 4 AS A MAIN COURSE

⅔ cup dried white beans, such as cannellini or flageolet, or 2 cups cooked or canned beans, drained and rinsed if canned

3 tablespoons extra-virgin olive oil, plus more for drizzling

1 yellow onion, diced

2 carrots, diced

2 celery stalks, diced

3 garlic cloves, minced

1 teaspoon kosher salt

¼ teaspoon red pepper flakes

5 cups Potager Vegetable Broth (page 70) or water

4 slices stale, crusty bread, such as French or Italian, cut into 1- to 2-inch cubes

1 (15-ounce) can diced tomatoes with their juices

1 bunch lacinato (Tuscan) kale, leaves stemmed and cut into ribbons

Grated Parmigiano-Reggiano cheese, for serving

In earlier times, no self-respecting cook would waste bread—the very staff of life. All over the Mediterranean, recipes were invented as a way to make use of stale or day-old bread, from Fatteh (page 117) to Sour Cherry Bread Pudding (page 173). Ribollita, a hearty bread-and-vegetable soup, is the Tuscan way to repurpose yesterday's loaf. With beans for protein, lots of vegetables, and chunks of stale bread that become almost dumpling-like after being soaked in the soup, ribollita is a thoroughly satisfying vegetarian meal. Potager Vegetable Broth (page 70) works especially well with these ingredients. Lacinato (also known as Tuscan or dinosaur) kale is most authentic here and looks beautiful in the bowl. I recommend soaking the beans overnight so they cook in the same amount of time as the other ingredients and hold their shape in the finished dish.

1. Place the beans in a bowl and cover with several cups of cold water. Soak for at least 8 hours or overnight. Drain and set aside.

2. Pour the olive oil into the inner pot of your electric pressure cooker. Select the Sauté function and set the heat level to "Normal." When the oil is shimmering, after about 2 minutes, add the onion and sauté, stirring frequently, until softened, about 3 minutes. Add the carrots, celery, and garlic and sauté for 3 to 5 minutes, until softened. Season with the salt and red pepper flakes and sauté for an additional minute, until fragrant. Press Cancel to turn off the Sauté function.

3. Add the beans, broth, bread cubes, tomatoes, and kale. Close the lid and make sure the pressure release valve is closed. Select the Pressure Cook function and set the cooking time to 9 minutes at high pressure.

4. When the cooking program is complete, allow the pressure to release naturally for 10 minutes, then manually release the remaining pressure and remove the lid.

5. Taste and adjust the seasoning. Serve hot, topped with cheese and a drizzle of olive oil.

NOTE: Ribollita almost tastes better the next day. When reheating the soup, add additional liquid, as the bread will continue to absorb the broth overnight.

Avgolemono Soup with Chicken

**SERVES 4 AS A
MAIN COURSE,
OR 6 AS A FIRST
COURSE**

---

2 boneless, skinless
chicken breasts
(about 1½ pounds
total)

1 yellow onion, halved

1 carrot, peeled and
halved

1 celery stalk, halved

3 garlic cloves, smashed

1 teaspoon kosher salt,
plus more if needed

1 bay leaf

3 tablespoons extra-
virgin olive oil

3 cups Chicken Broth
(page 72)

1 cup orzo

4 large eggs

½ cup freshly squeezed
lemon juice

Freshly ground black
pepper

Several sprigs fresh dill,
for garnish (optional)

Avgolemono—a sauce made of eggs and lemon juice—is practically omnipresent in Greek cuisine, where it is served alongside dolmades, artichokes, fish, and meat. The sauce is also used to thicken soups and stews, many of which contain rice or orzo because the grains help to stabilize the fragile emulsion of egg, lemon, and broth. In the United States, we know avgolemono primarily as a chicken soup, and as chicken soups go, it is among the best. The eggs make the soup silky smooth, and the lemon adds an appealing note of brightness to this otherwise simple dish.

As is often the case, the electric pressure cooker performs double duty in this recipe: First we use it to poach the chicken for the soup, which has the added benefit of giving us some nicely flavored broth. Then we use it to cook the orzo in an almost entirely hands-off manner. While this recipe starts with instructions for cooking the chicken, you can also substitute shredded cooked chicken, be it left over from another meal or from a supermarket rotisserie chicken.

1. Place the chicken, half the onion, the carrot, celery, garlic, salt, and bay leaf in the inner pot of your electric pressure cooker and cover with 1 cup cold water. Close the lid and make sure the pressure release valve is closed. Select the Pressure Cook function and set the cooking time to 10 minutes at high pressure.

2. When the cooking program is complete, release the pressure manually and remove the lid. Remove the inner pot and transfer the chicken to a plate.

3. Set a strainer over a bowl. Strain the liquid from the pot into the bowl, discarding the solids (you should have about 2 cups of liquid); set aside. Wipe out the inner pot and return it to the pressure cooker.

4. When the chicken is cool enough to handle, shred the meat using two forks or your hands and set aside.

5. Pour the olive oil into the inner pot of the pressure cooker. Select the Sauté function and set the heat level to "Normal." Dice the remaining onion half. When the oil is shimmering, after about 2 minutes, add the remaining onion and sauté, stirring frequently, until softened, about 3 minutes. Press Cancel to turn off the Sauté function.

6. Add enough additional broth or water to the reserved cooking liquid to make 5 cups of liquid total, then add the liquid to the pot. Add the orzo and stir to cover the pasta with the liquid. Close the lid and make sure the pressure release valve is closed. Select the Pressure Cook function and set the cooking time to 3 minutes at high pressure.

7. Meanwhile, whisk together the eggs and lemon juice in a heatproof bowl.

8. When the cooking program is complete, allow the pressure to release naturally for 10 minutes, then manually release the remaining pressure and remove the lid.

9. While whisking continuously, slowly ladle 1 cup of the hot broth from the pot into the egg mixture to temper the eggs. (This will prevent the eggs from curdling in the hot liquid.) Then slowly pour the tempered egg mixture back into the pot with the remaining broth. Add the chicken and stir to combine. Taste and adjust the seasoning, adding more salt, if needed, and the pepper. (Use the Keep Warm function to maintain the soup's temperature. Do not turn on the Sauté function or allow the soup to come to a boil at any point after adding the eggs, which could cause the soup to break or curdle.)

10. Serve the soup immediately, garnished with dill, if desired.

Loubia (Moroccan White Bean & Tomato Soup)

**SERVES 4 AS A
MAIN COURSE**

1 pound dried white
beans, such as
cannellini, great
northern, or navy

2 teaspoons kosher salt

2 tablespoons extra-
virgin olive oil

1 yellow onion, diced

1 tablespoon tomato
paste

1 teaspoon diced
preserved lemon rind
(optional; see Note)

3 garlic cloves, minced

1 tablespoon ground
cumin

2 teaspoons ground
ginger

1 teaspoon paprika

¼ teaspoon cayenne
pepper

¼ teaspoon ground
cinnamon

2 large tomatoes

3 cups Chicken Broth
(page 72), Potager
Vegetable Broth
(page 70), or water

You would not likely see this rustic, homey dish of white beans stewed in tomato sauce on the menu of an elegant Moroccan restaurant, but it is exactly the kind of dish that a Moroccan grandmother would prepare at home for her family. The overnight soak helps the beans cook quickly in an electric pressure cooker and still retain their shape. This is a lovely, protein-packed, main-course soup for chilly nights. Serve with Focaccia with Roasted Garlic (page 66) or Whole Wheat Pita (page 58).

1. Place the beans in a large bowl and cover with cold water and 1 teaspoon of salt. Let soak overnight.

2. Pour the olive oil into the inner pot of your electric pressure cooker. Select the Sauté function and set the heat level to "Less." When the oil is shimmering, after about 2 minutes, add the onion and sauté, stirring frequently until softened, about 5 minutes.

3. Add the tomato paste, preserved lemon (if using), garlic, spices, and the remaining teaspoon of salt and stir to combine. Sauté until fragrant, about 3 minutes. Press Cancel to turn off the Sauté function.

4. Cut the tomatoes in half horizontally and grate the cut side on the coarse side

of a box grater into a shallow bowl until you reach the skin. Discard the skin. Add the tomato pulp to the pressure cooker and stir to combine.

5. Add the soaked beans and the broth. Stir to combine. Close the lid and make sure the pressure release valve is closed. Select the Pressure Cook function and set the cooking time to 10 minutes at high pressure.

6. When the cooking program is complete, allow the pressure to release naturally for as long as possible, then remove the lid.

7. Taste the soup, adding more salt, if needed, and serve hot.

NOTE: Preserved lemons are lemons that have been pickled in salt and their own juices. They add a briny tartness to many North African dishes. With preserved lemons, you use just the lemon rind, not the pulp, which is usually discarded. Preserved lemons are easy to make at home, but the process takes about 3 weeks. You can also find them in grocery stores with a good selection of international ingredients. If you cannot source preserved lemons, you can omit them here without affecting the final dish too much.

Pumpkin & Red Lentil Soup with Dukkah

SERVES 4 AS A MAIN COURSE, OR 6 AS A FIRST COURSE

3 tablespoons extra-virgin olive oil

1 yellow onion, diced

2 garlic cloves, minced

2 tablespoons tomato paste

2 teaspoons ground cumin

2 teaspoons ground cinnamon

1 teaspoon ground coriander

1 teaspoon ground allspice

1 teaspoon mild ground red chile, such as Aleppo pepper, or ½ teaspoon spicy red pepper flakes

1 teaspoon kosher salt

1 cup dried red lentils

4 cups Chicken Broth (page 72), Potager Vegetable Broth (page 70), or water

2 cups pumpkin purée, canned or homemade (see page 48)

3 tablespoons honey

Juice of 1 lemon

Labneh (page 52), Quick Labneh (page 191), or plain Greek yogurt, for serving

Dukkah (recipe follows), for serving

Pumpkin did not arrive in the Mediterranean until well after Europeans landed on the shores of the Americas and learned about this New World vegetable from the region's indigenous peoples. But in the intervening centuries, several Mediterranean cuisines, particularly those of Italy, North Africa, and the eastern Mediterranean, found that they appreciated pumpkin for its natural sweetness and meaty texture. In Turkey, for example, you will find desserts made from pumpkin, chunks of roast pumpkin folded into rice dishes, and sweet, earthy pumpkin soups like this one.

With plant-based protein from the lentils, this soup makes for a satisfying meatless lunch or dinner on a chilly day. (To make the soup vegetarian, not just meatless, be sure to use vegetable broth or water.) Or serve it as an easy make-ahead first course for an autumn dinner party with freshly baked Whole Wheat Pita (page 58) alongside.

1. Pour the olive oil into the inner pot of your electric pressure cooker. Select the Sauté function and set the heat level to "Less." When the oil is shimmering, after about 2 minutes, add the onion and sauté until softened, about 5 minutes.

2. Add the garlic, tomato paste, spices, and salt and sauté for a few minutes more, until fragrant. Press Cancel to turn off the Sauté function.

3. Add the lentils and broth. Close the lid and make sure the pressure release valve is closed. Select the Pressure Cook function and set the cooking time to 6 minutes at high pressure.

4. When the cooking program is complete, allow the pressure to release naturally for 10 minutes, then manually release the remaining pressure and remove the lid. Press Cancel to turn off the Keep Warm function. (Red lentils break down when cooked, so the texture of the soup will be thick and chunky.)

5. Select the Sauté function and set the heat level to "Less." Add the pumpkin and honey to the soup. Stir to combine. Cook until the soup is simmering and the pumpkin is heated through. Add the lemon juice. Taste and adjust the seasoning, adding more salt or honey as needed.

6. To serve, ladle the soup into four bowls. Top each with a dollop of labneh and sprinkle dukkah over the soup. Serve hot.

Dukkah

**MAKES ABOUT
1¾ CUPS**

---

1 cup blanched whole
  hazelnuts

½ cup shelled
  pistachios, preferably
  unsalted

¼ cup raw white
  sesame seeds

1 tablespoon fennel
  seeds

2 teaspoons cumin
  seeds

2 teaspoons coriander
  seeds

1 teaspoon kosher salt

Dukkah is an Egyptian nut and seed mixture that is used to add crunch and flavor to dips, spreads, and soups. The simplest way to enjoy dukkah is to sprinkle some on bread that has been dredged in olive oil. But that is only the beginning. Use it as a coating for fish, sprinkle it on salads, or use it to top Labneh (page 52) or Smooth and Creamy Hummus (page 41). And dukkah is absolute heaven on avocado toast.

Hazelnuts are the most traditional nut to use, but feel free to create your own house blend with almonds, walnuts, or pecans. Sesame, cumin, fennel, and coriander seeds are all part of an authentic dukkah, but what else you add is entirely up to you. Add sugar for a sweeter mixture or cayenne for a fiery one.

1. Place the hazelnuts and pistachios in a large skillet and toast over medium heat until fragrant, 2 to 3 minutes. Add the sesame, fennel, cumin, and coriander seeds and toast, stirring continuously, for a few minutes more, until everything smells toasty. (Do not let the nuts or seeds burn or get dark.)

2. Remove from the heat and allow the mixture to cool, then transfer to a food processor or spice grinder, working in batches as necessary, and pulse until the mixture resembles a coarse meal with some slightly larger pieces of nuts remaining. (Do not process too much or the mixture will turn into nut butter.)

3. Transfer the mixture to an airtight container and stir in the salt. Store dukkah in the freezer (to prevent rancidity) for up to 6 months.

Vegetable & Chickpea Tagine with Pickled Raisins

**SERVES 4 AS A
MAIN COURSE**

PICKLED RAISINS
½ cup golden raisins

½ cup apple cider vinegar

2 tablespoons sugar

TAGINE
3 tablespoons ghee or
  extra-virgin olive oil

1 large yellow onion, diced

2 garlic cloves, minced

1 tablespoon tomato paste

2 teaspoons ground cumin

1 teaspoon paprika

1 teaspoon ground coriander

1 teaspoon ground
  cinnamon

1 teaspoon kosher salt

2 red bell peppers, chopped

2 small to medium
  zucchini, halved and
  cut into wedges

2 small turnips, peeled
  and cut into wedges

1 bunch carrots, chopped

2 sweet potatoes, peeled
  and cubed

1 (15-ounce) can diced
  tomatoes with their juices

2 cups Potager Vegetable
  Broth (page 70) or water

1 (15-ounce) can chickpeas,
  drained and rinsed

2 teaspoons ras el hanout
  (optional)

¼ cup slivered almonds,
  for garnish (optional)

2 tablespoons chopped
  fresh flat-leaf parsley,
  for garnish

Rice with Vermicelli (page
  101) or cooked couscous,
  for serving (optional)

This Moroccan-inspired vegetable and chickpea stew is so healthy, satisfying, and full of flavor that no one will notice it is vegetarian. While this dish is easy enough to prepare on a busy weeknight, it is also elegant enough to serve to vegetarian guests at a dinner party, especially with its unusual pickled raisin garnish. Moroccan food is highly seasoned—but not spicy—so you will notice a wide range of spices in this recipe, from paprika to cinnamon. I highly recommend seeking out the North African spice blend ras el hanout. A mix of many different ingredients including pepper, cinnamon, nutmeg, allspice, cumin, cardamom pods, rose petals, and grains of paradise, ras el hanout adds sweet, earthy, and even floral notes to this vegetarian tagine and other North African–inspired dishes.

1. Make the pickled raisins: Place the raisins in a heatproof bowl. Combine the vinegar and sugar in a small saucepan and bring to a boil over high heat, stirring to dissolve the sugar. Pour the vinegar mixture over the raisins and set aside to cool to room temperature.

2. Make the tagine: Put the ghee in the inner pot of your electric pressure cooker. Select the Sauté function and set the heat level to "Normal." When the ghee has melted, after about 2 minutes, add the onion and sauté, stirring frequently, until softened, about 5 minutes.

3. Add the garlic, tomato paste, cumin, paprika, coriander, cinnamon, and salt and stir to combine. Sauté the mixture, stirring frequently to prevent scorching, for a few minutes more, until fragrant. Press Cancel to turn off the Sauté function.

4. Add the bell peppers, zucchini, turnips, carrots, sweet potatoes, and tomatoes and stir to combine. Add the broth.

5. Close the lid and make sure the pressure release valve is closed. Select the Pressure Cook function and set the cooking time to 5 minutes at high pressure. When the cooking program is complete, allow the pressure to release naturally for 10 minutes, then manually release the remaining pressure and remove the lid.

6. Add the chickpeas and ras el hanout (if using) to the stew. Simmer on the Keep Warm setting until the chickpeas are heated through, 5 to 10 minutes.

7. Divide the stew evenly among four bowls. Garnish with the pickled raisins, almonds, if desired, and parsley. Serve with rice or couscous, if you like.

NOTE: I suggest using ghee, or a type of clarified butter that comes from India, to sauté the vegetables for this dish as a nod to *smen*, a fermented butter used in traditional Moroccan tagines that can be hard to source in the United States. Ghee adds a rich, nutty flavor to this dish, as smen would, but feel free to use olive oil if that is easier or if you wish to keep the dish vegan.

Soupe au Pistou

SERVES 4 TO 6 AS A MAIN COURSE

SOUP

1 pound dried cannellini, great northern, or other white beans, 2 cups cooked beans, or 1 (15-ounce) can, drained and rinsed if canned

6 garlic cloves: 2 smashed and 4 minced

1 sprig rosemary

5 tablespoons extra-virgin olive oil

2 teaspoons kosher salt

1 yellow onion, diced

3 carrots, diced

1 leek, white and light green parts only, halved lengthwise and thinly sliced

1 medium zucchini, chopped

2 Roma (plum) tomatoes, diced

2 cups sliced green beans (1-inch pieces)

1 cup elbow macaroni or other small pasta

Freshly ground black pepper

Juice of 1 to 2 lemons

PISTOU

2 garlic cloves

Kosher salt

1¼ ounces fresh basil leaves, cut into ribbons

½ cup grated Parmigiano-Reggiano cheese, plus more for serving

¼ cup extra-virgin olive oil, plus more for drizzling

Soupe au pistou is a Provençal vegetable soup similar to Italian minestrone. Pistou is actually the Provençal version of pesto, which is similar to the Italian version but without any nuts or pine nuts. The pistou is used to garnish the soup, and diners swirl it into their bowls just before eating. In Provence, cooks often have summer and winter versions of this soup, making use of seasonal vegetables for each. This recipe, with zucchini, tomatoes, and green beans, is definitely a summer version, but I make it all year long using Roma (plum) tomatoes. With protein from the beans and water instead of broth as the soup's base, which is the authentic Provençal way, this soup is a satisfying vegetarian meal, especially when paired with a crusty baguette or Focaccia with Roasted Garlic (page 66).

1. If starting with dried beans, place the beans, the smashed garlic cloves, the rosemary, 2 tablespoons of the olive oil, and 1 teaspoon of the salt in the inner pot of your electric pressure cooker and cover with 7 cups cold water. Close the lid and make sure the pressure release valve is closed. Select the Pressure Cook function and set the cooking time to 30 minutes at high pressure.

2. When the cooking program is complete, allow the pressure to release naturally for at least 10 minutes, then manually release the remaining pressure and remove the lid. Transfer the beans and their cooking liquid to a bowl and set aside. (This may be done up to 5 days in advance; let cool, then refrigerate the beans in an airtight container with their cooking liquid.) Press Cancel to turn off the Keep Warm function.

3. Pour the remaining 3 tablespoons olive oil into the inner pot. Select the Sauté function and set the heat level to "Less." When the oil is shimmering, after about 2 minutes, add the onion and sauté until softened, about 3 minutes. Add the minced garlic, carrots, and leek and sauté until softened, 5 minutes more. Press Cancel to turn off the Sauté function.

4. Add the zucchini and tomatoes. If you started with dried beans, drain the beans, reserving as much of the cooking liquid as possible, then measure the liquid. Add

enough water to make 3 cups of liquid total and add the liquid to the pot. (If using cooked or canned beans, simply add 3 cups cold water to the pot.) Add 2 cups of the beans, the green beans, macaroni, remaining 1 teaspoon salt, and pepper to taste and stir to combine. (Reserve any remaining cooked beans for another use.)

5. Close the lid and make sure the pressure release valve is closed. Select the Pressure Cook function and set the cooking time to 3 minutes at high pressure.

6. While the soup is cooking, prepare the pistou. Place the garlic cloves in a mortar with a pinch of salt. Mash into a paste using the pestle. Add the basil and mash until the leaves have broken down. Using a fork, whisk in the grated cheese and olive oil. Taste and adjust the seasoning, adding more salt if necessary. Set aside.

7. When the cooking program is complete, allow the pressure to release naturally for 10 minutes, then manually release the remaining pressure and remove the lid. Add the lemon juice to the soup and taste. Adjust the seasoning if necessary, adding more lemon juice, salt, or pepper as needed.

8. To serve, ladle the soup into bowls and add a dollop of pistou and a drizzle of olive oil to each bowl. Serve topped with additional cheese.

Sopa de Ajo (Castilian Garlic Soup)

SERVES 2 AS A MAIN COURSE, OR 4 AS A FIRST COURSE

3 tablespoons extra-virgin olive oil, plus more for drizzling

6 garlic cloves, sliced

2 teaspoons Spanish smoked paprika

1 teaspoon kosher salt

4 cups 1-inch bread cubes, from a loaf of French or Italian bread, preferably day-old

5 to 6 cups Chicken Broth (page 72) or Potager Vegetable Broth (page 70)

2 large eggs, beaten

2 tablespoons chopped fresh flat-leaf parsley, for garnish

Freshly ground black pepper

This smoky, garlicky soup, known for its restorative powers, is a traditional Spanish dish for Semana Santa, the week leading up to Easter. Like Ribollita (page 74), *sopa de ajo* is true peasant food and an ingenious way to make use of leftover stale bread. In *The Food of Spain*, Claudia Roden notes that the more elegant version of garlic soup—which, like this version, includes egg—used to appear on the menus of Madrid cafés frequented by writers, artists, and other bohemians.

Even when you think you have no food in the house, you probably have the ingredients for sopa de ajo, and the whole thing comes together in mere minutes in an electric pressure cooker. When combined, the humble ingredients—bread, garlic, and eggs—become far more than the sum of their parts. For a heartier soup, stir in 4 ounces chopped cooked ham at the end of cooking.

1. Pour the olive oil into the inner pot of your electric pressure cooker. Select the Sauté function and set the heat level to "Less." When the oil is shimmering, after about 2 minutes, add the garlic and sauté until softened, about 2 minutes.

2. Add the paprika, salt, and bread cubes and toss to coat the bread with the oil and spices. Toast the bread for a few minutes more. Press Cancel to turn off the Sauté function.

3. Add 5 cups of the broth. Close the lid and make sure the pressure release valve is closed. Select the Pressure Cook function and set the cooking time to 5 minutes at high pressure.

4. When the cooking program is complete, allow the pressure to release naturally for 5 minutes, then manually release the remaining pressure and remove the lid. Press Cancel to turn off the Keep Warm function.

5. Select the Sauté function and set the heat level to "Less." If the soup appears to be too thick, thin it out with the remaining cup of broth. When the soup is simmering, pour in the beaten eggs and stir. Simmer just until the eggs are cooked, 30 to 60 seconds.

6. To serve, divide the soup evenly among two or four bowls. Drizzle each bowl with olive oil, garnish with the parsley, and season with pepper.

NOTE: If you have it in your pantry, smoked olive oil is especially delicious drizzled over this soup just prior to serving.

Bouillabaisse with Rouille & Garlic Toasts

**SERVES 4 AS
A MAIN COURSE**

ROUILLE

2 garlic cloves, smashed and peeled

1 tablespoon freshly squeezed lemon juice

1 large egg yolk

½ roasted red pepper, fresh or jarred

½ teaspoon kosher salt

⅛ teaspoon cayenne pepper

Pinch of saffron

¾ cup extra-virgin olive oil

¼ cup neutral oil, such as vegetable, grapeseed, or canola

GARLIC TOASTS

½ baguette, cut into ¼-inch-thick slices

2 to 3 tablespoons extra-virgin olive oil

3 garlic cloves, peeled

BOUILLABAISSE

2 tablespoons extra-virgin olive oil

2 tablespoons unsalted butter

1 yellow onion, sliced

1 leek, white and light green parts only, halved lengthwise and thinly sliced

1 bulb fennel, cored and sliced, fronds reserved

3 garlic cloves, smashed

1 tablespoon tomato paste

1 teaspoon kosher salt

½ teaspoon freshly ground black pepper

¼ teaspoon red pepper flakes

¼ teaspoon saffron

2 tablespoons anise-flavored liqueur, such as ouzo or pastis (optional)

1 (15-ounce) can diced tomatoes with their juices

1½ cups Fish Stock (page 88), seafood stock, or clam juice

Several long strips of orange zest

2 pounds flaky, white-fleshed fish fillets, such as cod, halibut, snapper, branzino, sea bass, or monkfish (aim for a combination of at least two or preferably three different fish)

2 tablespoons chopped fresh flat-leaf parsley, for garnish

This is one of the more elaborate recipes in the book, but imagine how satisfying it is to make a beautiful bouillabaisse, complete with garlic toasts and homemade red pepper mayonnaise—known as *rouille* in French—in your own kitchen. This electric pressure cooker bouillabaisse is eminently doable, especially because you do not need to bring home the whole fish counter. Pick two or three varieties of fish from the ones I list, depending on what is available near you, and you will come close enough to replicating a true bouillabaisse from Marseilles.

You will notice that this recipe does not include shellfish. Bouillabaisse is traditionally a fish stew, designed to use up the parts of the catch that the fisherman was unable to sell that day. The flavors of fennel and saffron, combined with fish, are the key elements for authentic bouillabaisse.

1. Make the rouille: Place the garlic, lemon juice, egg yolk, roasted pepper, salt, cayenne, and saffron in a food processor and blend until smooth. With the motor running, slowly pour in the oils in a thin, steady stream. Keep blending until the mixture emulsifies and become thick like mayonnaise. Refrigerate until needed. (This may be done up to 1 week in advance; store the rouille in an airtight container in the refrigerator.)

2. To make the garlic toasts, preheat the oven to 450°F. Brush both sides of the bread slices with olive oil and arrange them in a single layer on a baking sheet. Bake until the bread is firm, crisp, and golden brown, 9 to 12 minutes. When the bread is cool enough to handle, rub one side of each slice with a whole, raw garlic clove. When one clove gets too small to hold, use a new clove. (The rough surface of the bread will act like a grater, breaking down the garlic cloves.) Set aside until needed.

3. To make the bouillabaisse, add the olive oil and butter to the electric pressure cooker. Select the Sauté function and set the heat level to "Normal." When the oil is shimmering and the butter is melted, after about 2 minutes, add the onion and sauté until softened, about 3 minutes. Add the leek, fennel, and garlic and sauté until they have softened and are beginning to take on a little color, about 5 minutes. Add the tomato paste, salt, black pepper, red pepper flakes, saffron, and anise-

flavored liqueur (if using) and sauté for an additional minute, until fragrant and most of the liquid has evaporated. Press Cancel to turn off the Sauté function.

4. Add the tomatoes, stock, and several long strips of zest from the orange and stir to combine. Lay the fish on top of the vegetables, but do not stir it in. Close the lid and make sure the pressure release valve is closed. Select the Pressure Cook function and set the cooking time to 0 minutes at low pressure. (It will take the pressure cooker about 14 minutes to come to pressure and the fish will cook through during that time.)

5. When the cooking program is complete, release the pressure manually and remove the lid. If any of your fish fillets came with skin attached, remove them with a slotted spoon, peel off the skin, and discard it. Return the fish to the pressure cooker. At this point, you can break the fillets up into smaller pieces for easier serving if desired.

6. Taste the soup and adjust the seasoning, adding more salt, black pepper, or orange zest if needed.

7. To serve, divide the soup among four bowls, making sure each bowl gets some of each variety of fish. Garnish each bowl with the parsley and some of the reserved fennel fronds. Pass the garlic toasts and rouille separately.

Fish Stock

MAKES 2 QUARTS

1 leek, white and light green parts only, sliced

1 bulb fennel, quartered

1 yellow onion, quartered

3 pounds bones or heads from white-fleshed fish, such as halibut, cod, or sea bass, rinsed

Several sprigs fresh flat-leaf parsley

Several sprigs fresh thyme

1 bay leaf

½ teaspoon whole black peppercorns

If you would like to try making your own fish stock—for Bouillabaisse or to use in other seafood soups and stews—it is very easy to do in an electric pressure cooker. Ask your fishmonger for bones or heads from white-fleshed fish. (Oily fishes like salmon are too strong.) You may have to request them a day in advance, but the vendor should give them to you for free or quite cheaply.

1. Place all the ingredients in the inner pot of your electric pressure cooker and cover with 8 cups cold water. (Do not fill the inner pot more than two-thirds full.)

2. Close the lid and make sure the pressure release valve is closed. Select the Pressure Cook function and set the cooking time to 30 minutes at high pressure.

3. When the cooking program is complete, allow the pressure to release naturally for at least 20 minutes, then manually release the remaining pressure and remove the lid. Use a large strainer to scoop the bones and vegetables out of the stock and discard the solids.

4. Line a fine-mesh strainer with cheesecloth or muslin and place it over a large bowl. Strain the broth into the bowl to catch the remaining solids or any impurities.

5. Fish stock tastes best when freshly made, but it will keep in a large airtight glass or plastic container in the refrigerator for up to 3 days or in the freezer for up to 2 months.

Chraime (North African Spicy Fish Stew)

**SERVES 4 AS A
MAIN COURSE**

3 tablespoons extra-
virgin olive oil

1 yellow onion, sliced

1 red bell pepper, sliced

1 jalapeño, seeded and
sliced

8 garlic cloves, thinly
sliced

1 tablespoon tomato
paste

1 tablespoon harissa
(optional)

1½ teaspoons ground
cumin

1 teaspoon sweet
paprika

1 teaspoon smoked
paprika

½ teaspoon ground
turmeric

½ teaspoon kosher
salt, plus more for
seasoning

1 (15-ounce) can diced
tomatoes, with their
juices

1 cup Fish Stock
(page 88), seafood
stock, clam juice, or
water

1 teaspoon sugar

1¼ pounds flaky,
white-fleshed fish
fillets, such as
snapper, halibut,
grouper, or cod

Several sprigs fresh
cilantro, stems
removed, for garnish

Whole Wheat Pita
(page 58) or cooked
couscous, for serving
(optional)

This type of spicy tomato-and-pepper fish stew is common all over North Africa, from Libya to Morocco, where it is known as *dag hareef*. Chraime, the Libyan name, was a traditional Friday-night and holiday dish among Sephardic Jews. Today, it is quite popular in Israel, where there is a large North African population. This stew offers bold flavors and is a complete one-dish meal, especially when served with Whole Wheat Pita (page 58), a crusty baguette, or couscous. The electric pressure cooker gently poaches the fish in the liquid and prevents the smell of fish from permeating your entire kitchen.

1. Pour the olive oil into the inner pot of your electric pressure cooker. Select the Sauté function and set the heat level to "Normal." When the oil is shimmering, after about 2 minutes, add the onion and sauté until softened, about 3 minutes. Add the bell pepper, jalapeño, and garlic and sauté until softened, about 5 minutes. Add the tomato paste, harissa (if using), cumin, sweet paprika, smoked paprika, turmeric, and salt and sauté for an additional minute, until fragrant. Press Cancel to turn off the Sauté function.

2. Add the tomatoes with their juices, stock, and sugar and stir to combine. Lay the fish fillets on top of the other ingredients (do not stir). Close the lid and make sure the pressure release valve is closed. Select the Pressure Cook function and set the cooking time to 0 minutes at low pressure. (The pressure cooker will take about 13 minutes to come to pressure, during which time the fish will cook.) When the cooking program is complete, release the pressure manually and remove the lid.

3. If your fish came with the skin attached, remove it from the pot with a slotted spoon, and peel off and discard the skin. Return the fish to the soup.

4. Taste the soup and adjust the seasoning, adding more salt, if needed.

5. Divide the soup among four bowls, making sure each bowl gets a good amount of fish. Garnish with cilantro and serve with pita or couscous, if desired.

4

GRAINS, VEGETABLES & PULSES

Classic Tabbouleh with Parsley & Mint

SERVES 6 TO 8 AS A SIDE DISH

1 cup bulgur wheat

6 tablespoons freshly squeezed lemon juice

3 cups chopped fresh flat-leaf parsley

3 cups diced fresh tomatoes

1 cup finely diced red onion

1 cup chopped fresh mint

3 tablespoons extra-virgin olive oil

1 teaspoon kosher salt

Freshly ground black pepper

Some tabbouleh recipes call for you to rinse bulgur in cold water; others instruct you to soak the bulgur in warm water—or maybe boiling water—for 10 minutes or 30 minutes or even an hour. Why all the different instructions? It's because bulgur comes in different grinds, including coarse, medium, and fine. A cold-water rinse might soften finely ground bulgur, but it will do little for coarser grinds. Rather than try to guess what variety your bulgur is, I recommend cooking it in an electric pressure cooker for a mere 12 minutes. The grains come out tender but firm and not at all gummy—perfect for tossing with lots of fresh herbs and tomatoes to make a classic tabbouleh.

This recipe calls for a lot of knife work, but do not be tempted to use a food processor to chop the parsley and mint. It will bruise the herbs, making them taste grassy and bitter. Use your sharpest blade to chop them finely and practice those knife skills!

1. Place the bulgur and 1¼ cups water in the inner pot of your electric pressure cooker and stir to combine. Close the lid and make sure the pressure release valve is closed. Select the Rice function or the Pressure Cook function and set the cooking time to 12 minutes at low pressure.

2. When the cooking program is complete, release the pressure manually and remove the lid. Fluff the bulgur with a fork, transfer the inner pot to a cooling rack, and allow the bulgur to cool slightly.

3. While the bulgur is still warm, sprinkle ¼ cup of the lemon juice over it and toss to combine. (The warm grains will absorb the liquid, giving the whole dish extra flavor.)

4. Combine the parsley, tomatoes, onion, and mint in a large bowl. Add the bulgur and toss gently to combine.

5. Whisk together the remaining 2 tablespoons lemon juice, the olive oil, and salt in a small bowl and pour the dressing over the salad. Toss to coat. Taste and season with pepper and additional salt if needed.

6. Allow the salad to stand for at least 30 minutes prior to serving for the flavors to develop.

Jeweled Barley Salad with Apricot, Pine Nuts & Pomegranate

SERVES 6 TO 8 AS A SIDE DISH

1½ cups pearl barley

Zest and juice of 2 lemons

1 tablespoon honey

½ teaspoon kosher salt

Freshly ground black pepper

⅓ cup extra-virgin olive oil

1 shallot, minced

1 bunch scallions, white and light green parts only, sliced

¾ cup chopped dried Turkish apricots

⅓ cup pine nuts, toasted

Seeds of 1 pomegranate

Barley is an ancient grain treasured in the Mediterranean for its nutty flavor and toothsome texture. When cooked in soup, barley breaks down and becomes thick and creamy. But when cooled and tossed in a salad, as here, the grains stay distinct and pleasantly chewy. An electric pressure cooker takes all the guesswork out of cooking whole grains like barley, and ensures a perfect result every time. Just be sure to use pearl barley, as specified, not hulled barley, which takes much longer to cook.

With jewel-like pops of color from the golden apricots and ruby-red pomegranate seeds, this barley salad is exceptionally pretty, as well as healthy and satisfying. Add the sweet-tart lemon-honey dressing to the barley while it is still warm to help the grains soak it up. This salad can sit at room temperature for hours, making it a perfect potluck dish.

1. Place the barley in the inner pot of your electric pressure cooker and cover with 2¼ cups cold water. Close the lid and make sure the pressure release valve is closed. Select the Pressure Cook function and set the cooking time to 25 minutes at high pressure.

2. Meanwhile, whisk together the zest from one of the lemons, the juice from both lemons, honey, salt, and pepper to taste in a small bowl. While whisking, slowly pour in the olive oil and continue whisking until emulsified. Set aside.

3. When the cooking program is complete, allow the pressure to release naturally for 10 minutes, then manually release any remaining pressure and remove the lid.

4. Spread the barley on a rimmed baking sheet and while the grains are still warm, pour the dressing over them. Carefully toss the grains so they are all coated with the dressing and separated. Allow to cool.

5. Transfer the cooled barley to a large serving bowl. Add the shallot, scallions, apricots, pine nuts, and pomegranate seeds and stir to combine. Serve at room temperature.

Tomato Bulgur Pilaf

**SERVES 4 AS
A SIDE DISH**

3 tablespoons extra-
virgin olive oil

1 yellow onion, diced

1 tablespoon tomato
paste

2 to 3 tomatoes, diced

1 teaspoon kosher salt

1 teaspoon smoked
paprika

1 cup coarse to medium
bulgur wheat

1¼ cups Chicken Broth
(page 72), Potager
Vegetable Broth
(page 70), or water

Labneh (page 52),
Cucumber Tzatziki
(page 56), or plain
Greek yogurt, for
serving

Homey bulgur pilaf is eaten as a side dish throughout Turkey and Lebanon. Rice is not grown in Turkey, and until recent times, it was considered a luxury ingredient. Thus, bulgur is the traditional grain in Turkish cuisine. This kind of simple bulgur pilaf is commonly served alongside grilled meats and kebabs. As noted on page 92, bulgur comes in many grinds, from coarse to extra fine. For salads and other cold dishes, Turkish cooks prefer finely ground bulgur, but for a cooked pilaf such as this, they use a coarse to medium grind. When shopping, look for whole-grain bulgur that is close to the size of short-grain rice versus finely ground bulgur, which is as small as grains of sand. An electric pressure cooker cooks whole grains exceptionally well, and bulgur is no exception.

1. Pour the olive oil into the inner pot of your electric pressure cooker. Select the Sauté function and set the heat level to "Less." When the oil is shimmering, after about 2 minutes, add the onion and sauté until softened, about 5 minutes. Add the tomato paste, tomatoes, salt, and smoked paprika and stir to combine. Sauté for a few minutes more, until fragrant.

2. Add the bulgur, stir to combine, and sauté for 2 minutes. Press Cancel to turn off the Sauté function.

3. Add the broth. Close the lid and make sure the pressure release valve is closed.

Select the Rice function or the Pressure Cook function and set the cooking time to 12 minutes at low pressure. When the cooking program is complete, release the pressure manually and remove the lid.

4. Bulgur pilaf is often served in individual portions. To serve it the traditional way, place some pilaf in a small bowl or ramekin and pack it tightly. Place a plate on top of the bowl and flip it over. The pilaf should hold its shape and remain in a dome. Garnish with labneh, tzatziki, or yogurt, as desired.

NOTE: Bob's Red Mill whole grain red bulgur, which is available at grocery stores with a good selection of international ingredients or whole grains, is suitable for this recipe.

Squash Blossom Risotto

SERVES 4 AS A SIDE DISH OR FIRST COURSE, OR 2 AS A MAIN COURSE

3 tablespoons unsalted butter

2 tablespoons extra-virgin olive oil

2 shallots, minced

Kosher salt

1½ cups Arborio rice or other short-grain Italian rice

¼ cup white wine

3¼ cups Chicken Broth (page 72), warm or at room temperature

¾ cup grated Parmigiano-Reggiano or Grana Padano cheese, plus more for serving

Zest and juice of 1 lemon

Kosher salt and freshly ground black pepper

12 squash blossoms, cut into ribbons

8 fresh basil leaves, cut into ribbons

I love the creamy texture and comforting simplicity of a bowl of risotto. But standing over the stove, stirring continuously for 20, 30, or even 40 minutes, is hardly my idea of a good time—especially on a busy weeknight. Thankfully, an electric pressure cooker takes all the work out of risotto, making this Italian comfort food accessible any day of the week. This version of risotto highlights fragile squash blossoms, a favorite midsummer farmers' market find. While squash blossoms are most often served fried, in Italy they are also incorporated into pasta, used to top pizza, and folded into risotto. This dish is all about subtlety—the delicate zucchini flavor of the squash blossoms married with the ethereal texture of risotto. Serve it as a starter for an elegant summer dinner party or enjoy it as a meatless main course for two.

1. Place 2 tablespoons of the butter and the olive oil in the inner pot of your electric pressure cooker. Select the Sauté function and set the heat level to "Less." When the butter has melted and the oil is shimmering, after about 2 minutes, add the shallots and sauté until softened, about 3 minutes. Season with a pinch of salt.

2. Add the rice and stir to coat the grains. Toast the rice until fragrant, about 3 minutes. Add the wine and simmer until the liquid has been absorbed, about 1 minute. Press Cancel to turn off the Sauté function.

3. Add 3 cups of the broth and stir to combine. Close the lid and make sure the pressure release valve is closed. Select the Pressure Cook function and set the cooking time to 6 minutes at high pressure. When the cooking program is complete, release the pressure manually and remove the lid.

4. Add the cheese and stir briskly until the rice has absorbed the remaining liquid. Add the lemon zest and juice and season with salt and pepper.

5. Add the squash blossoms and basil and stir gently to combine. Taste and adjust the seasoning. For added richness, stir in the remaining tablespoon of butter. If the risotto is too thick, stir in the remaining broth a little bit at a time.

6. Serve immediately with additional grated cheese.

NOTE: Leftover risotto does not reheat especially well, so if you have some extra, consider making Arancini di Riso (page 194).

Butternut Squash & Kale Farrotto

**SERVES 4 TO 6 AS
A STARTER OR SIDE,
OR 2 OR 3 AS A
MAIN COURSE**

1 butternut squash

3 tablespoons extra-
virgin olive oil, plus
more for drizzling

¾ cup minced shallots

2 garlic cloves, minced

1 teaspoon kosher
salt, plus more for
seasoning

½ teaspoon freshly
ground black
pepper, plus more
for seasoning

Pinch of red pepper
flakes

1½ cups farro perlato

¼ cup white wine

3 cups Chicken Broth
(page 72) or Potager
Vegetable Broth
(page 70)

3 cups chopped kale
leaves (woody stems
removed)

1 cup grated
Parmigiano-Reggiano
cheese, plus more for
serving

Juice of ½ lemon

Farro is nothing more than an ancient form of wheat, which is sometimes also known as emmer. Small but powerful, farro has a nutty flavor and a springy, al dente texture and is exactly the kind of nutritious whole grain that makes Mediterranean food so healthy. My favorite way to prepare farro is to cook it like risotto by gradually adding warm broth to the toasted grains until they are tender. The grains stay perfectly toothsome and separate, yet the final dish is creamy and deeply comforting, especially on a cold night. As you might imagine, a farro risotto, or *farrotto*, can take as long as 45 minutes on the stove—with constant attention required—but an electric pressure cooker streamlines the whole process. You even cook the butternut squash in the pressure cooker for easier cleanup.

1. To prepare the squash, cut off the stem and cut the squash in half lengthwise. Scoop out the seeds. Cut both pieces in half cross-wise, then cut the pieces from the top of the squash—the thicker unscooped part—in half again.

2. Place the trivet in the electric pressure cooker and add 1½ cups water. Arrange the pieces of squash on the trivet in as close to a single layer as possible. Close the lid and make sure the pressure release valve is closed. Select the Pressure Cook function and set the cooking time to 12 minutes at high pressure.

3. When the cooking program is complete, release the pressure manually and remove the lid. Remove the squash using tongs and place the pieces on a cutting board until cool enough to handle. Turn off the pressure cooker and dump out the water.

4. Cut or peel off the skin of the squash; it should come off quite easily. Cut half of the squash into cubes and set aside, reserving the remaining squash for another use.

5. To make the farrotto, add the olive oil to the inner pot. Select the Sauté function and set the heat level to "Less." When the oil is shimmering, after about 2 minutes, add the shallots and sauté until softened, about 3 minutes.

6. Add the garlic and sauté for a few minutes more. Season with the salt, black pepper, and red pepper flakes.

7. Add the farro and toss to coat with the oil. Toast the farro grains until slightly darkened and fragrant, about 3 minutes.

8. Add the white wine and cook until nearly evaporated, about 30 seconds. Press Cancel to turn off the Sauté function.

9. Add the broth to the farro and stir to combine. Add the cubed squash, close the lid and make sure the pressure release valve is closed. Select the Pressure Cook function and set the cooking time to 12 minutes at high pressure.

10. When the cooking program is complete, release the pressure manually and remove the lid. Turn off the pressure cooker and then select the Sauté function and set the heat level to "Less."

11. Add the chopped kale and grated cheese and stir to combine. Taste and adjust the seasoning, adding more salt and black pepper as needed. Sauté, stirring, until most of the remaining liquid has been absorbed or has evaporated. Add the lemon juice and stir to combine.

12. Spoon the farrotto into shallow pasta bowls. Drizzle olive oil over each bowl and pass more grated cheese at the table. Serve immediately.

Polenta with Butter & Cheese

SERVES 4 TO 6 AS A SIDE DISH

6 tablespoons (¾ stick) unsalted butter

1½ cups polenta, yellow corn grits (not instant), or coarse stone-ground cornmeal

1 teaspoon kosher salt, plus more for seasoning

½ cup grated Parmigiano-Reggiano or pecorino cheese, plus more for serving

Freshly ground black pepper

In America, pasta, potatoes, and rice are staple side dishes, and we tend to overlook Italian's beloved cornmeal porridge, polenta. But what a side dish it is! Polenta is creamy, comforting, and the perfect bed for stews, braises, and all manner of tomato-based sauces. It even makes dreamy leftovers, especially if you cut the cold polenta into slices and pan-fry it—or, better yet, make Polenta Fries in the air fryer (see page 206).

I think part of the reason we hesitate to cook polenta at home is the same reason we hesitate to cook risotto at home: we just don't have time to stand over the stove, stirring continuously for 30 to 40 minutes. But as with risotto, an electric pressure cooker makes cooking polenta easy and almost entirely hands-off. I especially like to serve this polenta with Italian Sausage Ragù (page 137).

1. Add 2 tablespoons of the butter to the electric pressure cooker. Select the Sauté function and set the heat level to "Less." When the butter has melted, after about 2 minutes, add the polenta and stir to coat the grains with the butter. Toast the polenta for 1 minute.

2. Press Cancel to turn off the Sauté function. Add 5 cups water and the salt to the polenta and stir to combine.

3. Close the lid and make sure the pressure release valve is closed. Select the Pressure Cook function and set the cooking time to 12 minutes at high pressure. When the cooking program is complete, allow the pressure to release naturally for at least 15 minutes, then manually release the remaining pressure and remove the lid.

4. Stir the polenta thoroughly with a spatula, scraping up anything stuck to the bottom of the pot. (Typically, the top layer of the polenta will be thin with more liquid, while the bottom layer will be thick and might be sticking to the pot. Continue to stir until the polenta is an even consistency throughout.)

5. Cut the remaining 4 tablespoons (½ stick) butter into pieces and add it to the polenta, stirring until the butter is melted. Stir in the cheese. Taste and adjust the seasoning, adding more salt and pepper if needed.

6. Transfer the polenta to a bowl for serving, passing more grated cheese at the table. Polenta will keep for several days in an airtight container in the refrigerator. Reheat in the microwave or in a pan on the stovetop, adding water, milk, or broth as needed to thin the polenta.

NOTE: If left to sit, cooked polenta will stick to the bottom of the inner pot and create a mess. I recommend soaking the pot as soon as you remove the polenta for easier cleanup.

Rice with Vermicelli

3 tablespoons clarified
butter, ghee, or extra-
virgin olive oil

½ cup vermicelli or
angel hair pasta
(broken into pieces
1 to 2 inches long)

1 garlic clove, minced

1½ cups long-grain
white rice, such as
basmati or jasmine

2½ cups Chicken Broth
(page 72) or water

Pinch of kosher salt

⅓ cup chopped fresh
flat-leaf parsley, for
garnish

¼ cup pine nuts,
toasted, for garnish

Rice is the staple grain of the Levant, and this simple rice and noodle pilaf is one of the most common side dishes throughout the Middle East, but especially in Lebanon. Broken pieces of thin pasta, such as angel hair or vermicelli, are toasted until golden brown and then cooked with rice to make a versatile side dish that puts plain rice to shame. Serve alongside grilled meats and vegetables, or Middle Eastern- and North African-inspired dishes.

In Lebanon, clarified butter is the preferred fat for toasting the vermicelli. Ghee, a form of clarified butter that is readily available in grocery stores, works very well here, despite being more typically known as an Indian ingredient. To keep this dish dairy-free, however, it is perfectly acceptable to use olive oil to toast the pasta.

1. Place the clarified butter in the inner pot of your electric pressure cooker. Select the Sauté function and set the heat level to "Normal." When the butter has melted, after about 2 minutes, add the vermicelli and toast the pasta, stirring frequently, until golden brown, about 3 minutes. Add the garlic and sauté until fragrant, about 30 seconds. Press Cancel to turn off the Sauté function.

2. Add the rice and stir to coat the grains with the butter. Cover the rice mixture with the broth and add the salt. Close the lid and make sure the pressure release valve is closed.

3. Select the Rice function or the Pressure Cook function and set the cooking time to 12 minutes at low pressure.

4. When the cooking program is complete, allow the pressure to release naturally for 10 minutes and remove the lid. Fluff the rice with a fork. Cover the inner pot with a clean dish towel and allow the rice to steam for 10 additional minutes.

5. Garnish with the parsley and pine nuts. Serve warm or at room temperature.

NOTE: Some Middle Eastern markets sell vermicelli broken into small pieces for this very purpose. I find that it is just as easy to use angel hair or capellini pasta and break it into pieces by hand.

Fasolakia (Braised Green Beans with Tomato)

SERVES 4 TO 6 AS A SIDE DISH

¼ cup extra-virgin olive oil, plus more for drizzling

1 yellow onion, diced

3 garlic cloves, minced

2 teaspoons kosher salt, plus more for seasoning

1½ teaspoons baharat (see Note)

Pinch of red pepper flakes

1½ pounds green beans, trimmed

1 (28-ounce) can whole tomatoes, with their juices

1 teaspoon sugar

Juice of 1 lemon

We have become so fixated on crisp-tender as the only proper texture for cooked vegetables that we have forgotten the pleasure of tender, velvety long-cooked vegetables. Let this recipe remind you. Long-simmered green beans, stewed with onion and tomato, is a homey, Grandma-style dish that you find with slight variations all over the Mediterranean, from Italy and Greece to Egypt and Lebanon. While braising green beans until meltingly tender can take as long as an hour, or even more, on the stove, you can achieve the same texture with just a few minutes of pressure cooking. Serve these green beans over rice or couscous, with Whole Wheat Pita (page 58), or alongside grilled chicken or lamb. They are equally good hot or at room temperature. I like to drizzle them with a fruity olive oil before serving.

1. Pour the olive oil into the inner pot of your electric pressure cooker. Select the Sauté function and set the heat level to "Less." When the oil is shimmering, after about 2 minutes, add the onion and sauté until softened, about 3 minutes.

2. Add the garlic, salt, baharat, and red pepper flakes and sauté for a few minutes more, until fragrant. Press Cancel to turn off the Sauté function.

3. Add the green beans, tomatoes with their juices, and sugar. Close the lid and make sure the pressure release valve is closed. Select the Pressure Cook function and set the cooking time to 5 minutes at high pressure.

4. When the cooking program is complete, release the pressure manually and remove the lid.

5. Add the lemon juice and taste and adjust the seasoning, adding more salt or spices as needed.

6. Before serving, drizzle the green beans with olive oil. Serve hot or at room temperature.

NOTE: Baharat is a warm, earthy Middle Eastern spice blend that typically contains paprika, coriander, cumin, cardamom, allspice, cloves, nutmeg, cinnamon, and black pepper. You can find it at grocery stores with a good spice section, Middle Eastern grocers, and online.

Goat Cheese–Stuffed Tomatoes

SERVES 4 TO 6 AS A SIDE DISH, OR 3 OR 4 AS A MAIN COURSE

12 ounces fresh goat cheese

¼ cup heavy cream

2 garlic cloves, minced

¼ cup chopped fresh herbs, such as basil, flat-leaf parsley, and oregano

½ teaspoon kosher salt

½ teaspoon freshly ground black pepper

7 or 8 medium tomatoes on the vine

¼ cup extra-virgin olive oil

Luscious, late-season tomatoes stuffed with bread crumbs, herbs, and cheese and baked in a hot oven is an iconic side dish in the South of France. Here, I have updated the classic Provençal stuffed tomato for quick cooking in an electric pressure cooker. Instead of bread crumbs, I fill these tomatoes with a seasoned herb-and-goat-cheese mixture for a gluten-free version of this beloved dish. After just a few minutes in the electric pressure cooker, the tomatoes become soft and the goat cheese filling turns deliciously smooth and runny, almost like a sauce. These quick and easy stuffed tomatoes are a delightful accompaniment to grilled meats in the summertime or serve them any time of year alongside a green salad as a light lunch. I recommend using tomatoes on the vine, which are often the most flavorful variety of supermarket tomatoes, for an especially elegant presentation.

1. Mix together the goat cheese, heavy cream, garlic, herbs, salt, and pepper in a medium bowl and mash with a fork to combine.

2. Cut the tops off the tomatoes and set aside. Scoop the tomato cores and seeds into a large bowl and set aside.

3. Strain the liquid from the reserved tomato cores into a measuring cup and add water as needed to make 1 cup of liquid total. Add the liquid to the inner pot of the pressure cooker.

4. Spoon the goat cheese mixture into the tomatoes, mounding the filling over the tops. Place the trivet in your electric pressure cooker and arrange the tomatoes on the trivet. Place the tops back on the tomatoes and drizzle with the olive oil.

5. Close the lid and make sure the pressure release valve is closed. Select the Pressure Cook function and set the cooking time to 2 minutes at high pressure.

6. When the cooking program is complete, release the pressure manually and remove the lid. Carefully remove the tomatoes with a slotted spoon and arrange on a platter. Serve immediately.

Mujadara

SERVES 2 AS A MAIN COURSE, OR 4 AS A SIDE DISH

1 cup long-grain white rice, such as basmati

2 tablespoons extra-virgin olive oil

1 yellow onion, diced

3 garlic cloves, minced

1½ teaspoons ground cumin

1 teaspoon ground coriander

½ teaspoon ground cinnamon

½ teaspoon ground allspice

½ teaspoon ground ginger

1 teaspoon kosher salt

Zest and juice of 1 lemon

1 cup brown or green lentils

¼ cup chopped fresh flat-leaf parsley

6 ounces shallots (optional; see Note)

Cucumber Tzatziki (page 56) or Tahini Sauce (page 121), for serving (optional)

One of most iconic and beloved comfort food dishes in the Middle East is *mujadara* (sometimes written *mejadra*), which is simply rice and lentils cooked together and gently flavored with sweet and earthy spices. Mujadara is not only delicious and healthy, but it is also extremely versatile. You can serve it hot or at room temperature. Mujadara can be both the base for a satisfying and complete vegetarian main course or a side dish for Middle Eastern–inspired meals. And did I mention it is both gluten-free and vegan?

Mujadara is traditionally topped with a tangle of fried onions. If you own an air fryer—or an air fryer lid for your pressure cooker—you can make deliciously crispy fried shallots with almost no oil, and they make an outstanding garnish for a bowl of mujadara. A drizzle of Tahini Sauce (page 121) or Cucumber Tzatziki (page 56) is the perfect finishing touch.

1. Rinse the rice in several changes of cold water. If time permits, soak the rice in water for 1 hour and drain.

2. Pour the olive oil into the inner pot of your electric pressure cooker. Select the Sauté function and set the heat level to "Less." When the oil is shimmering, after about 2 minutes, add the onion and sauté until softened, about 5 minutes. Add the garlic, spices, salt, and lemon zest and sauté an additional minute until fragrant. Press Cancel to turn off the Sauté function.

3. Add the drained rice and the lentils and cover with 2½ cups of cold water. Close the lid and make sure the pressure release valve is closed. Select the Rice function or the Pressure Cook function and set the cooking time to 12 minutes at low pressure. When the cooking program is complete, allow the pressure to release naturally for 10 minutes.

4. Open the lid and fluff the mujadara with a fork. Add the lemon juice and parsley and stir gently to combine.

5. Serve warm or at room temperature with an optional garnish of fried shallots, if desired, and a sauce such as tzatziki or tahini sauce.

NOTE: To make fried shallots in the air fryer, peel the shallots and slice them as thinly as possible. Place the sliced shallots in the basket of the air fryer. Cook at 250°F for 5 minutes, then open the air fryer and shake the basket to toss the shallots. Repeat, cooking the shallots at 250°F and shaking and tossing them every 5 minutes, until they become brown and crispy, 30 to 35 minutes. Halfway through the cooking time, after 15 to 20 minutes, spray the shallots with oil. Once all the shallots are browned, remove them from the air fryer. They will crisp up as they cool.

Braised Fennel

3 bulbs fennel

4 tablespoons (½ stick)
unsalted butter

1 teaspoon kosher
salt, plus more for
seasoning

1 teaspoon sugar

2 tablespoons licorice-
flavored liqueur,
such as ouzo, pastis,
anisette, or sambuca
(optional)

½ cup white wine

½ cup Chicken Broth
(page 72)

1 tablespoon orange
zest

Freshly ground black
pepper

Fennel is native to the Mediterranean, and indeed, wild fennel grows all over the region, from southern France to Sicily to the Greek Isles. While every Mediterranean cuisine uses fennel to some extent, the Italians are especially fond of this bulbous vegetable for salads, soups, and as a *contorno*, or side dish.

Fennel can be divisive. Some people love its licorice-like flavor and others cannot stand it. Many of us have only tried fennel raw—in a salad, for example—where the flavor is especially pronounced. But cooking fennel tends to sweeten it and mellow the licorice bite. When cooking fennel, I actually double down on the anise flavor by adding a splash of a licorice-flavored spirit, which abound in the Mediterranean, to the braising liquid. Feel free to skip that step if you don't have one of these spirits in your liquor cabinet or prefer a milder licorice flavor.

1. Trim the stalks and bottom of the fennel bulbs, reserving a small amount of the fronds for garnish. Cut the bulbs in half lengthwise through the core, then cut each half into quarters, leaving some of the core intact so the wedges hold together. Set aside.

2. Place the butter in the inner pot of your electric pressure cooker. Select the Sauté function and set the heat level to "Normal." When the butter has melted, after about 3 minutes, add the fennel, salt, and sugar and stir to coat the fennel in the butter. Sauté the fennel, stirring occasionally, until it begins to brown and caramelize, about 8 minutes. Add the liqueur (if using) and let the liquid bubble away until it has almost completely evaporated. Press Cancel to turn off the Sauté function.

3. Add the wine and broth to the pot. Close the lid and make sure the pressure release valve is closed. Select the Pressure Cook function and set the cooking time to 2 minutes at high pressure. When the cooking program is complete, release the pressure manually and remove the lid. Remove the fennel to a serving platter using a slotted spoon, leaving the liquid behind.

4. Select the Sauté function and set the heat level to "Normal." Simmer the liquid until reduced, about 5 minutes.

5. Spoon the sauce over the fennel. Garnish with the reserved fennel fronds and the orange zest. Season with pepper and additional salt, if needed, and serve.

Ratatouille

**SERVES 4 AS A
SIDE DISH, OR
2 OR 3 AS A MAIN
COURSE**

½ cup plus
2 tablespoons extra-
virgin olive oil, plus
more for drizzling

1 yellow onion, halved
and sliced

1¾ to 2 teaspoons
kosher salt

3 garlic cloves, minced

1 large or 2 small red
bell peppers, sliced

1 large zucchini, sliced
into ¼-inch-thick
rounds

1 medium eggplant,
cut into 1-inch cubes

2 tomatoes, preferably
Roma (plum) or
on-the-vine, if out
of season

½ cup Potager
Vegetable Broth
(page 70), white wine,
or water

Freshly ground black
pepper

3 tablespoons sliced
fresh basil leaves

Ratatouille, the famous Provençal vegetable stew, lets glorious summer produce take center stage. Tomatoes, zucchini, and eggplant combine harmoniously with onion, garlic, and lots of olive oil for a perfect summer side dish or luscious vegetarian meal. While ratatouille may be French, you will find similar vegetable stews all over the Mediterranean, from the Catalonia region of Spain to Turkey to Egypt. Ratatouille has a reputation for being difficult to prepare, in part because the traditional method has you browning each ingredient separately before layering them all together in the pot for a long, slow cook. For the pressure cooker version of ratatouille, I keep the tradition of sautéing each vegetable separately—in part so as not to overcrowd the pot—and then combine everything for a very quick cook under pressure. I think you will find that this method preserves the silky-smooth texture and gorgeous flavors of traditional ratatouille but takes a lot less time.

1. Pour 2 tablespoons of the olive oil into the inner pot of your electric pressure cooker. Select the Sauté function and set the heat level to "Normal." When the oil is shimmering, after about 2 minutes, add the onion and season with ½ teaspoon of the salt. Sauté, stirring frequently, until the onion is lightly browned and very soft, 8 to 10 minutes. Add the garlic and sauté just until fragrant, about 30 seconds. Transfer the onion and garlic to a bowl and set aside.

2. Add another 2 tablespoons of the olive oil and the bell peppers to the pot and season with ½ teaspoon of the salt. Sauté, stirring frequently, until the peppers are softened and browned in places, 8 to 10 minutes. Transfer the peppers to the bowl with the onion and garlic and set aside.

3. Add another 2 tablespoons of the olive oil and the zucchini to the pot and season with ½ teaspoon of the salt. Sauté, stirring frequently, until the zucchini is softened, about 5 minutes. Transfer the zucchini to the bowl with the other vegetables and set aside.

4. Add 2 tablespoons of the olive oil and half the eggplant to the pot. Sauté, stirring frequently, until very soft, about 6 minutes. If the eggplant starts to stick to the bottom

of the pot, add 2 tablespoons water and sauté, scraping up any browned pieces stuck to the bottom of the pot. Transfer the first batch of eggplant to a bowl and repeat with the remaining eggplant and remaining 2 tablespoons olive oil.

5. Cut the tomatoes in half horizontally and grate each half on the coarse side of a box grater set over a bowl to catch the flesh and juice. Discard the skins.

6. Return all the vegetables to the pressure cooker and add the tomatoes with their juices, and the broth, wine, or water. Taste and season with the remaining ½ teaspoon of salt, if desired, and black pepper.

7. Close the lid and make sure the pressure release valve is closed. Select the Pressure Cook function and set the cooking time to 3 minutes at high pressure. When the cooking program is complete, release the pressure manually and remove the lid.

8. If the ratatouille is too liquid for your liking at this point, select the Sauté function and set the heat level to "Normal." Sauté for 5 minutes, or until reduced and thickened.

9. Stir in the basil and drizzle with additional olive oil. Serve warm or at room temperature.

Lebanese Potato Salad with Mint

SERVES 4 TO 6 AS A SIDE DISH

3 pounds waxy potatoes, such as Yukon Gold or Red Bliss, cut into 1-inch pieces

Juice of 2 to 3 lemons

¼ cup extra-virgin olive oil

1 teaspoon kosher salt, plus more for seasoning

Freshly ground black pepper

½ red onion, diced

½ cup fresh mint leaves, cut into ribbons

Around the Mediterranean, potato salad means potatoes tossed with fresh herbs in a tangy, flavorful vinaigrette. This kind of vinaigrette-based potato salad is light and refreshing and, because it has no mayonnaise, can sit out at your picnic or backyard barbecue without risk of spoilage. Lebanese potato salad is distinctive for its bright lemony dressing and generous use of mint, which adds sweetness. A pressure cooker makes quick work of steaming the potatoes without having to stand over a pot of boiling water. And the potatoes emerge perfectly tender—not gummy—while maintaining their shape. For the best flavor, be sure to add the lemon juice and olive oil to the potatoes while they are still hot, as warm potatoes absorb dressing better. Allow the salad to cool slightly before adding the herbs, however, or the heat will cause the mint to discolor. *Photo on page 112.*

1. Pour 1 cup water into the inner pot of your electric pressure cooker. Place the potatoes in a steamer basket and place the basket in the pressure cooker.

2. Close the lid and make sure the pressure release valve is closed. Select the Steam function or Pressure Cook function and set the cooking time to 3 minutes at high pressure.

3. When the cooking program is complete, release the pressure manually and remove the lid. Remove the steamer basket and allow the potatoes to drain.

4. Place the potatoes in a large bowl. (Leave the skins on for a more rustic look or remove them if you prefer.) Gently toss the still-warm potatoes with the juice of two of the lemons (about ½ cup), the olive oil, salt, and pepper to taste.

5. Let the potatoes cool to room temperature. Taste and adjust the seasoning if necessary, by adding up to 2 tablespoons more lemon juice, drizzling with additional olive oil, or adding more salt and pepper. Add the red onion and mint leaves and toss gently to combine. Serve at room temperature.

NOTE: Mint is one of my favorite herbs and is very common throughout the eastern Mediterranean in particular. But if mint is not your favorite, you can substitute flat-leaf parsley, basil, or a combination of the two in this salad.

Olive Oil & Garlic Mashed Potatoes

SERVES 4

3 pounds waxy potatoes, such as Yukon Gold, peeled and cut into 1-inch cubes

6 tablespoons extra-virgin olive oil

9 garlic cloves, peeled

2 sprigs rosemary

1 teaspoon kosher salt, plus more for seasoning

Freshly ground black pepper

There may be an occasion when you need a dairy-free version of mashed potatoes, and this recipe—inspired by Italian flavors and enriched with that signature Mediterranean ingredient, olive oil—will more than satisfy. The garlic-and-rosemary-infused olive oil will add subtle flavor, but for a stronger hit of garlic, crush some or all of the oil-poached garlic cloves and add them to the potatoes. The Keep Warm function on your electric pressure cooker will keep your mashed potatoes warm for up to an hour without drying them out or scorching the bottom, which is very helpful for large holiday gatherings or just a busy weeknight when family members are coming and going at different times. *Photo on page 113.*

1. Pour 1 cup water into the inner pot of your electric pressure cooker. Place the potatoes in a steamer basket and place the basket in the pot.

2. Close the lid and make sure the pressure release valve is closed. Select the Pressure Cook function and set the cooking time to 8 minutes at high pressure.

3. While the potatoes are cooking, heat the olive oil in a small saucepan over medium heat. Add the garlic and rosemary and toss to coat with the oil. Turn the heat down to low and cook, allowing the garlic and herbs to infuse the oil, for about 20 minutes. Remove the rosemary and garlic cloves with a slotted spoon. Discard the rosemary but reserve the garlic.

4. When the cooking program is complete, release the pressure manually and remove the lid. Press Cancel to turn off the Keep Warm function. Remove the steamer basket. Drain the potatoes, reserving 1 cup of the cooking water.

5. Return the drained potatoes to the pot. Select the Sauté function and set the heat level to "Normal." Cook the potatoes, tossing them gently, for 1 to 2 minutes to dry them out.

6. Select the Keep Warm function and mash the potatoes directly in the pot. Season with the salt and pepper to taste. Gradually add the infused olive oil to the potatoes while mashing. If the mashed potatoes seem too thick, add a splash of the reserved cooking water and continue to mash.

7. Smash some or all of the oil-poached garlic cloves, as desired, and stir them into the potatoes. Taste and adjust the seasoning, if needed.

8. Serve immediately, or hold the potatoes, covered, on the Keep Warm setting for up to 1 hour before serving.

French Lentil Salad with Walnuts & Feta

SERVES 4

SALAD

2 tablespoons extra-virgin olive oil

1 small red onion, finely diced

2 carrots, finely diced

1 celery stalk, finely diced

1½ cups green lentils, preferably French

3 cups Chicken Broth (page 72), Potager Vegetable Broth (page 70), or water

1 bay leaf

1 garlic clove, smashed and peeled

1 cup walnuts, lightly toasted and chopped

Juice of 1 lemon

4 ounces feta cheese, crumbled

¼ cup chopped fresh flat-leaf parsley

DRESSING

1 shallot, minced

1 teaspoon Dijon mustard

2 tablespoons red wine vinegar

⅓ cup extra-virgin olive oil, walnut oil, or a combination

1 teaspoon kosher salt, plus more for seasoning

Freshly ground black pepper

Quick-cooking and nutritious, lentils are an essential part of many of the plant-forward cuisines around the Mediterranean. While the enormous variety of lentils may be overwhelming at first, the important thing to keep in mind is that different types of lentils are suited to different purposes. For example, red lentils are ideal for soups because they break down when cooked, making those soups thick and creamy. French green lentils, on the other hand, are perfect for salads because they hold their shape during cooking and retain a pleasantly firm texture. Cooking lentils in an electric pressure cooker is hands-off and foolproof, and will help you incorporate these healthy pulses into your regular repertoire. This classic French lentil salad is the perfect high-protein meatless meal or side dish. Make a big batch over the weekend and enjoy it for lunch all week long. This salad travels exceptionally well, so bring it to the office—or a potluck!

1. Pour the olive oil into the inner pot of your electric pressure cooker. Select the Sauté function and set the heat level to "Normal." When the oil is shimmering, after about 2 minutes, add the onion, carrots, and celery and sauté until softened, about 5 minutes. Using a slotted spoon, remove the vegetables to a large serving bowl and set aside. Press Cancel to turn off the Sauté function.

2. Add the lentils, broth, bay leaf, and garlic. Close the lid and make sure the pressure release valve is closed. Select the Pressure Cook function and set the cooking time to 9 minutes at high pressure.

3. Meanwhile, make the dressing: In a small bowl, whisk together the shallot, mustard, and vinegar. While whisking, slowly add the oil in a steady stream and continue whisking until emulsified. Add the salt and pepper to taste. Set aside.

4. When the cooking program is complete, release the pressure manually and remove the lid. Drain the lentils, discarding the bay leaf, and add them to the bowl with the vegetables. Add the dressing to the lentils while they are still warm and toss to combine.

5. Let the lentils cool to room temperature before adding the walnuts, lemon juice, feta, and parsley. Taste and adjust the seasoning, adding more salt and pepper if necessary. Serve at room temperature.

Braised Savoy Cabbage

**SERVES 4 AS A
SIDE DISH**

1 large head savoy
   cabbage (about
   2 pounds)

3 tablespoons extra-
   virgin olive oil, plus
   more for drizzling

4 garlic cloves, minced

¼ teaspoon red pepper
   flakes

Pinch of kosher salt

¼ cup grated
   Parmigiano-Reggiano
   cheese

Savoy cabbage, known as *cavolo verza* in Italian, is a beloved late-fall and winter vegetable. It resembles regular green cabbage, but with a darker color and tightly crinkled leaves that make the whole head feel a bit bouncy. The mild taste and tender leaves of savoy cabbage make it popular even among those who claim not to like cabbage. This braised savoy cabbage with garlic and red pepper flakes is ready for the table in just minutes, making it one of the easiest—and healthiest—side dishes you can throw together. Try it as an accompaniment to your cold-weather stews and braises.

1. Remove any tough or wilted outer leaves from the cabbage. Trim the stem. Quarter the cabbage and remove the core. Coarsely chop the cabbage, removing any thick ribs. Set aside.

2. Pour the olive oil into the inner pot of your electric pressure cooker. Select the Sauté function and set the heat level to "Less." When the oil is shimmering, after about 2 minutes, add the garlic and red pepper flakes and sauté just until fragrant, about 30 seconds. Add the cabbage and salt and stir to coat the cabbage with the oil. Sauté for a few minutes more.

3. Press Cancel to turn off the Sauté function. Add ¾ cup water.

4. Close the lid and make sure the pressure release valve is closed. Select the Pressure Cook function and set the cooking time to 3 minutes at high pressure. When the cooking program is complete, release the pressure manually and remove the lid. Use a slotted spoon to remove the cabbage and garlic, leaving behind any remaining liquid, and transfer to a serving dish.

5. Drizzle olive oil over the cabbage and sprinkle with the cheese. Serve warm.

Fatteh (Toasted Pita with Chickpeas & Yogurt)

**SERVES 4 TO 6 AS
AN APPETIZER,
OR 3 OR 4 AS A
MAIN COURSE**

FATTEH

1 cup dried chickpeas

1 teaspoon kosher salt

3 or 4 pita breads,
homemade (page 58)
or store-bought,
preferably day-old

¼ cup extra-virgin olive
oil, plus more for
drizzling

YOGURT SAUCE

1 cup plain yogurt,
preferably full-fat

2 garlic cloves, minced

2 tablespoons tahini

Juice of 1 lemon

½ teaspoon ground
cumin

½ teaspoon kosher salt

1 tablespoon extra-
virgin olive oil

¼ cup pine nuts, lightly
toasted

2 tablespoons chopped
fresh flat-leaf parsley
or cilantro

½ teaspoon ground
sumac

At its most basic, *fatteh* is a Lebanese dish of toasted or fried pitas topped with chickpeas and a yogurt-tahini sauce. You see many variations on this theme all over the Levant—some made with meat or chicken, for example—but, in sum, fatteh is a dish intended to be thrown together quickly and to make use of leftover or stale pita. Indeed, *fatteh* simply means "crushed" or "crumbs" in Arabic. In that vein, if you have cooked chickpeas, yogurt, or pitas left over from the other recipes in this book, this is the perfect dish to put them to good use. In the Middle East, fatteh is typically served for breakfast or brunch, but I recommend it as a snack or appetizer for a crowd or a satisfying vegetarian lunch.

1. Place the chickpeas and 1 teaspoon of the salt in the inner pot of your electric pressure cooker and cover with 4 cups cold water. Close the lid and make sure the pressure release valve is closed. Select the Pressure Cook function and set the cooking time to 40 minutes at high pressure.

2. Meanwhile, toast the pitas: Preheat the oven to 350°F. Cut each round of pita into six wedges and cut the wedges in half through the middle if the pitas are thick. Toss the pita wedges with the olive oil in a medium bowl. Arrange the pitas in a single layer on a baking sheet and bake in the oven until completely crisp and browned, 20 to 25 minutes.

3. When the cooking program is complete, allow the pressure to release naturally for at least 15 minutes, then manually release the remaining pressure and remove the lid. Drain the chickpeas, reserving ¼ cup of the cooking water.

4. Prepare the yogurt sauce: Combine the yogurt, garlic, tahini, lemon juice, cumin, salt, and olive oil in a medium bowl and whisk until smooth. Set aside. (If the yogurt sauce is too thick to pour, thin it with a bit of the reserved cooking water from the chickpeas.)

5. To assemble the fatteh, arrange the toasted pita chips in the bottom of a shallow bowl or on a platter. Top with 1½ cups of cooked chickpeas, setting aside the extra for another use. Ladle the yogurt sauce over the warm chickpeas.

6. Top the fatteh with the pine nuts, parsley, a drizzle of olive oil, and a dusting of sumac. Serve immediately.

Gigantes Plaki

**SERVES 4 TO 6 AS
AN APPETIZER,
OR 3 OR 4 AS
A MAIN COURSE**

1 pound gigante beans
(see Note)

4 garlic cloves:
2 smashed and
2 minced

¼ cup extra-virgin olive
oil, plus more for
drizzling

2 teaspoons kosher salt

1 bay leaf

1 yellow onion, diced

1 tablespoon tomato
paste

1 teaspoon ground
cinnamon

1 teaspoon Aleppo
pepper

1 (28-ounce) can whole
tomatoes, with their
juices

1 tablespoon sugar

2 tablespoons chopped
fresh flat-leaf
parsley, for garnish

Crumbled feta cheese,
for garnish (optional)

Gigantes are large, broad white beans, also known as Greek butter beans, that are prized for their meaty texture, mild flavor, and ability to hold their shape through long cooking. *Gigantes plaki* is a classic Greek small plate, known as a *mezede*, and a healthy dish with lots of plant-based protein. (*Plaki* simply means cooked in a skillet or flat dish.) Here we cook the beans in an electric pressure cooker until softened but still firm, with no soaking required—an enormous shortcut from the traditional overnight soak plus long cooking time. But we finish the beans, and their tomato-based sauce, in the oven as is traditional. Serve gigantes plaki as a starter like the Greeks do, or as a vegetarian main course with a loaf of crusty bread.

1. Place the gigantes, smashed garlic cloves, 1 tablespoon of the olive oil, the salt, and the bay leaf in the inner pot of your electric pressure cooker and cover with 8 cups cold water. Close the lid and make sure the pressure release valve is closed. Select the Pressure Cook function and set the cooking time to 25 minutes at high pressure.

2. When the cooking program is complete, allow the pressure to release naturally for at least 10 minutes, then manually release the remaining pressure and remove the lid. Drain the beans, reserving a small amount of the cooking water, and set aside. Wipe out the inner pot. (This may be done up to 5 days in advance. Store the cooked gigantes and the reserved liquid in an airtight container in the refrigerator.)

3. Preheat the oven to 350°F.

4. Add the remaining 3 tablespoons olive oil to the pressure cooker. Select the

Sauté function and set the heat level to "Normal." When the oil is shimmering, after about 2 minutes, add the onion and sauté until softened, about 3 minutes.

5. Add the minced garlic, tomato paste, cinnamon, and Aleppo pepper and sauté for a few minutes more, until fragrant. Add the tomatoes with their juices, crushing them with a wooden spoon, and the sugar and sauté until the sauce is thickened, about 5 minutes. Add the drained beans and stir to combine. Press Cancel to turn off the Sauté function.

6. Pour the bean mixture into a large baking dish and bake in the oven until the sauce is thickened and the beans are tender and creamy, about 1 hour. If the beans start to get too dry, add a splash of the reserved cooking water.

7. Garnish with parsley, a drizzle of olive oil, and feta, if using. Serve warm or at room temperature with crusty bread.

NOTE: Gigante beans are available in grocery stores with a large selection of dried beans and online. If you cannot source gigantes, large lima beans are an acceptable substitute, but the cooking times may be shorter.

Ful Medames with Tahini Sauce

SERVES 2 AS A MAIN COURSE, OR 4 AS A STARTER OR DIP

2 large eggs

2 tablespoons extra-virgin olive oil, plus more for drizzling

1 yellow onion, diced

4 garlic cloves, minced

2 teaspoons ground cumin

1 teaspoon ground coriander

1 teaspoon kosher salt, plus more for seasoning

1 teaspoon paprika

¼ teaspoon cayenne pepper

2 (15-ounce) cans fava beans, drained and rinsed

Juice of 1 lemon

¼ cup chopped fresh flat-leaf parsley

1 tomato, diced

3 scallions, white and light green parts only, sliced

FOR SERVING (OPTIONAL)
Harissa

Tahini Sauce (recipe follows)

Whole Wheat Pita (page 58)

Ful medames is a staple throughout the Middle East, but especially in Egypt, where it is considered the national dish. This vegetarian stew, made from fava beans, dates back to antiquity, when it was an important source of protein for the masses. As you might imagine for such an ancient dish, there are many ways to prepare and serve ful. In some places, ful is served as a main course—like a stew—with a variety of toppings and a hard-boiled egg for added heft. Alternatively, you can serve ful as a dip, similar to hummus, with pita bread for scooping. This recipe gives you options for both. (To keep this recipe vegan, by the way, simply omit the hard-boiled eggs.)

I recommend canned beans here because dried fava beans—especially the smaller ones needed for ful—can be hard to source, and they need to be peeled after cooking, which is tedious. Happily, canned fava beans are readily available and make this dish quick and easy to prepare.

1. Place the trivet in your electric pressure cooker and pour 1 cup water into the inner pot. Arrange the eggs on the trivet. Close the lid and make sure the pressure release valve is closed. Select the Pressure Cook function and set the cooking time to 7 minutes at low pressure. While the eggs are cooking, fill a medium bowl with ice and cold water. When the cooking program is complete, release the pressure manually and immediately move the eggs to the ice water. Once the eggs are cool enough to handle, drain and peel them. Quarter the eggs and set them aside until needed.

2. Pour the olive oil into the inner pot of the pressure cooker. Select the Sauté function and set the heat level to "Normal." When the oil is shimmering, after about 2 minutes, add the onion and sauté until softened, about 5 minutes.

3. Add the garlic, cumin, coriander, salt, paprika, and cayenne and sauté for a few minutes more, until fragrant. Press Cancel to turn off the Sauté function.

4. Add the drained beans and 1 cup water and stir to combine. Close the lid and make sure the pressure release valve is closed. Select the Pressure Cook function and set the cooking time to 1 minute at high pressure. When the cooking program is complete, allow the pressure to release naturally for at least 5 minutes, then manually release the remaining pressure and remove the lid.

5. Mash the fava beans with a potato masher but leave some beans whole for texture. Add the lemon juice and stir to combine. Taste and adjust the seasoning, adding more salt or lemon juice as needed.

6. To serve the ful as a stew, divide the beans equally between two bowls. Top each bowl with 2 tablespoons of the parsley, half the diced tomato and scallions, and one of the eggs. Drizzle each bowl with olive oil. Serve warm, with harissa or tahini sauce on the side, if desired. To serve ful as a dip, arrange the beans in a shallow bowl or on a platter. Sprinkle with the parsley, tomato, and scallions and drizzle with olive oil. Place the eggs around the outside of the platter. Drizzle with harissa or tahini sauce, if desired, and serve with pita.

Tahini Sauce

**MAKES ABOUT
1½ CUPS**

¾ cup tahini

⅓ cup freshly squeezed
  lemon juice

2 or 3 garlic cloves,
  coarsely chopped

½ teaspoon kosher salt

½ to ¾ cup cold water

Place the tahini, lemon juice, garlic, and salt in a blender or food processor and pulse a few times until the mixture forms a paste. With the motor running, slowly pour in ½ cup of the water and blend until the sauce is lighter in color and fluffy, 1 to 2 minutes. If the mixture is still quite thick, which will depend on the consistency of your tahini, add the remaining water in the same manner and blend until the mixture is completely smooth and thin enough to drizzle. The tahini sauce will keep in an airtight container in the refrigerator for up to 2 weeks.

5

MAIN COURSES WITH MEAT & FISH

Beef-&-Rice-Stuffed Peppers with Pine Nuts & Barberries

SERVES 4

2 tablespoons extra-virgin olive oil

1 yellow onion, diced

12 ounces ground beef

2 garlic cloves, minced

1½ teaspoons kosher salt

1 teaspoon ground cumin

1 teaspoon paprika

⅛ teaspoon ground allspice

2 medium tomatoes or 1 large tomato

¼ cup pine nuts

¼ cup barberries or dried cranberries

1 cup cooked long-grain white rice, such as basmati (see Note)

1½ cups Chicken Broth (page 72)

4 red bell peppers

¼ cup canned tomato sauce

1 cup fresh mint leaves, sliced into ribbons

Known as *mahshi*, vegetables stuffed with rice (and sometimes meat) are common throughout the Levant and North Africa. Stuffed peppers are certainly a favorite in the United States as well, but in the oven, it can take as long as an hour for bell peppers to soften. In an electric pressure cooker, however, the peppers are fork-tender after a mere 8 minutes. This recipe calls for barberries, a small berry that, in their dried form, are an important ingredient in Persian cuisine, especially in the many fragrant rice dishes. Barberries have a distinctive taste that starts sweet but ends on a concentrated sour note. Here they add a tart fruitiness and authentic Persian flavor to these stuffed peppers. Look for barberries at Middle Eastern markets or online. If you cannot source them, dried cranberries are an acceptable substitute, but cut them in half, as they are larger than barberries.

1. Pour the olive oil into the inner pot of your electric pressure cooker. Select the Sauté function and set the heat level to "Normal." When the oil is shimmering, after about 2 minutes, add the onion and sauté until softened, about 3 minutes. Add the ground beef, garlic, salt, and spices and cook, stirring, until the meat is no longer pink, 3 to 5 minutes.

2. Meanwhile, slice off the stem end of the tomatoes and grate the flesh using the coarse side of a box grater. Discard the skin.

3. Add the tomato pulp, pine nuts, and barberries to the meat mixture and sauté for a few minutes more to thicken. Press Cancel to turn off the Sauté function.

4. Transfer the meat mixture to a bowl and mix in the cup of rice. Set aside.

5. Return the inner pot to the pressure cooker. Place the trivet inside the inner pot and add the broth.

6. Cut off the tops of the bell peppers and remove the seeds and inner membranes. Divide the meat mixture evenly among the four peppers. Add 1 tablespoon of tomato sauce to each pepper and place the tops back on the peppers.

7. Arrange the peppers on the trivet. Close the lid and make sure the pressure release valve is closed. Select the Pressure Cook function and set the cooking time to 8 minutes at high pressure.

8. When the cooking program is complete, allow the pressure to release naturally for 5 minutes, then manually release the remaining pressure and remove the lid.

9. Carefully remove the peppers and top with the mint. Serve warm.

NOTE: If you do not have cooked rice on hand, you can begin the recipe by making rice in your pressure cooker and it will not add too much time to the overall dish. Start with 2 cups uncooked rice (this will make more rice than you will need, but most pressure cookers do not cook smaller amounts of rice well). Rinse the rice under cold water, add it to the inner pot of your electric pressure cooker, and cover with 2 cups cold water. Close the lid and make sure the pressure release valve is closed. Select the Pressure Cook function and set the cooking time to 8 minutes at low pressure. When the cooking program is complete, allow the pressure to release naturally, then remove the lid. Measure out 1 cup of the cooked rice for the stuffed peppers and reserve the remainder for another use.

Albóndigas (Catalonian Meatballs in Tomato Sauce)

**SERVES 4 AS A
MAIN COURSE,
OR 6 TO 8 AS AN
HORS D'OEUVRE**

MEATBALLS
½ cup milk, preferably
    whole

3 slices white bread,
    crusts removed, torn
    into pieces

1 yellow onion

1 pound ground meat,
    such as beef chuck,
    veal, pork, or a
    combination

1 large egg, beaten

½ cup grated Manchego
    or Parmigiano-
    Reggiano cheese

2 garlic cloves, grated
    on a Microplane

1 teaspoon kosher salt

½ teaspoon paprika

2 tablespoons chopped
    fresh flat-leaf parsley

Vegetable oil

SAUCE
2 tablespoons extra-
    virgin olive oil

3 garlic cloves, minced

½ teaspoon kosher salt

½ teaspoon paprika

¼ teaspoon red pepper
    flakes

1 (28-ounce) can
    crushed tomatoes

1 cup Chicken Broth
    (page 72), Potager
    Vegetable Broth
    (page 70), or water

1 teaspoon sugar

1 bay leaf

Meatballs served in different types of sauces are a popular Spanish tapa, or small plate. These *albóndigas* are an easy and family-friendly main course, especially when served with crusty bread or over Polenta with Butter and Cheese (page 100). But you can also serve them as a hot hors d'oeuvre for a small gathering, much like a tapas bar would: simply place the meatballs and a small amount of sauce in a large serving dish and add a toothpick to each meatball. Their small size makes these albóndigas easy to eat in just one bite.

Many meatball recipes advise you not to handle the meat too much for fear of making the meatballs tough. I take the opposite approach, and recommend that you knead the meat mixture thoroughly before forming the meatballs. The egg and soaked bread, which were originally intended as filler to make a small amount of meat stretch to feed a whole family, make these meatballs exceptionally tender, no matter how much you handle them.

1. Make the meatballs: Place the milk in a bowl or shallow dish and add the bread. Allow the bread to soak for several minutes, until it becomes soft enough to mash into a paste. Grate half of the onion on the coarse side of a box grater, or dice it very finely, reserving the remaining half for the sauce.

2. In a large bowl, combine the grated onion, ground meat, egg, cheese, garlic, salt, paprika, and parsley. Mash the bread until it forms a paste with no large chunks remaining. Add the bread to the meat mixture. Knead the meat mixture thoroughly with your hands until all the ingredients are completely incorporated. With damp hands, shape into balls the size of a large walnut. (You should end up with about 32 meatballs.) Cover and refrigerate the meatballs. (This may be done up to 1 day in advance.)

3. Make the sauce: Pour the olive oil into the inner pot of your electric pressure cooker. Select the Sauté function and set the heat level to "Less." Dice the remaining half of the onion. When the oil is shimmering, after about 2 minutes, add the onion and sauté until softened, about 5 minutes. Add the garlic, salt, paprika, and red pepper flakes and sauté an additional minute until fragrant. Press Cancel to turn off the Sauté function.

4. Add the crushed tomatoes, broth, sugar, and bay leaf and stir to combine. Set aside while you brown the meatballs.

5. Heat ½ inch of vegetable oil in a large heavy skillet over medium-high heat. When the oil is shimmering, add as many meatballs as will fit in a single layer without crowding. Brown the meatballs on all sides, but do not worry about cooking them all the way through as they will finish cooking in the sauce. Once browned, remove the meatballs to a paper towel–lined plate to drain. Repeat with the remaining meatballs.

6. Add the browned meatballs to the sauce in the pressure cooker. Close the lid and make sure the pressure release valve is closed. Select the Pressure Cook function and set the cooking time to 5 minutes at high pressure. When the cooking program is complete, allow the pressure to release naturally for at least 10 minutes, then manually release the remaining pressure and remove the lid. Taste the sauce and adjust the seasoning, adding more salt if needed. Discard the bay leaf.

7. Serve the meatballs hot with the sauce.

NOTE: Even though it requires an extra step, it is worthwhile to brown the meatballs on the stove before adding them to the sauce. Adding the meatballs raw can make the sauce greasy. If you want to streamline the process and skip browning the meatballs to save time, however, you may add them to the sauce raw. Just use a lean ground beef and increase the cooking time to 8 minutes at high pressure.

Veal Marengo

SERVES 4

---

2 pounds veal stew meat

2 teaspoons kosher salt

½ teaspoon freshly ground black pepper, plus more for seasoning

¼ cup all-purpose flour

¼ cup extra-virgin olive oil

2 tablespoons unsalted butter

3 shallots, minced

2 carrots, diced

2 garlic cloves, minced

½ teaspoon dried thyme leaves (not ground thyme)

½ cup dry white wine

1 (15-ounce) can diced tomatoes, with their juices

2 bay leaves

1 cup Chicken Broth (page 72) or Potager Vegetable Broth (page 70)

Zest of 1 orange

Chopped fresh flat-leaf parsley, for garnish (optional)

Cooked egg noodles, cooked rice, or Polenta with Butter and Cheese (page 100), for serving

Veal Marengo sounds Italian but is, in fact, classic French bistro fare. The legend is that Napoleon's chef prepared this stew for him after he defeated the Austrians at the Battle of Marengo. This was one of my favorite special-occasion dishes when I was growing up, especially when served over egg noodles. As an adult, I tried to re-create that veal Marengo, but often, when I would make this stew on the stove, the veal would turn out tough and chewy, which was definitely not how I remembered it. Since I have started making veal Marengo in my electric pressure cooker, however, the veal always comes out perfectly fork-tender. Now this is one of my family's favorite meals. Do not skip the final step of adding orange zest to the stew—it brightens the whole dish.

1. Season the meat with 1 teaspoon of the salt and the pepper. Spread the flour on a plate and dredge the veal pieces in the flour, shaking off any excess. (Excess flour can burn and scorch the bottom of an electric pressure cooker.) Add 2 tablespoons of olive oil and the butter to the inner pot of your pressure cooker. Select the Sauté function and set the heat level to "Less." When the butter is melted and the oil is shimmering, after about 2 minutes, add as many veal pieces as will fit comfortably in a single layer. (You will need to brown the meat in batches so as not to overcrowd the pan, which will cause the meat to steam, not brown.) Brown the meat on one side and then turn and brown on the other side. Transfer the browned meat to a plate. Repeat, working in as many batches as necessary, until all the meat is browned. (You can speed up this process considerably by browning the meat in a large skillet on the stove, if time is a consideration.)

2. Add the remaining 2 tablespoons of olive oil to the inner pot followed by the shallots, carrots, and garlic. Sauté the aromatics until softened, about 2 minutes. Season with the remaining teaspoon salt and the dried thyme.

3. Add the wine to the inner pot and deglaze it by using a wooden spoon to scrape up any browned bits stuck to the bottom of the pot. Press Cancel to turn off the Sauté function.

4. Return the meat and any accumulated juices to the pot along with the tomatoes with their juices, bay leaves, and broth. Close the lid and make sure the pressure release valve is closed. Select the Pressure Cook function and set the cooking time to 18 minutes at high pressure.

5. When the cooking program is complete, allow the pressure to release naturally for at least 15 minutes, then manually release the remaining pressure and remove the lid.

6. Just prior to serving, add the orange zest to the stew and discard the bay leaves. Taste and adjust the seasoning, adding more salt or pepper as needed. Garnish with parsley, if using. Serve warm over the egg noodles, rice, or polenta.

Provençal Beef Daube

SERVES 4 TO 6

- 4 slices thick-cut bacon, chopped
- 2½ pounds boneless beef chuck, cut into 2-inch cubes
- 1½ teaspoons kosher salt, plus more for seasoning
- 1 teaspoon freshly ground black pepper, plus more for seasoning
- 1 to 2 tablespoons vegetable oil, if needed
- 1 yellow onion, halved and sliced
- 2 shallots, sliced
- 1 tablespoon tomato paste
- 6 carrots, cut into 2-inch chunks
- 1 head garlic, halved horizontally, papery outer skin removed
- 1½ cups red wine
- 1 bay leaf
- 3 or 4 sprigs fresh thyme
- 1 celery stalk, with leaves
- 3 or 4 sprigs fresh flat-leaf parsley
- 1 tablespoon cornstarch
- ¾ cup frozen peas
- 1 tablespoon red wine vinegar

Daube is the Provençal name for a slow-cooked stew with wine as the cooking liquid. For my version of a daube, I keep the wine, but speed up the cooking by using an electric pressure cooker. After just 25 minutes of pressure cooking, the meat is fork-tender and the rich sauce tastes as if it has simmered all day. You can also prepare this stew in advance and hold it on the Keep Warm setting until you're ready to serve it. The flavors will develop even further.

I prefer to buy boneless chuck roast and cut it into pieces myself rather than purchase beef stew meat. That way, I can cut the meat into large pieces, which hold up well to pressure cooking. This is one of my family's favorite cold-weather meals, especially when I serve it over Olive Oil and Garlic Mashed Potatoes (page 111), rice, or buttered egg noodles.

1. Put the bacon in the inner pot of your electric pressure cooker. Select the Sauté function and set the heat level to "Normal." Sauté, stirring, until lightly browned and crisp and the fat is rendered, about 7 minutes. Remove the bacon with a slotted spoon to a paper towel–lined plate.

2. Pat dry the pieces of beef using paper towels and season them with 1 teaspoon of the salt and ½ teaspoon of pepper. Working in batches, add as many pieces of beef as will fit in a single layer to the pressure cooker without crowding. Brown the meat on both sides, 2 to 3 minutes per side, and as they brown, transfer the pieces of meat to a plate. Repeat until all the meat is browned. If the pot begins to look dry, add oil, 1 tablespoon at a time. (This step may also be done in a large skillet on the stove, which may be quicker.)

3. Add the onion and shallots and season with the remaining ½ teaspoon each of salt and pepper. Cook, stirring, until the onions have softened, about 8 minutes. Add the tomato paste and stir to combine. Press Cancel to turn off the Sauté function.

4. Return the beef and bacon to the pot. Add the carrots, garlic, wine, and bay leaf. Tie the thyme, celery, and parsley together with twine and add the bundle to the pot.

5. Close the lid and make sure the pressure release valve is closed. Select the Pressure Cook function and set the cooking time to 25 minutes at high pressure. When the cooking program is complete, release the pressure manually and remove the lid. (This may be done up to several hours in advance.) Press Cancel to turn off the Keep Warm function.

6. Remove the garlic, bay leaf, and bundle of herbs with a slotted spoon. If desired, squeeze the softened cloves of garlic out of the husks and add some or all them back to the stew. Select the Sauté function and set the heat level to "Less."

7. Whisk together the cornstarch and 1 tablespoon cold water in a small bowl to make a slurry. Add the cornstarch slurry to the daube and stir to combine. Add the peas. Simmer the stew until the peas are heated through and the sauce has thickened slightly, about 5 minutes.

8. Add the vinegar and stir to combine. Taste and adjust the seasoning, adding more salt and pepper as needed. Serve warm.

Turkish Stuffed Cabbage with Lamb

SERVES 4 TO 6

SAUCE

3 tablespoons extra-virgin olive oil

1 yellow onion, diced

3 garlic cloves, minced

1 tablespoon tomato paste

1 teaspoon kosher salt

1 teaspoon ground cumin

1 teaspoon ground cinnamon

1 teaspoon ground allspice

½ teaspoon smoked paprika

½ teaspoon Aleppo pepper

1 (28-ounce) can crushed tomatoes

2 teaspoons sugar

The best stuffed cabbage I have ever tasted is served at Galit, Chicago's outstanding Israeli restaurant. Chef Zach Engel stuffs cabbage leaves with lamb, smothers them in a spicy tomato sauce seasoned with cinnamon and allspice, and tops the whole thing with a generous dollop of tangy labneh. This is my attempt to re-create that memorable dish at home. While many cultures have their own take on stuffed cabbage, this version—with its lamb-and-bulgur filling and earthy tomato sauce—is most commonly seen in Turkey and around the eastern Mediterranean.

An electric pressure cooker saves quite a bit of time over baking stuffed cabbage rolls in the oven, but this dish still has many steps. Luckily, the sauce can be prepared up to several days in advance, and you can blanch the cabbage the day before and refrigerate the leaves. You can also prepare the sauce in your electric pressure cooker as opposed to on the stove; just transfer the sauce to a bowl and wash the inner pot before proceeding.

1. To make the sauce, heat the olive oil in a Dutch oven over medium heat. Add the onion and sauté until translucent, about 3 minutes. Add the garlic and sauté an additional minute.

2. Add the tomato paste, salt, and spices and sauté for a few minutes more, until fragrant. Add the tomatoes and sugar and stir to combine. Raise the heat and bring the sauce to a boil. Turn down the heat and simmer until slightly thickened, 10 to 15 minutes. Set aside. (This may be done up to 2 days in advance. Refrigerate the sauce in an airtight container until needed.)

3. To blanch the cabbage, place the trivet in the bottom of the electric pressure cooker and add 1½ cups water. Place the cabbage on the trivet and close the lid and make sure the pressure release valve is closed. Select the Pressure Cook function and set the cooking time to 9 minutes at high pressure.

4. When the cooking program is complete, allow the pressure to release naturally for at least 5 minutes, then manually release the remaining pressure and remove the lid. Remove the cabbage and let cool. Dump out the water and return the inner pot to the pressure cooker.

5. Place the bulgur in a bowl and cover it with warm water. Let rest for 20 minutes while you prepare the cabbage. Drain any excess water before proceeding.

6. Once the cabbage is cool, carefully peel off the individual leaves, doing your best not to tear them. Once you reach the inside of the cabbage, where the leaves are too small to stuff, stop. Using a sharp paring knife, cut out the thick center vein of each leaf. Set aside the leaves. (This may be done up to 1 day in advance. Refrigerate the leaves, covered, until needed.)

7. In a large mixing bowl, combine the soaked bulgur, ground lamb, garlic, pine nuts, dried apricots, salt, and spices. Stir with a fork or your hands until thoroughly mixed.

Ingredients & recipe continue

STUFFED CABBAGE

1 head green cabbage, tough outer leaves removed

1 cup fine bulgur wheat

1 pound ground lamb

2 garlic cloves, minced

½ cup pine nuts, plus more for garnish

¼ cup chopped dried apricots

2 teaspoons kosher salt

2 teaspoons ground cumin

1 teaspoon ground coriander

1 teaspoon ground sumac

½ teaspoon ground cinnamon

½ teaspoon Aleppo pepper or other mild ground red chile

1 cup Chicken Broth (page 72) or Potager Vegetable Broth (page 70)

Labneh (page 52), Quick Labneh (page 191), or plain Greek yogurt, for serving

Chopped fresh mint or flat-leaf parsley, for garnish

8. To stuff the cabbage, place one of the larger leaves on a clean board with the cut-out part at the top. Add ⅓ cup of the filling to the bottom half of the leaf. Fold the bottom of the cabbage leaf over the filling, tuck in the sides, and roll away from you. Place the stuffed cabbage roll seam-side down on a clean plate. Repeat with the remaining leaves. As the leaves get smaller, reduce the amount of filling in each, first to ¼ cup, then 3 tablespoons, and so on. Continue until you have used all the filling or run out of usable leaves. (If needed, two of the smaller leaves can be overlapped and used to make one roll. Cabbage leaves may be stuffed in advance and the rolls refrigerated, covered, until needed for up to a day.)

9. Place the trivet in the electric pressure cooker and add the broth. Arrange a layer of cabbage rolls on top of the trivet. Spoon half the tomato sauce over the rolls. Place the remaining rolls on top of the first layer and spoon the remaining sauce over the second layer.

10. Close the lid and make sure the pressure release valve is closed. Select the Pressure Cook function and set the cooking time to 22 minutes at high pressure.

11. When the cooking program is complete, allow the pressure to release naturally for at least 15 minutes, then manually release the remaining pressure and remove the lid.

12. Serve the cabbage rolls immediately with labneh or yogurt and garnish with additional pine nuts, if desired, and mint or flat-leaf parsley.

Wine-Braised Lamb Shanks with Dried Fruit

SERVES 4 TO 6

- 4 (12- to 16-ounce) lamb shanks
- 2 teaspoons kosher salt
- 1 teaspoon freshly ground black pepper
- 2 tablespoons extra-virgin olive oil
- 1 yellow onion, coarsely chopped
- 2 carrots, chopped
- 1 leek, white and light green parts only, coarsely chopped
- 2 celery stalks, coarsely chopped
- Several sprigs fresh thyme
- 1 cup red wine
- 1 cinnamon stick
- 1 star anise pod
- 1 dried red chile
- 1 whole clove
- 1 tablespoon cornstarch
- 1 cup dried fruit, such as apricots, prunes, and golden raisins, chopped, if large
- 2 tablespoons pomegranate molasses or balsamic vinegar

This North African–inspired braised lamb is an impressive dish suitable for company or even for a holiday celebration. It used to take hours of long slow cooking to turn tough lamb shanks into juicy, succulent meat that practically falls off the bone, but an electric pressure cooker gets the job done in a fraction of the time. Even so, you may want to make this dish a day in advance and reheat it on the stove just prior to serving, which, if anything, will only make it more flavorful. (See the note for reheating instructions.) The key to making this stew lick-the-spoon delicious is to remove the grease so that you can turn the liquid into a flavorful—but not greasy—sauce for the meat. I suggest a few different ways to do this, but a fat separator that pours from the bottom makes it especially easy.

1. Pat the lamb shanks dry and season them on both sides with the salt and the pepper.

2. Pour the olive oil into the inner pot of your electric pressure cooker. Select the Sauté function and set the heat level to "More." When the oil is shimmering, after about 2 minutes, add 2 of the lamb shanks. Brown the lamb shanks on both sides, about 5 minutes per side, then transfer them to a plate. Repeat with the remaining lamb shanks. Set aside.

3. Add the onion, carrots, leek, celery, and thyme to the pot and stir to coat with the oil. Sauté the vegetables until softened, about 5 minutes. Press Cancel to turn off the Sauté function.

4. Add the wine and scrape up any browned bits from the bottom of the pot. Add the cinnamon stick, star anise, chile, and clove and stir to combine. Lay the lamb shanks on top of the vegetables.

5. Close the lid and make sure the pressure release valve is closed. Select the Pressure Cook function and set the cooking time to 40 minutes at high pressure.

6. When the cooking program is complete, allow the pressure to release naturally for at least 15 minutes, then manually release the remaining pressure and remove the lid. Transfer the lamb shanks to a plate and tent with foil to keep warm.

7. Set a fine-mesh strainer over a large bowl. Remove the inner pot and pour the cooking liquid through the strainer to remove the solids. Press on the vegetables with a spatula to extract as much liquid as possible, then discard the solids.

8. The next step is to remove the fat from the cooking liquid, which, if not removed, could make the final dish greasy. The fat naturally rises to the top and sits above the liquid, so you can skim it off with a spoon. Alternatively, pour the liquid into a fat separator, if you have one. Return the inner pot to the pressure cooker and pour the cooking liquid, leaving behind the grease, into the pot. Select the Sauté function and set the heat level to "Normal."

9. Whisk together the cornstarch and 1 tablespoon cold water in a small bowl. Add the cornstarch slurry to the cooking liquid and stir to combine. Add the dried fruit. Simmer the sauce until it has thickened slightly, about 5 minutes. If the lamb shanks have gotten cold, you can return them to the sauce and simmer until they are warmed through.

10. Just prior to serving, stir the pomegranate molasses into the sauce. Serve the lamb shanks, with the sauce, over rice or couscous.

INSTANTLY MEDITERRANEAN

NOTE: Like many stews and braises, these lamb shanks can be prepared a day in advance, which is helpful if you're making them for company. After removing the lamb shanks and straining the sauce, transfer the meat and sauce to separate airtight containers and refrigerate. The fat in the sauce will rise to the top and congeal, making it easy to remove and discard. To reheat, place the sauce and the lamb shanks in a large saucepan or Dutch oven and add the dried fruit. Cover and cook over medium heat until the meat is heated through. Then remove the lid and simmer the sauce until slightly reduced and thickened. (You should not need the cornstarch slurry.)

Italian Sausage Ragù

SERVES 4 TO 6

2 tablespoons extra-virgin olive oil

1 yellow onion, diced

2 carrots, diced

2 celery stalks, diced

4 garlic cloves, minced

1 tablespoon tomato paste

1 teaspoon kosher salt

1 teaspoon fennel seeds (optional)

⅛ teaspoon red pepper flakes

1 pound Italian sausage, sweet or hot, casings removed (see Note)

½ cup red wine

1 (28-ounce) can whole tomatoes, with their juices

1 teaspoon sugar

1 bay leaf

Polenta with Butter and Cheese (page 100), Olive Oil and Garlic Mashed potatoes (page 111), or pasta, for serving

One of the greatest advantages of an electric pressure cooker is that it delivers the richness and depth of flavor of a long-simmered sauce without the hours of low, slow cooking. This hearty sausage ragù, for example, tastes like it bubbled away on the back of the stove for an entire Sunday afternoon, when in reality, it is ready to eat in under an hour. I especially like to serve this ragù over polenta, which I also make in the pressure cooker (see page 100). Simply make the ragù first, or in advance, and transfer it to a pot; keep it warm on the stovetop while you make the polenta in the pressure cooker. (Those who have two pressure cookers—and there are a surprising number of you who do—can make the ragù and polenta simultaneously.)

1. Pour the olive oil into the inner pot of your electric pressure cooker. Select the Sauté function and set the heat level to "Normal." When the oil is shimmering, after about 2 minutes, add the onion and sauté until translucent, about 3 minutes. Add the carrots and celery and sauté until the vegetables are softened, about 5 minutes. Add the garlic, tomato paste, salt, fennel seeds (if using), and red pepper flakes and stir to combine. Sauté for an additional minute, just until fragrant.

2. Add the sausage and stir to combine. Sauté the sausage, breaking it up with a wooden spoon, until cooked through and no longer pink, 4 to 6 minutes. Press Cancel to turn off the Sauté function.

3. Add the red wine, tomatoes with their juices, sugar, and bay leaf and stir to combine. Break up the tomatoes with a wooden spoon.

4. Close the lid and make sure the pressure release valve is closed. Select the Pressure Cook function and set the cooking time to 35 minutes at high pressure.

5. When the cooking program is complete, you can release the pressure manually, if that is more convenient, or allow the pressure to release naturally. (You can also make the ragù in advance and hold on the Keep Warm setting until needed.)

6. If the sauce seems thin, select the Sauté function and simmer for 5 to 10 minutes, until slightly reduced and thickened.

7. Serve warm, over polenta, mashed potatoes, or pasta.

NOTE: For a lighter take on this dish, or for those of you who do not eat pork, substitute Italian-flavored chicken or turkey sausage.

Circassian Chicken

SERVES 4 TO 6

2½ pounds boneless, skinless chicken breasts

1 cup Chicken Broth (page 72) or water

1 teaspoon kosher salt

Assorted aromatics, such as an onion, a carrot, a celery stalk, and sprigs of fresh parsley or thyme (optional)

⅔ cup milk (any kind)

3 slices white sandwich bread

1½ cups whole walnuts, lightly toasted

3 garlic cloves, peeled

2 tablespoons unsalted butter

1 teaspoon mild ground red chile, such as Aleppo pepper

1 small head butter lettuce or Boston lettuce, leaves separated, for serving (optional)

½ cup fresh cilantro leaves, for garnish

Circassian chicken is a Turkish chicken salad in which poached chicken is tossed in a creamy walnut sauce and drizzled with red-flecked chile butter. This salad is often served as a mezze, or appetizer, in Turkey, but it makes an outstanding main course, especially in the summer months. This is a wonderful dish for entertaining—or to bring to a potluck—because it tastes equally good warm or at room temperature. You can serve the chicken over lettuce, as I suggest here, or with bread or crackers.

Poaching chicken in an electric pressure cooker is foolproof and entirely hands-off. Some of the poaching liquid is then used to enrich and thin out the walnut sauce. For an especially flavorful broth that can be saved to use in other dishes, start with homemade or canned chicken broth and add some aromatics to the pot when poaching the chicken.

1. Place the chicken in the inner pot of your electric pressure cooker, cover with the broth, and add the salt. If desired, add some or all of the suggested aromatics. (Adding aromatics will create a more flavorful broth, but it is not necessary to cook the chicken.)

2. Close the lid and make sure the pressure release valve is closed. Select the Poultry function or the Pressure Cook function and set the cooking time to 15 minutes at high pressure.

3. When the cooking program is complete, release the pressure manually and remove the lid. Transfer the chicken to a large bowl and allow it to cool. If you cooked the chicken with any aromatics, strain the cooking liquid and set aside; discard the solids. When the chicken is cool enough to handle, tear it into strips with your hands or two forks.

4. Place the milk in a bowl or shallow dish and add the bread. Allow the bread to soak for several minutes, until it becomes soft enough to mash into a paste.

5. Place the soaked bread, walnuts (reserving a few to garnish the final dish), and garlic in a food processor and process until they have formed a rough paste. With the motor of the food processor running, slowly pour in about ¼ cup of the reserved cooking liquid to create a smooth, creamy sauce with a mayonnaise-like consistency. If the sauce is too thick, add more liquid, 1 tablespoon at a time up to an additional ¼ cup, and process until very smooth. (Reserve the remaining broth for another use.)

6. Add the walnut sauce to the shredded chicken and toss to coat the chicken with the sauce. (This may be done up to 1 day in advance; store the chicken in an airtight container in the refrigerator.)

7. Just prior to serving, melt the butter in a small saucepan on the stovetop (or in a microwave-safe bowl using the microwave) and stir in ground chile.

8. To serve, arrange the lettuce (if using) on a platter, then arrange the chicken over the lettuce. Drizzle the chile butter over the chicken and garnish with the cilantro and reserved walnuts. Serve warm or at room temperature.

NOTE: Circassian chicken has been a part of Turkish cuisine dating back to the days of the Ottoman Empire. The Circassian people who lent their name to this dish were not Turkish, but rather came from an area of the Caucasus Mountains along the northeastern coast of the Black Sea. They were exiled in the middle of the nineteenth century following the loss of their land to Russia, and most settled in parts of the Ottoman Empire. Perhaps not surprisingly, a very similar dish exists in Georgian cuisine.

Chicken Musakhan (Sumac-Scented Chicken with Onion Flatbread)

SERVES 4 TO 6

CARAMELIZED ONIONS

4 tablespoons (½ stick) unsalted butter

4 yellow onions, halved and sliced

1 teaspoon kosher salt

2 teaspoons ground sumac

½ teaspoon freshly ground black pepper

CHICKEN

1 tablespoon ground sumac

1 teaspoon ground cumin

½ teaspoon ground cinnamon

½ teaspoon ground allspice

¼ teaspoon ground coriander

⅛ teaspoon ground nutmeg

3 tablespoons extra-virgin olive oil

6 to 8 bone-in, skin-on chicken thighs (2 pounds total)

1 teaspoon kosher salt

1 cup Chicken Broth (page 72) or water

Chicken musakhan is considered the national dish of Palestine. It's a combination of roast chicken, heavily seasoned with sumac and warm spices, served on top of—or alongside—flatbreads topped with caramelized onions, which are also seasoned with sumac. Once again, an electric pressure cooker does double duty: I use it both to caramelize the onions for the flatbread and to cook the chicken. Bone-in chicken pieces are traditional, so I use bone-in thighs, which have great flavor but cook quickly. I like to serve chicken musakhan with an Israeli salad (see page 207) on the side. The bright, fresh flavors and acidity of the salad are a nice contrast to the sweetness of the caramelized onion flatbread.

1. If you are making the flatbreads from scratch, do that first, using the recipe on page 142.

2. Caramelize the onions: Add the butter to the inner pot of your electric pressure cooker. Select the Sauté function and set the heat level to "More." When the butter is melted, after about 2 minutes, add the onions and salt and stir to coat with the butter.

3. Cover the inner pot with a tempered glass lid designed for the Instant Pot or another lid that fits. Cook the onions, covered, for 10 minutes to soften them. Remove the lid and continue to cook the onions until they are very soft, light brown, and beginning to melt, about 20 additional minutes. Stir occasionally at first, then more frequently as the onions cook down. Make sure to scrape up any onions or browned bits that are sticking to the bottom. (If the Sauté cycle shuts off automatically before the onions are caramelized, turn it back on and continue cooking until they are.) Toward the end of cooking, add the sumac and pepper. (This may be done up to 4 days in advance. Refrigerate the onions in an airtight container until needed or freeze for up to 3 months.)

4. Make the chicken: Press Cancel to turn off the Sauté function. Transfer the onions to a bowl and let cool. Wash or wipe out the inner pot. In a small bowl whisk together the sumac, cumin, cinnamon, allspice, coriander, and nutmeg to create a spice mix. Set aside 1 teaspoon of the spice mix.

5. Brush 2 tablespoons of the olive oil on the chicken and rub the spice mix all over the pieces, including under the skin. Sprinkle with the salt. (This may be done up to 8 hours in advance. Place the seasoned chicken in a bowl, cover, and refrigerate until needed.)

6. Add the remaining tablespoon of olive oil to the pressure cooker. Select the Sauté function and set the heat level to "Normal." When the oil is shimmering, after about 2 minutes, add as many of the chicken thighs as will fit comfortably in a single layer, skin-side down. (You may have to work in two batches.)

7. Cook the chicken without disturbing it until the skin is golden brown and the chicken releases easily from the pan, about 7 minutes. Flip the chicken and cook the second side until browned, 3 to 4 minutes. (The chicken will not be cooked through at this point.) Transfer the chicken to a plate and set aside. Repeat with the remaining chicken thighs, if needed. (Because the pot is hotter, the second batch often takes less long to cook.)

FOR SERVING

6 flatbreads, such as Laffa Bread (recipe follows), Whole Wheat Pita (page 58), or naan, homemade or store-bought

¼ cup pine nuts, lightly toasted

2 tablespoons chopped fresh flat-leaf parsley

1 lemon, cut into wedges

8. Add the broth to the pressure cooker and scrape up the browned bits on the bottom of the pot with a spatula or wooden spoon. Place the trivet inside and arrange the chicken on top of the trivet. Close the lid and make sure the pressure release valve is closed.

9. Select the Pressure Cook function and set the cooking time to 12 minutes at high pressure. When the cooking program is complete, allow the pressure to release naturally for at least 10 minutes, then manually release the remaining pressure and remove the lid. Transfer the chicken to a platter and tent with foil to keep warm. (If you like, you can serve the cooking liquid alongside the chicken as a sauce. Be sure to taste it first to make sure there is no bitter flavor from the scorched spices.)

10. Assemble the flatbreads: Divide the caramelized onions among the flatbreads and spread them in an even layer. Sprinkle each with a bit of the reserved spice mix. Preheat the broiler on your oven. Arrange the flatbreads on two baking sheets and place them under the broiler, one sheet at a time, until the edges are brown and the onions are warmed through, 2 to 4 minutes. Top the flatbreads with the pine nuts and parsley.

11. To serve, place a piece of chicken directly on top of the flatbreads or serve them next to each other. Alternatively, you can shred the chicken off the bone and top each flatbread with a portion of the shredded chicken (this works especially well for children). Give each diner a wedge of lemon for squeezing over their chicken, and if you reserved the cooking liquid, pass it separately at the table.

Laffa Bread

MAKES 6 FLATBREADS

2 teaspoons instant or
active dry yeast

⅞ to 1 cup warm water

2 cups all-purpose flour,
plus more for dusting

½ cup whole wheat
flour

1½ teaspoons kosher
salt

1½ teaspoons sugar

Laffa is a soft and chewy Middle Eastern flatbread similar to pita, but without a pocket. Traditionally, laffa is baked in a special wood-fired oven called a *taboon*, the bottom of which is lined with pebbles or stones that become incredibly hot. Bread cooked in a taboon, which is sometimes simply called taboon bread, is known for its bumpy texture, which comes from being cooked on the pebbles.

Bumpy taboon bread is the traditional base for Chicken Musakhan (page 140), but there are some foods that we simply cannot re-create in a home oven. This laffa bread, cooked on a hot baking sheet or pizza stone in your home oven, is a reasonable substitute. Steaming the laffa when it comes out of the oven and storing it in a bag is important for achieving its soft texture—a trick I learned from the book *Breaking Breads* by Uri Scheft.

1. If using active dry yeast, whisk together the yeast and warm water (start with ⅞ cup) in a small bowl and let it sit until foamy, about 10 minutes.

2. Combine the all-purpose flour, whole wheat flour, salt, and sugar in the bowl of a stand mixer or in a large bowl and stir to combine. If using instant yeast, add it to the flour mixture.

3. Gradually add the water-yeast mixture (or just the warm water, if using instant yeast) to the flour and stir with a fork until a dry, shaggy dough comes together. If the dough seems dry, add the remaining water 1 tablespoon at a time. If it seems too wet, add more flour, also 1 tablespoon at a time.

4. If using a stand mixer, attach the dough hook and beat the dough for 1 minute on low speed and then on medium speed for 3 minutes, or until the dough begins to clear the sides of the bowl. If kneading by hand, turn the dough out onto a lightly floured surface and knead until it is smooth and elastic, 8 to 10 minutes. (The dough should be a little tacky but not so sticky that it is hard to work with.)

5. Cover the dough and allow it to rise in a warm place until it is about 50 percent bigger, about 30 minutes. (You can use the yogurt cycle of the electric pressure cooker to proof the bread as described on page 66 if you do not need it to make other parts of this recipe at the same time.)

6. Turn the dough out onto a lightly floured surface and divide it into 6 equal pieces. Roll each piece into a ball and cover with a clean towel. Allow the dough to proof until, when you press it lightly with a finger, the depression springs back slowly and fills in halfway, about 30 minutes.

7. Preheat the oven to 500°F. Place a baking stone or an upside-down rimmed baking sheet directly on the oven floor, adjusting the oven racks or moving them out of the way as necessary. Line a second upside-down rimmed baking sheet (or a rimless cookie sheet) with parchment paper. (You will use this baking sheet to transfer the dough to the oven.)

8. Roll each dough ball out on a lightly floured surface until it is a thin circle of approximately 8 inches in diameter. Poke the dough all over with a fork. (This will prevent the bread from puffing up in the oven like a pita does.)

9. Carefully transfer one of the flatbreads to the parchment paper–lined baking sheet. Open the oven and slide the parchment paper onto the baking sheet on the bottom of the oven.

10. Bake the flatbread until the edges are golden brown, about 5 minutes. Remove the bread and wrap it in a clean towel so that it steams and stays soft. Bake the remaining flatbreads in the same manner, wrapping them in the towel. When the breads are cool enough to handle, transfer them to a plastic bag to store until needed, up to 2 days.

Chicken Tagine with Preserved Lemon & Olives

SERVES 4

3 tablespoons ghee or extra-virgin olive oil

3 pounds bone-in, skin-on chicken parts, such as thighs, drumsticks, and split breasts (cut in half if large)

1 teaspoon kosher salt, plus more for seasoning

1 teaspoon freshly ground black pepper

2 yellow onions, halved and sliced

5 garlic cloves, sliced

1 teaspoon paprika

½ teaspoon ground ginger

½ teaspoon ground cumin

1 cinnamon stick

¼ teaspoon saffron threads, dissolved in 1 tablespoon warm water

1 cup Chicken Broth (page 72)

¼ cup freshly squeezed lemon juice

Rind from ½ preserved lemon, cut into strips (see Note, page 78)

16 green olives

1 tablespoon cornstarch

1 tablespoon chopped fresh flat-leaf parsley, for garnish

Couscous or rice, for serving

On a trip to Morocco a few years ago, my mother took a cooking class at her hotel in Marrakesh. She brought me back a book of recipes, which included a dish much like this one. The combination of preserved lemons and green olives is quite traditional in Morocco. While it would also be traditional to cook a dish such as this in a clay tagine, an electric pressure cooker is actually very effective at producing juicy chicken and flavorful sauce in a fraction of the time. As is typical of Moroccan cuisine, this dish is highly seasoned with warm, earthy spices, but is not spicy. Preserved lemons and olives are both quite salty, so you may not need to add any additional salt to the tagine. I like to make this dish with a mix of white- and dark-meat chicken pieces. If using split breasts that are particularly large, cut them in half through the bone using a heavy knife to fit them in the pressure cooker.

1. Add the ghee to the inner pot of your electric pressure cooker. Select the Sauté function and set the heat level to "Normal." Season the chicken pieces with the salt and pepper. When the ghee is shimmering, after about 2 minutes, add half of the chicken pieces, skin-side down. Brown the chicken on the first side, then turn it over and brown it on the second side, about 5 minutes per side. Transfer the chicken to a plate and repeat with the remaining chicken pieces. Set aside.

2. Add the onions to the inner pot and stir to coat with the oil. Sauté the onions, until softened, about 3 minutes. Add the garlic and spices and sauté for an additional minute until fragrant. Press Cancel to turn off the Sauté function.

3. Add the broth and lemon juice and stir to combine. Nestle the chicken pieces among the onions. Add the preserved lemon and olives. Close the lid and make sure the pressure release valve is closed.

4. Select the Pressure Cook function and set the cooking time to 13 minutes at high pressure. When the cooking program is complete, release the pressure manually and remove the lid. Press Cancel to turn off the Keep Warm function.

5. Select the Sauté function and set the heat level to "Less." Whisk together the cornstarch and 1 tablespoon cold water in a small bowl to make a slurry. Add the cornstarch slurry to the sauce and stir to combine. Simmer the sauce, uncovered, until thickened, about 5 minutes. Taste and adjust the seasoning, adding salt if necessary.

6. Garnish with the parsley. Serve warm, over couscous or rice. Remind everyone to be careful of the olive pits.

Chicken & Chorizo Paella

SERVES 6 TO 8

2 tablespoons extra-virgin olive oil

1 yellow onion, diced

1 red bell pepper, diced

1 green bell pepper, diced

3 garlic cloves, minced

1 tablespoon tomato paste

2 teaspoons smoked paprika

½ teaspoon saffron threads

1 teaspoon kosher salt, plus more for seasoning

1 teaspoon freshly ground black pepper, plus more for seasoning

2 cups Calasparra, bomba, or other short-grain paella rice

½ cup dry white wine

1 (14.5-ounce) can crushed tomatoes

4 cups Chicken Broth (page 72)

8 boneless, skinless chicken thighs

12 ounces Spanish chorizo, sliced (see Note)

1 cup frozen peas

Chopped fresh flat-leaf parsley, for serving (optional)

Lemon wedges, for serving (optional)

This pressure cooker version of paella, made with chicken and chorizo, is the very definition of a one-dish meal. The vegetables, rice, and meat cook together all at once without needing any intervention. The paella will be ready to eat as soon as the pressure cooking cycle is complete, but for a more authentic texture, sauté the rice for a few additional minutes to achieve a crispy bottom layer, known as *socarrat*, as you would if making traditional paella on the stove. Seek out a Spanish short-grain rice, such as bomba or Calasparra. You can order imported varieties online or find them at international markets. I have also seen this type of rice at grocery stores in the Latin foods aisle, labeled "pearl rice." Arborio rice, the Italian short-grain rice used for risotto, is not a good substitute, because it is designed to be creamy, while paella rice is not.

1. Pour the olive oil into the inner pot of your electric pressure cooker. Select the Sauté function and set the heat level to "Less." When the oil is shimmering, after about 2 minutes, add the onion and bell peppers and sauté until softened, about 3 minutes. Add the garlic and sauté an additional minute. Add the tomato paste, paprika, saffron, salt, and black pepper and sauté for a few minutes more, until fragrant.

2. Add the rice and stir to coat the grains with the oil. Toast the rice until fragrant, about 3 minutes. Add the wine and simmer until the liquid has been absorbed, about 1 minute. Press Cancel to turn off the Sauté function.

3. Add the crushed tomatoes and broth and stir to combine. Place the chicken thighs and chorizo on top of the rice. Close the lid and make sure the pressure release valve is closed. Select the Pressure Cook function and set the cooking time to 10 minutes at high pressure. When the cooking program is complete, release the pressure manually and remove the lid.

4. Press Cancel to reset the program. Select the Sauté function and set the heat level to "Normal." Add the peas and stir them in gently to the top layer of rice without disturbing the rice on the bottom of the pan. Cook until the peas are heated through and the rice at the bottom of the pot is browned and crispy, 12 to 15 minutes.

5. Transfer the paella to a serving dish. Use a spatula to loosen the socarrat, the crunchy, golden rice at the bottom of the pot, and stir it into the rest of the paella. Taste and adjust the seasoning, adding additional salt and black pepper as needed.

6. Garnish with parsley and serve with lemon wedges, if desired.

NOTE: Spanish chorizo is a hard, cured pork sausage seasoned heavily with paprika, which gives the meat its characteristic red hue. Mexican chorizo, which is a fresh, uncooked sausage, is quite different and is not a suitable substitute here. If you are unable to find Spanish chorizo, andouille sausage will work, as it will lend the paella a smoky flavor, which is the goal.

Chicken Sofrito

SERVES 4

8 bone-in, skin-on chicken thighs

1½ teaspoons kosher salt, plus more for seasoning

1 teaspoon freshly ground black pepper, plus more for seasoning

3 tablespoons extra-virgin olive oil

2 large russet potatoes, peeled and cut into 1-inch chunks

1 yellow onion, halved and sliced

1¼ cups Chicken Broth (page 72)

1 teaspoon paprika

¼ teaspoon ground turmeric

¼ teaspoon ground cinnamon

Juice of 1 lemon

In Israel, chicken sofrito is a beloved comfort food dish among the country's Sephardic population. Indeed, the word *sofrito* comes from the Spanish verb *sofreír*, which means "to fry lightly." Traditionally, the chicken is cooked low and slow for hours, with only a small amount of braising liquid. As a result, the chicken effectively steams in its own juices, making the meat exceptionally tender and flavorful. We can achieve these same results—tender, juicy, falling-off-the-bone meat in a flavorful gravy—in a fraction of the time using an electric pressure cooker. This dish does have several steps: the chicken, potatoes, and onions are all cooked separately using the Sauté function before they are ultimately combined and cooked under pressure. But at the end, you will have a comforting, one-dish meal that tastes like it simmered on the stove all day.

1. Pat the chicken thighs dry and season both sides with 1 teaspoon of the salt and ½ teaspoon of pepper.

2. Pour the olive oil into the inner pot of your electric pressure cooker. Select the Sauté function and set the heat level to "Normal." When the oil is shimmering, after about 2 minutes, add 4 of the chicken thighs, skin-side down.

3. Cook the chicken without disturbing it until the skin is golden brown and the chicken releases easily from the pan, about 7 minutes. Flip the chicken and cook the second side until browned, 3 to 4 minutes. (The chicken will not be cooked through at this point.) Transfer the chicken to a plate and set aside. Repeat with the remaining chicken thighs. (Because the pot is hotter, the second batch often takes less time to cook.)

4. Add the potatoes to the pressure cooker. Toss to coat the potatoes with the oil and season with the remaining teaspoon salt and ½ teaspoon pepper. Arrange the potatoes in as close to a single layer as possible and cook without disturbing until the bottoms are browned and the potatoes release easily from the pot, about 5 minutes. Toss and cook for a few minutes more. Then, using a slotted spoon, remove the potatoes to a plate or bowl and set aside.

5. Add the onion to the pressure cooker and sauté until softened, about 3 minutes.

6. Whisk together the broth, paprika, turmeric, and cinnamon and add it to the pot. Using a wooden spoon, deglaze the pot by scraping up any browned bits stuck to the bottom. Press Cancel to turn off the Sauté function.

7. Return the potatoes to the pot. Arrange the chicken thighs in a single layer on top of the potatoes, overlapping them slightly as needed.

8. Close the lid and make sure the pressure release valve is closed. Select the Pressure Cook function and set the cooking time to 12 minutes at high pressure. When the cooking program is complete, allow the pressure to release naturally for at least 5 minutes, then manually release the remaining pressure and remove the lid.

9. Taste the sauce and adjust the seasoning, adding more salt and pepper if needed. Add the lemon juice and stir to combine.

10. Divide the potatoes and onions evenly among four shallow bowls. Place two chicken thighs in each bowl. Spoon the gravy over the potatoes and chicken. Serve immediately.

Seafood Paella

SERVES 6 TO 8

2 tablespoons extra-
virgin olive oil

1 yellow onion, diced

1 red bell pepper, diced

1 green bell pepper,
diced

3 garlic cloves, minced

1 tablespoon tomato
paste

2 teaspoons smoked
paprika

½ teaspoon saffron
threads

1 teaspoon red pepper
flakes

1 teaspoon kosher salt

1 teaspoon freshly
ground black pepper

2 cups Calasparra,
bomba, or other
short-grain paella
rice (see page 146)

½ cup dry white wine

1 (14.5-ounce) can
crushed tomatoes

4 cups Fish Stock
(page 88) or
seafood stock

1 pound littleneck or
other small clams

1 pound large
(21/25-count) shrimp,
peeled and deveined

1 cup frozen peas

Chopped fresh flat-leaf
parsley, for garnish

Lemon wedges, for
serving

The hallmark of an authentic Spanish paella is the presence of *socarrat*, the crispy, savory crust of rice that forms on the bottom of the pot when the paella is cooked properly. Forming a proper socarrat in an electric pressure cooker requires employing the Sauté function at the end of the recipe after pressure cooking the rice, and doing so can take some trial and error. No matter what, resist the urge to scrape the rice from the bottom of the pan until the paella is finished cooking! Your patience will be rewarded with unparalleled flavor and the paella rice's unique crispy, crunchy texture. If the socarrat sticks to the bottom of the pressure cooker pot, use a spatula to loosen it, then simply stir it into the rest of rice before serving.

1. Pour the olive oil into the inner pot of your electric pressure cooker. Select the Sauté function and set the heat level to "Less." When the oil is shimmering, after about 2 minutes, add the onion and bell peppers and sauté until softened, about 3 minutes. Add the garlic and sauté for an additional minute. Add the tomato paste, spices, salt, and black pepper and sauté for a few minutes more, until fragrant.

2. Add the rice and stir to coat the grains with the oil. Toast the rice until fragrant, about 3 minutes. Add the wine and simmer until the liquid has been absorbed, about 1 minute. Press Cancel to turn off the Sauté function.

3. Add the crushed tomatoes and stock and stir to combine. Arrange the clams on top of the rice, discarding any clams that are open and fail to close when touched. Close the lid and make sure the pressure release valve is closed. Select the Pressure Cook function and set the cooking time to 4 minutes at high pressure. When the cooking program is complete, release the pressure manually and remove the lid.

4. Press Cancel to reset the program. Select the Sauté function and set the heat level to "Normal."

5. Add the shrimp to the pot, pushing them into the broth and rice without stirring or disturbing the rice at the bottom of the pot. Add the peas on top and cook until the shrimp are opaque throughout, the peas are heated through, and the rice at the bottom of the pot is browned and crispy, 12 to 15 minutes.

6. Transfer the paella to a serving dish, discarding any clams that failed to open. Use a spatula to loosen the socarrat, the crunchy, golden rice at the bottom of the pot, and stir it into the rest of the paella. Taste and adjust the seasoning, adding additional salt and black pepper as needed. Garnish with the parsley and serve with lemon wedges.

Mussels with Fennel, Saffron & Tomato

SERVES 2 AS A MAIN COURSE, OR 4 AS A FIRST COURSE

2 pounds mussels in their shells

2 tablespoons extra-virgin olive oil

1 tablespoon unsalted butter

1 small or ½ large yellow onion, halved and thinly sliced

1 bulb fennel, cored and sliced

3 garlic cloves, minced

1 (15-ounce) can diced tomatoes, with their juices

½ teaspoon kosher salt

¼ teaspoon saffron threads

Pinch of red pepper flakes

Several long strips of orange zest

2 tablespoons anise-flavored liqueur, such as ouzo or pastis (optional)

1 cup white wine

Focaccia with Roasted Garlic (page 66) or other crusty bread, for serving (optional)

Many of us love to order a bowl of mussels as a starter—or even a main course—when dining out, yet we rarely think to cook mussels at home. Why is that? Farm-raised mussels are readily available, inexpensive, sustainable, and, best of all, a snap to prepare. A pressure cooker makes cooking mussels especially quick and foolproof. This French-inspired dish of mussels steamed in a heady tomato-and-fennel-scented broth will rival anything you've sampled at your favorite bistro. Serve them with homemade focaccia or a crusty baguette to soak up all the luscious broth.

1. Rinse the mussels in cold water and discard any that are cracked or open and do not close when tapped. Set aside. (If your mussels are not farm-raised, they may require additional scrubbing and debearding.)

2. Put the olive oil and butter in the inner pot of your electric pressure cooker. Select the Sauté function and set the heat level to "Less." When the butter is melted and the oil is shimmering, after about 2 minutes, add the onion and fennel and sauté until softened, about 5 minutes. Add the garlic, tomatoes with their juices, salt, saffron, red pepper flakes, and orange zest and sauté an additional minute. Add the anise liqueur (if using) and wine and bring the liquid to a simmer. Press Cancel to turn off the Sauté function.

3. Add the mussels to the pressure cooker. Close the lid and make sure the pressure release valve is closed. Select the Pressure Cook function and set the cooking time to 1 minute at low pressure. When the cooking program is complete, release the pressure manually and remove the lid. Discard any mussels that have not opened.

4. Divide the mussels evenly among two or four shallow serving bowls. Pour the liquid and vegetables over the mussels and serve immediately, with focaccia or other bread, if desired, for soaking up the broth.

Shrimp with Herbed Orzo & Rice

**SERVES 4 TO 6 AS
A MAIN COURSE**

2 cups basmati or other
long-grain white rice

3 tablespoons extra-
virgin olive oil

½ cup orzo

1 yellow onion, diced

2 garlic cloves, minced

Zest and juice of 1
lemon, plus 1 lemon,
cut into wedges, for
serving

3 cups Chicken Broth
(page 72) or Potager
Vegetable Broth
(page 70)

1 teaspoon red pepper
flakes

1 teaspoon kosher salt

1 teaspoon freshly
ground black pepper

1 pound large
(21/25-count) shrimp,
peeled and deveined

1 cup chopped fresh
flat-leaf parsley

1 teaspoon fresh dill,
minced

1 cup grape tomatoes,
quartered

½ cup crumbled feta
cheese, preferably
Greek

¼ cup chopped pitted
kalamata olives

3 tablespoons chopped
or sliced peperoncini
peppers

Bright herbs, briny olives, and spicy peperoncini peppers add wonderful depth to this Greek-inspired shrimp dish, which is equally delicious served hot or cold. By cooking the grains and shrimp together, you have a one-pot meal that is ready to serve in under 30 minutes—perfect for busy weeknights. You may even use frozen shrimp, which are especially convenient; just thaw them according to the package instructions before proceeding. The key to cooking shrimp in an electric pressure cooker without overcooking them is to start with large or jumbo shrimp and release the pressure manually as soon as the cooking program is complete.

1. Rinse the rice and then soak it for 15 to 20 minutes in enough cold water to cover the rice by 1 inch. Drain and set aside.

2. Pour 2 tablespoons of the olive oil into the inner pot of your electric pressure cooker. Select the Sauté function and set the heat level to "Normal." When the oil is shimmering, after about 2 minutes, add the orzo. Toast the orzo, stirring, until fragrant and beginning to brown, about 3 minutes. Add the onion and garlic, stir to combine, and sauté until softened, about 3 minutes. Press Cancel to turn off the Sauté function.

3. Add the rice, lemon zest, lemon juice, broth, red pepper flakes, salt, and black pepper and stir to combine. Arrange the shrimp on top of rice mixture. Close the lid and make sure the pressure release valve is closed. Select the Pressure Cook function and set the cooking time to 2 minutes at high pressure. When the cooking program is complete, release the pressure manually and remove the lid.

4. Fluff the rice mixture with a fork. Add the parsley, dill, tomatoes, feta, olives, and peperoncini peppers and stir to combine. Drizzle the rice with the remaining 1 tablespoon olive oil. Serve with the lemon wedges.

Cod with Tomatoes, Olives & Capers

SERVES 4

- 2 tablespoons extra-virgin olive oil
- 1 yellow onion, halved and thinly sliced
- 1 pint cherry tomatoes or grape tomatoes, halved
- 3 garlic cloves, minced
- ½ cup marinated black olives, such as kalamata, pitted
- 1 tablespoon capers
- Pinch of red pepper flakes
- ½ cup white wine
- 4 (6- to 8-ounce) cod fillets
- ½ teaspoon kosher salt
- Freshly ground black pepper
- 2 tablespoons chopped fresh basil, for garnish

Many people are reluctant to cook fish at home because they fear over- or undercooking it, and who wants to ruin such an expensive ingredient? Moreover, no one enjoys the lingering odor that cooking fish seems to leave behind. Pressure cooking, however, addresses both of these concerns. Gentle poaching in a pressure cooker results in perfectly cooked, flaky fish every time, and the machine does an outstanding job of containing the fishy smell. This Provençal-inspired fish dish pairs classic Mediterranean ingredients like wine, tomato, and olives with Atlantic cod—a mild-tasting and readily available fish—to take all the anxiety out of cooking fish. Serve the final dish over rice or orzo, or with a crusty loaf, so as not to waste a drop of the lovely tomato-scented broth.

1. Pour the olive oil into the inner pot of your electric pressure cooker. Select the Sauté function and set the heat level to "Normal." When the oil is shimmering, after about 2 minutes, add the onion and sauté until softened, about 3 minutes. Add the tomatoes, garlic, olives, capers, and red pepper flakes and sauté for a few minutes more, until the tomatoes are softened. Press Cancel to turn off the Sauté function.

2. Add the wine to the vegetable mixture and stir to combine.

3. Season the cod with the salt and black pepper. Arrange the cod fillets on top of the vegetables.

4. Close the lid and make sure the pressure release valve is closed. Select the Pressure Cook function and set the cooking time to 2 minutes at low pressure.

5. When the cooking program is complete, allow the pressure to release naturally. (This will take about 5 minutes.) Taste the broth and adjust the seasoning if necessary. (Both olives and capers are salty ingredients, so taste before adding any additional salt.)

6. To serve, divide the cod among four plates or shallow bowls. Top each fillet with several spoonfuls of the vegetables and broth. Garnish with the basil. Serve immediately.

Poached Halibut with Chermoula

SERVES 4

2 cups fresh cilantro leaves

1 cup fresh flat-leaf parsley leaves

3 garlic cloves, peeled and halved

Zest and juice of 1 lemon, plus 1 lemon, cut into wedges, for serving

1 teaspoon chopped preserved lemon rind (optional; see Note, page 78)

½ teaspoon ground cumin

½ teaspoon ground coriander

½ teaspoon paprika

⅛ teaspoon red pepper flakes

Kosher salt

½ cup plus 2 tablespoons extra-virgin olive oil

4 (6- to 8-ounce) halibut fillets

Freshly ground black pepper

1 cup Fish Stock (page 88) or water

Chermoula is a piquant Moroccan herb paste—enriched with lemon juice and olive oil—reminiscent of South America's chimichurri. In Morocco, chermoula is used as both a marinade for grilled fish and a condiment passed at the table. We do the same in this recipe—marinating the fish briefly in the chermoula before poaching it gently in the pressure cooker *and* using the chermoula as a sauce for the finished dish. While this halibut is quick enough to prepare on a busy weeknight, it is certainly elegant enough for a special occasion. Couscous or Rice with Vermicelli (page 101) would make a nice accompaniment.

1. To make the chermoula, place the cilantro, parsley, garlic, lemon zest and juice, preserved lemon (if using), spices, and a pinch of salt in a food processor and pulse until the mixture forms a coarse paste. With the motor running, slowly pour in the olive oil and process until the mixture is smooth and has a thin, liquid consistency. Taste and adjust the seasoning. If you did not include the preserved lemon, you will likely need to add more salt. (This may be done up to 2 days in advance. Refrigerate in an airtight container until needed.)

2. Brush each piece of fish with a thin layer of chermoula and season with a pinch of salt and black pepper. Cover and refrigerate the fish for at least 15 and up to 30 minutes.

3. Add the stock to the electric pressure cooker and place the trivet inside the inner pot. Arrange the halibut fillets on top of the trivet, skin-side down.

4. Close the lid and make sure the pressure release valve is closed. Select the Pressure Cook function and set the cooking time to 2 minutes at low pressure. When the cooking program is complete, allow the pressure to release naturally. Remove the fillets and serve immediately.

5. To serve, drizzle the fish with additional chermoula. Pass wedges from the remaining lemon at the table.

Salade Niçoise with Tuna

SERVES 4

DRESSING

6 tablespoons white wine vinegar

1½ teaspoons Dijon mustard

2 garlic cloves, minced or grated on a Microplane

1 teaspoon kosher salt

½ teaspoon freshly ground black pepper

Pinch of sugar

½ cup extra-virgin olive oil

SALAD

4 large eggs

1 pound fingerling potatoes

1 (8-ounce) bag green beans or haricots verts

1 (5-ounce) bag salad greens, such as butter lettuce or Little Gem

12 ounces tuna packed in oil, drained

4 Roma (plum) or on-the-vine tomatoes, cut into wedges

½ cup Niçoise olives (or substitute kalamata)

Elegant, timeless salade Niçoise is perhaps the Mediterranean's best-loved main-course salad. To eat a Niçoise salad is to feel transported—if only for a moment—to a seaside restaurant on the French Riviera, a bottle of rosé chilling in a bucket beside you. As elegant as it is, however, this French bistro staple is surprisingly easy to prepare at home, and it makes a delightfully light, healthy warm-weather meal. Here I use an electric pressure cooker to cook each element of the traditional Niçoise salad to perfection, with a minimum of effort and dirty dishes. The first secret to a restaurant-quality Niçoise salad is dressing each element separately and then arranging them in sections on top of the greens— what the French call a *salade composée*. The second secret is using high-quality tuna packed in olive oil. I like to splurge on imported brands such as Ortiz, Genova, Bela, and Tonnino that use traditional pole-and-line fishing, which is more sustainable than other methods.

1. Make the dressing: Whisk together the vinegar, mustard, garlic, salt, pepper, and sugar in a medium bowl. While whisking, slowly pour in the olive oil in a steady stream and continue whisking until emulsified. Set aside.

2. Make the salad: Pour 1 cup water into the inner pot of your electric pressure cooker. Place the trivet in the pot and arrange the eggs on the trivet. Close the lid and make sure the pressure release valve is closed. Select the Pressure Cook function and set the cooking time to 7 minutes at low pressure.

3. Meanwhile, fill a large bowl with ice and cold water. When the cooking program is complete, release the pressure manually and remove the lid. Press Cancel to turn off the Keep Warm setting. Transfer the eggs to the bowl of ice water to cool; drain the inner pot and return it to the pressure cooker. When the eggs are cool enough to handle, peel them and cut them in half; set aside.

4. Pour 1 cup water into the inner pot of the pressure cooker and return the trivet to the pot. Place the potatoes in a steamer basket or small colander and place the basket on top of the trivet. Close the lid

and make sure the pressure release valve is closed. Select the Pressure Cook function and set the cooking time to 10 minutes at high pressure.

5. When the cooking program is complete, release the pressure manually and remove the lid. Remove the steamer basket with the potatoes and pour out the water. Press Cancel to turn off the Keep Warm setting.

6. As soon as the potatoes are cool enough to handle, halve or quarter them, depending on their size, and place them in a medium bowl. While the potatoes are still warm, add 3 tablespoons of the dressing and toss gently to coat. Set aside.

7. Pour 1 cup water into the inner pot of the pressure cooker and return the trivet to the pot. Place the green beans in the steamer basket or small colander and place the basket on top of the trivet. Close the lid and make sure the pressure release valve is closed. Select the Pressure Cook function and set the cooking time to 0 minutes at high pressure. (The pressure cooker will take around 10 minutes to come up to pressure, during which time the green beans will cook.)

8. Meanwhile, fill a large bowl with ice and cold water. When the cooking program is complete, release the pressure manually and remove the lid. Transfer the green beans to the bowl of ice water. When the green beans are cool, drain them and dry them well. Place the green beans in a separate medium bowl and toss with 2 tablespoons of the dressing.

9. Place the lettuce in a large bowl and toss with about ¼ cup of the dressing.

10. To assemble the salad, divide the lettuce evenly among four plates or shallow bowls. To each plate, add one-quarter of the potatoes, green beans, and tuna, arranging them in sections with the tuna in the middle. Add one egg and one tomato to each plate. Drizzle additional dressing over each plate, making sure to dress the tuna and tomatoes. Add 1 to 2 tablespoons of olives to each plate. Serve immediately with additional salt and pepper.

DESSERTS

Prosecco-Poached Pears

SERVES 4

1 bottle Prosecco

¾ cup sugar

2 cinnamon sticks

1 teaspoon whole cloves

4 firm or slightly underripe pears that hold their shape well, such as Bosc or Anjou

Poached pears are the little black dress of desserts because they are both elegant and versatile. Poaching in an electric pressure cooker is especially quick and foolproof. Prepare these pears a day or two in advance for a no-stress dessert for your next dinner party or holiday gathering—especially if you or any of your guests are gluten-free. Speaking of versatility, you can serve these poached pears any number of ways, such as with a scoop of vanilla ice cream and a drizzle of dark chocolate sauce, which is known as *poire Belle Hélène* in France. Alternatively, you could serve them with a dollop of mascarpone, a drizzle of honey, and a sprinkle of toasted almonds, which would lean Italian. Perhaps you will even use them to top a scoop of Labneh (page 52) at breakfast like an Israeli. If gluten is not a concern, these cinnamon-and-clove-infused pears are also wonderful alongside a piece of spice cake or gingerbread.

1. Combine the Prosecco, sugar, cinnamon sticks, and cloves in the inner pot of your electric pressure cooker. Select the Sauté function and set the heat level to "Normal." Bring the mixture to a simmer; this will take 5 to 7 minutes.

2. Meanwhile, peel the pears, halve them lengthwise, and scoop out the core with a melon baller or metal tablespoon.

3. Place the peeled pears in the poaching liquid and press Cancel to turn off the Sauté function. Close the lid and make sure the pressure release valve is closed. Select the Steam function and set the cooking time to 3 minutes at low pressure.

4. When the cooking program is complete, release the pressure manually and remove the lid. Press Cancel to turn off the Keep Warm function. Using a slotted spoon, transfer the pear halves to a bowl and set aside.

5. Select the Sauté function and set the heat level to "Normal." Bring the poaching liquid to a simmer. Simmer until the poaching liquid is golden, syrupy, and reduced to about 1 cup, 20 to 25 minutes. Strain the syrup to remove the solids.

6. If not serving right away, transfer the pears to an airtight container, pour the syrup over the pears, and store in the refrigerator for up to 5 days.

Poached Turkish Apricots with Labneh

SERVES 4

1 cup white wine

½ cup sugar

½ cup honey

1 vanilla bean, split lengthwise

1 cinnamon stick

4 whole cloves

3 green cardamom pods, lightly crushed

Zest of 1 lemon, cut into long strips

14 ounces dried apricots, preferably Turkish or Mediterranean

Labneh (page 52), for serving

The dead of winter, when there is no local fruit in season in many parts of United States, is the perfect moment to turn to dried fruit. Dried apricots are delightful to eat out of hand, but they become even more luscious when poached in a honey-sweetened white wine syrup until plump and juicy. Poaching in an electric pressure cooker is quick and easy and infuses the fruit with the flavors of the syrup. A few of these poached apricots topped with their syrup makes an elegant, light dessert, especially when served with a dollop of tangy homemade labneh. Or enjoy these for breakfast, sprinkled with Pistachio-Honey Granola (page 37) for a bit of crunch.

1. Combine the wine, sugar, honey, vanilla bean, cinnamon stick, cloves, cardamom pods, lemon zest, and 1½ cups water in the inner pot of your electric pressure cooker. Select the Sauté function and set the heat level to "Normal." Bring the mixture to a simmer.

2. Add the apricots and stir to combine. Press Cancel to turn off the Sauté function. Close the lid and make sure the pressure release valve is closed. Select the Steam function and set the cooking time to 12 minutes at high pressure. When the cooking program is complete, release the pressure manually and remove the lid. Press Cancel to turn off the Keep Warm function. Using a slotted spoon, transfer the apricots to a bowl and set aside.

3. Select the Sauté function and set the heat level to "Normal." Bring the poaching liquid to a simmer. Simmer until the syrup has reduced to about 1 cup, about 10 minutes. Strain the syrup to remove the solids. Allow the strained syrup to cool, then pour over the fruit and refrigerate in an airtight container until needed.

4. To serve, place about 8 apricots in a small dish. Spoon some of the syrup over the fruit and top with a dollop of labneh.

NOTE: Turkish or Mediterranean apricots are dried whole and then pitted. As a result, the apricots tend to be plumper and retain more of their moisture than California apricots, which are halved, pitted, and then dried. For best results, use whole Turkish apricots for poaching.

No-Bake Israeli Cheesecake

SERVES 4

Baking spray

1 (8.8-ounce) package Biscoff cookies

4 tablespoons (½ stick) unsalted butter, melted

1 cup plain 2% Greek yogurt

1 cup sour cream

3 large eggs

½ cup sugar

2 tablespoons cornstarch

1 teaspoon pure vanilla extract

Zest of 1 lemon

Cheesecakes are common throughout the Mediterranean, but they do not resemble the dense, New York–style cheesecakes we typically see in the United States. Made with soft, fresh, spreadable cheeses like quark or Israel's *gvina levana*, Mediterranean cheesecakes are light and airy, with an almost mousse-like texture. As gvina levana and other European-style fresh cheeses can be hard to source in America, I have substituted a combination of plain Greek yogurt and sour cream in this Israeli-inspired cheesecake. I think you will be won over by its pillowy texture and how quickly it comes together in an electric pressure cooker. For the crust, which does not require any baking, I use pulverized Biscoff cookies, which are a crunchy, caramel-flavored spice cookie beloved throughout Europe. I like to serve this with fresh berries or a dollop of lemon curd. *Photo on page 167.*

1. Spray a 7-inch springform pan (or a 7-inch cheesecake pan with a removable bottom) with baking spray. Line the bottom with parchment paper cut to fit, if necessary, and spray the parchment as well. If using a springform pan, wrap the bottom in aluminum foil to ensure a tight seal.

2. Place the trivet in the inner pot of your electric pressure cooker and pour in 1½ cups water.

3. Pulse the cookies in a food processor until reduced to fine crumbs. Measure 2 cups of the crumbs and place them in a large bowl; transfer the remaining crumbs to a separate dish and set aside. Wipe out the bowl of the food processor.

4. Drizzle the melted butter over the crumbs in the large bowl and stir with a fork until the crumbs are moistened and starting to clump together.

5. Pour the crumbs into the prepared pan and press the mixture firmly over the bottom and up the sides of the pan. Use a heavy-bottomed glass to tamp down the crumbs even further, making sure the crust is even on the bottom and the same thickness all around the sides. Place the crust in the freezer to firm up for at least 20 minutes while you make the filling. (This may be done up to a day in advance.)

6. Meanwhile, combine the yogurt, sour cream, eggs, sugar, cornstarch, vanilla, and lemon zest in a food processor. Pulse until the mixture is completely smooth, stopping to scrape down the sides as necessary.

7. Pour the filling onto the prepared crust. Cover the top of the pan with foil. (This will protect the cake from condensation dripping from the lid.) If using a bakeware sling, place the covered pan in the sling and lower it onto the trivet. Otherwise, carefully place the pan on top of the trivet.

8. Close the lid and make sure the pressure release valve is closed. Select the Pressure Cook function and set the cooking time to 30 minutes at high pressure. When the cooking program is complete, allow the pressure to release naturally for at least 15 minutes, then manually release the remaining pressure and remove the lid. Remove the pan and set it on a wire rack; carefully remove the foil covering. (The middle of the cake should still be wobbly at this point; it will set as it cools.)

9. Cool the cheesecake to room temperature, then cover and refrigerate overnight or for at least 8 hours prior to serving.

10. Sprinkle some of the reserved Biscoff crumbs over the top of the cheesecake, slice, and serve.

Orange Ricotta Cheesecake with Raspberries

SERVES 4

CRUST
Baking spray

½ cup slivered almonds, lightly toasted

¼ cup all-purpose flour

3 tablespoons granulated sugar

Pinch of fine sea salt

1 large egg yolk

2 tablespoons unsalted butter, melted

½ teaspoon pure vanilla extract

FILLING
16 ounces full-fat ricotta cheese, homemade (page 51) or store-bought, drained if watery

½ cup granulated sugar

3 large eggs

¼ cup sour cream

2 teaspoons cornstarch

2 teaspoons orange zest

1 teaspoon pure vanilla extract

1 tablespoon amaretto liqueur or Grand Marnier (optional)

TOPPING
⅓ cup raspberry jam

6 ounces fresh raspberries

Powdered sugar, for dusting

An electric pressure cooker is far superior to your oven for baking silky smooth, perfectly cooked cheesecake. No more messing around with a bulky water bath to create the moist, steamy environment your cheesecake needs—the pressure cooker creates that environment all on its own, and is faster at it, to boot. This particular cheesecake is fashioned after the Italian style and is made with ricotta cheese. The velvety filling, with its sunny orange flavor, sits atop a crumbly almond-shortbread crust. Decorated with raspberry jam and fresh raspberries, this elegant cheesecake is the perfect way to end an intimate, Mediterranean-inspired dinner party—especially because you make it the day before! *Photo on page 166.*

1. Make the crust: Preheat the oven to 325°F. Spray a 7-inch springform pan or a 7-inch cheesecake pan with a removable bottom with baking spray. Line the bottom with parchment paper cut to fit, if necessary, and spray the parchment as well.

2. Combine the almonds, flour, granulated sugar, and salt in a food processor and pulse until the mixture resembles fine crumbs.

3. Whisk together the egg yolk, melted butter, and vanilla in a small bowl and add the mixture to the dry ingredients in the food processor. Pulse several times, until the ingredients are moistened and crumbly.

4. Pour the mixture into the prepared pan and press it into an even layer over the bottom of the pan. Use a heavy-bottomed drinking glass to tamp down the crumbs even further. Place the crust in the freezer to firm up for at least 10 minutes.

5. Bake the crust for 10 to 15 minutes, until lightly golden in color. Cool on a wire rack while you prepare the filling. (This may be done up to a day in advance.)

6. Make the filling: Whisk together the ricotta, granulated sugar, eggs, sour cream, cornstarch, orange zest, vanilla, and liqueur (if using) in a medium bowl until smooth.

7. Pour the filling over the cooled crust and carefully tap the pan on the counter a few times to knock out any air bubbles. Cover the pan with foil. (This will protect the cake from condensation dripping from the lid.)

8. Place the trivet in the inner pot of your electric pressure cooker and pour in 1½ cups water. If using a bakeware sling, place the covered pan in the sling and lower it onto the trivet. Otherwise, carefully place the pan on top of the trivet.

9. Close the lid and make sure the pressure release valve is closed. Select the Pressure Cook function and set the cooking time to 35 minutes at high pressure. When the cooking program is complete, allow the pressure to release naturally for at least 15 minutes, then manually release the remaining pressure and remove the lid. Remove the pan, place it on a wire rack, and carefully remove the foil covering. (The middle of the cake should still be wobbly at this point; it will set as it cools.)

10. Cool the cheesecake to room temperature, then cover and refrigerate overnight or for at least 8 hours prior to serving.

11. Just before serving, spread the jam over the top of the cake using a small offset spatula. Arrange the raspberries on top of the jam, open-side down. Dust the top with powdered sugar and serve.

Basbousa (Semolina Yogurt Cake)

SERVES 4 TO 6

CAKE
Butter, for the pan

1¼ cups semolina flour

¾ teaspoon baking powder

½ teaspoon baking soda

½ teaspoon fine sea salt

⅓ cup sugar

2 large eggs

½ cup vegetable oil

½ teaspoon pure vanilla extract

½ cup plain yogurt, preferably full-fat

Zest of 1 lemon

SYRUP
1 cup sugar

1 tablespoon freshly squeezed lemon juice

Drop of rose water (optional)

1 cup plain yogurt, preferably full-fat, for topping

Cakes made with semolina flour, which is milled from durum wheat, are popular throughout North Africa, the Middle East, and the eastern Mediterranean. There are countless versions of this cake—coconut and almond being two of the most popular additions—and it goes by many names, depending on what country you are in. *Basbousa* is the Egyptian name. I first developed this recipe for my book *The Joys of Jewish Preserving.* When working on *this* book, I suspected that a semolina cake might do well in an electric pressure cooker, and I am happy to say that I was right. The combination of the yogurt in the batter and the steam cooking of the pressure cooker helps keep the cake moist despite the dry, almost gritty texture of semolina. The sugar syrup adds sweetness and the cake's characteristic saturated texture. Cakes cooked in a pressure cooker are not always the prettiest to look at, so the yogurt topping helps dress this one up.

1. Make the cake: Butter a 7-inch round cake pan or springform pan and line the bottom with parchment paper cut to fit. Butter the parchment as well.

2. Whisk together the semolina, baking powder, baking soda, and salt in a small bowl. Set aside.

3. Combine the sugar and eggs in a large bowl and beat with a handheld mixer on medium speed or whisk by hand until light and fluffy, about 3 minutes.

4. While mixing, slowly pour in the oil in a steady stream and continue to beat until combined. Add the vanilla.

5. Add the yogurt and mix until combined. Gradually add the dry ingredients and mix just until combined. Fold in the lemon zest.

6. Pour the batter into the prepared pan and smooth the top. Cover the pan with foil. (This will protect the cake from condensation dripping from the lid.)

7. Place the trivet in the inner pot of your electric pressure cooker and pour in 1½ cups water. If using a bakeware sling, place the covered pan in the sling and lower it onto the trivet. Otherwise, carefully place the pan on top of the trivet. Close the lid and make sure the pressure release valve is closed. Select the Pressure Cook function and set the cooking time to 40 minutes at high pressure.

8. Meanwhile, make the syrup: Combine the sugar and 1 cup water in a small saucepan. Bring to a boil over medium-high heat, stirring to dissolve the sugar. Add the lemon juice and rose water (if using) and reduce the heat to low. Simmer until the syrup has thickened, about 5 minutes. Remove from the heat and allow to cool. Transfer 2 tablespoons of the syrup to a small bowl and set aside.

9. When the cooking program is complete, allow the pressure to release naturally for at least 10 minutes, then manually release the remaining pressure and remove the lid. Remove the cake pan and carefully remove the foil.

10. While the cake is still warm, poke it all over with a toothpick or skewer. Ladle a spoonful of the syrup over the cake. Once the cake has absorbed the syrup, add another spoonful. Continue spooning syrup over the cake and allowing it to be absorbed until you have used all the syrup. Allow the cake to cool and absorb all the syrup before removing it from the pan. (This may be done up to 1 day in advance. Cover the cake and store at room temperature.)

11. Add the yogurt to the bowl with the reserved 2 tablespoons of syrup and stir to combine. Spread the yogurt over the cooled cake just prior to serving. Store any leftover cake with the yogurt topping, covered, in the refrigerator for up to 3 days.

Chocolate Olive Oil Cake
with Orange Ganache & Hazelnuts

SERVES 2 TO 4

CAKE

Butter, for the pan

⅔ cup all-purpose flour, plus more for dusting the pan

½ cup sugar

¼ cup unsweetened cocoa powder

½ teaspoon baking powder

½ teaspoon baking soda

½ teaspoon espresso powder (optional)

¼ teaspoon fine sea salt

1 large egg

½ cup whole milk

1 teaspoon pure vanilla extract

2½ tablespoons olive oil

GANACHE

4 ounces bittersweet chocolate, finely chopped

2 tablespoons unsalted butter, at room temperature

½ cup heavy cream

Zest of 1 orange

⅛ teaspoon ground allspice

⅛ teaspoon ground cloves

⅛ teaspoon fine sea salt

¼ cup hazelnuts, toasted and chopped

I love how quickly this cake comes together—don't even bother to pull out the electric mixer—and its petite size, which makes it a perfect indulgence for a couple or small group. The olive oil adds a pleasant savory note. Topped with a rich orange ganache and crunchy hazelnuts, this cake will transport you to Italy—if just for a moment. Why bake a cake in an electric pressure cooker if it does not save time over baking it in the oven? First, there are times that you may not want to turn on the oven, such as the hottest days of summer. Second, the steamy environment of the pressure cooker makes cakes turn out exceptionally moist and tender. While the pressure cooker will never replace your oven, using it to bake the occasional Mediterranean-inspired dessert is both fun and convenient.

1. Make the cake: Butter a 7-inch round cake pan or springform pan and dust with flour, tapping out any excess. Place the trivet in the electric pressure cooker and pour in 1½ cups water.

2. In a medium bowl, whisk together the flour, sugar, cocoa powder, baking powder, baking soda, espresso powder (if using), and salt. Set aside.

3. In a small bowl, whisk together the egg, milk, and vanilla. While mixing, slowly pour in the oil in a steady stream and continue to whisk until combined.

4. Add the liquid ingredients to the flour mixture and stir with a wooden spoon or spatula until smooth. Pour the batter into the prepared pan.

5. If using a bakeware sling, place the pan in the sling and lower it onto the trivet. Otherwise, carefully place the pan on top of the trivet. Close the lid and make sure the pressure release valve is closed. Select the Pressure Cook function and set the cooking time to 30 minutes at high pressure.

6. When the cooking program is complete, allow the pressure to release naturally for at least 10 minutes, then manually release the remaining pressure and remove the lid. Remove the cake pan, making sure not to drip any water on the cake. Place the cake on a wire rack and allow to cool for at least 15 minutes. Remove the cake from the pan and let cool completely before adding the ganache.

7. Make the ganache: Place the chocolate and butter in a heatproof bowl.

8. Combine the cream and orange zest in a small saucepan and bring just to a boil over medium heat. Remove from the heat and add the allspice, cloves, and salt. Set a fine-mesh strainer over the bowl with the chocolate and pour the warm cream mixture through the strainer to remove the zest. Stir together the cream and chocolate until smooth. Allow the ganache to cool and thicken slightly.

9. Ladle the ganache over the cooled cake, allowing the excess to drip down the sides. Top with the hazelnuts and serve.

Rice Pudding with Golden Raisins & Toasted Almonds

SERVES 6 TO 8

2½ cups whole milk

½ cup sugar

2 cinnamon sticks

1 vanilla bean, split lengthwise

1 teaspoon cardamom pods, lightly crushed

Pinch of fine sea salt

2 cups short-grain white rice, such as Arborio

2 tablespoons sweetened condensed milk (optional)

¾ cup golden raisins

⅓ cup sliced almonds, lightly toasted, plus more for garnish

½ teaspoon ground cinnamon, plus more for garnish

Sweet, creamy rice pudding is one of those dishes that you will find all around the Mediterranean, from France's *riz au lait* and Greece's *rizogalo* to *riz bi haleeb* in the Middle East. Whether served warm or cold, topped with dried fruits and nuts or just a dash of cinnamon, rice pudding is the very definition of comfort food no matter where you are from. My version of rice pudding has warm Middle Eastern spices, like cinnamon, cardamom, and vanilla, and is studded with golden raisins and almonds to add some texture to the creamy pudding. For added richness, and a particularly Middle Eastern touch, stir in some sweetened condensed milk. But if this is not an ingredient that is typically in your pantry, feel free to skip it.

1. Combine the milk, sugar, cinnamon sticks, vanilla bean, cardamom pods, and salt in a small saucepan and bring to a simmer over medium heat, stirring to dissolve the sugar. Remove from the heat, cover, and set aside to infuse while you cook the rice.

2. Place the rice in the inner pot of your electric pressure cooker, pour in 3 cups water, and stir to combine. Close the lid and make sure the pressure release valve is closed. Select the Pressure Cook function and set the cooking time to 3 minutes at high pressure. When the cooking program is complete, allow the pressure to release naturally for 10 minutes, then manually release the remaining pressure and remove the lid. Fluff the rice with a fork and leave the Keep Warm setting on.

3. Place a strainer over the inner pot. Gradually ladle the infused milk through the strainer onto the rice, stirring to combine, then discard the solids.

4. Once you have stirred in all the milk, add the sweetened condensed milk (if using), raisins, almonds, and cinnamon.

5. Serve warm, garnished with a sprinkle of sliced almonds and a dusting of cinnamon, or, to serve the rice pudding cold, store it covered in the refrigerator until needed. If the chilled rice pudding is too thick, thin it with a splash of milk prior to serving.

Sour Cherry Bread Pudding with Vanilla Sauce

SERVES 4 TO 6

BREAD PUDDING

1 tablespoon unsalted butter, at room temperature, for the dish

4 cups 1-inch bread cubes, from a loaf of sweet bread such as challah or brioche (preferably at least a day old)

1½ cups pitted fresh or frozen sour cherries

2 cups whole milk

4 large eggs

½ cup sugar

1 tablespoon pure vanilla extract

½ teaspoon ground cinnamon, plus more for dusting

VANILLA SAUCE

1 cup whole milk

4 large egg yolks

⅓ cup sugar

Pinch of fine sea salt

1 teaspoon pure vanilla extract

2 tablespoons fruit-flavored liqueur, such as Grand Marnier or kirsch, or brandy (optional)

This rich bread pudding studded with sour cherries is inspired by a Turkish recipe from Paula Wolfert's classic book *The Cooking of the Eastern Mediterranean*. Sour cherries are smaller and less shiny than their sweet cousins and are primarily used for baking and preserving. They are very fragile, so seek out fresh ones at a farmers' market in early summer—when they are in season—or use frozen sour cherries. Either works beautifully in this recipe. An electric pressure cooker steams bread pudding—rather than baking it as the oven does—so it stays velvety and custardy. The texture of the pudding is quite lovely by itself, but the luscious vanilla sauce, otherwise known as crème anglaise, elevates this somewhat rustic dessert to company-worthy. Follow the instructions about tempering the eggs carefully so you don't end up with scrambled eggs.

1. Make the bread pudding: Butter a 1½-quart soufflé dish. Place half the bread cubes in the dish, followed by half the cherries. Layer the remaining bread cubes on top of the cherries and top with the remaining cherries.

2. Whisk together the milk, eggs, sugar, vanilla, and cinnamon in a medium bowl. Pour the egg mixture over the bread and cherries in the soufflé dish and press down to submerge the bread. Cover with foil and refrigerate for at least 1 hour and up to overnight.

3. Place the trivet in the inner pot of your electric pressure cooker and pour in 1½ cups water. If using a bakeware sling, place the soufflé dish in the sling and lower it onto the trivet. Otherwise, carefully place the dish on top of the trivet. Close the lid and make sure the pressure release valve is closed. Select the Pressure Cook function and set the cooking time to 30 minutes at low pressure.

4. Meanwhile, make the vanilla sauce: Heat the milk in a 2-quart saucepan over medium-low heat just until steaming.

5. Whisk together the egg yolks, sugar, and salt in a heatproof bowl until lightened in color, about 2 minutes. While whisking, slowly ladle a generous spoonful of the warm milk into the egg mixture to temper the eggs. Then pour the egg mixture back into the saucepan. Gently cook the sauce over medium to medium-low heat, stirring continuously, until it thickens and coats the back of a spoon. (Do not allow the sauce to boil or it will curdle.)

6. Fill a bowl with ice and cold water. Remove the saucepan from the heat and strain the sauce through a fine-mesh strainer into a heatproof bowl. (Do not skip this step; it removes any bits of cooked egg that will ruin the sauce otherwise.) Add the vanilla and liqueur (if using). Place the bowl in the ice water and stir the sauce until it cools. Refrigerate the sauce in an airtight container until needed. (This may be done up to 5 days in advance.)

7. When the cooking program for the bread pudding is complete, allow the pressure to release naturally for at least 10 minutes, then manually release the remaining pressure and remove the lid. Remove the soufflé dish and remove the foil, making sure not to drip any water onto the bread pudding.

8. Dust the top with cinnamon. Serve the bread pudding warm or at room temperature with the vanilla sauce.

Lemon Pots de Crème

SERVES 4

1½ cups heavy cream

½ cup whole milk

Zest and juice of
   3 lemons (about
   ½ cup juice)

½ cup sugar

Fine sea salt

5 large egg yolks

Optional toppings:
   whipped cream,
   fresh berries,
   candied violets

Pot de crème is a baked French custard that is typically served in individual ramekins or custard cups. Unlike pudding, which is cooked on the stovetop, pot de crème is typically steamed in the oven and does not contain a thickener, such as cornstarch. While chocolate pot de crème is the most traditional variety, I enjoy applying the same technique to different flavors, such as lemon. To make this lemon version particularly aromatic, try making it with Meyer lemons when they are in season. Using an electric pressure cooker to steam the pots de crème simplifies the process and produces perfect results every time. Do not be alarmed that the custards are still wobbly when you take them out—they will firm up as they cool.

1. Combine the cream, milk, lemon zest and juice, ¼ cup of the sugar, and a pinch of salt in a small saucepan. Slowly bring to a simmer over medium-low heat, stirring frequently.

2. Meanwhile, in a large bowl, whisk the egg yolks with the remaining ¼ cup of sugar until pale yellow in color.

3. When the cream mixture is just at a simmer, remove from the heat. While whisking continuously, gradually and slowly pour the warm cream mixture into the egg yolks to temper the egg. (Do not rush this step or add too much cream at one time or you will scramble the eggs.)

4. Place a fine-mesh strainer or cheesecloth over a pitcher or large measuring cup with a spout. Strain the custard into the pitcher to remove the lemon zest and any bits of cooked egg.

5. Divide the custard evenly among four (8-ounce) ramekins or glass jars. Cover each ramekin with foil.

6. Place the trivet in the inner pot of the electric pressure cooker and pour in 1½ cups water. Arrange the ramekins on top of the trivet. Close the lid and make sure the pressure release valve is closed. Select the Pressure Cook function and set the cooking time to 6 minutes at low pressure.

7. When the cooking program is complete, allow the pressure to release naturally for 5 minutes, then manually release the remaining pressure and remove the lid.

8. Carefully remove the ramekins and place them on a wire rack. Remove the foil coverings and allow the pots de crème to cool to room temperature, then cover and refrigerate for at least 4 hours or overnight.

9. Remove the pots de crème from the refrigerator 30 minutes prior to serving. Serve plain or topped with a pretty garnish, such as whipped cream and fresh berries or a candied violet.

NOTE: For an especially adorable presentation, use pretty 8-ounce glass jars, such as those made by Weck, to steam and serve the pots de crème.

Crème Caramel

SERVES 6

1½ cups sugar

3 cups whole milk

1 vanilla bean, split lengthwise (optional)

Zest of 1 orange (optional)

2 large eggs

3 large egg yolks

Fine sea salt

NOTE: Straight-sided cylindrical ramekins work better here than pretty fluted ones, as you can fit all of them into the pressure cooker at once.

Crème caramel: You would be hard-pressed to think of a more classic French bistro dessert. Today, crème caramel (also known as flan in Spain or *flan au caramel* in the parts of France that are close to Spain) seems a bit old-fashioned, but I think it is time to bring back this iconic treat. When prepared properly, crème caramel is delightfully wobbly—not rubbery—with a fresh, eggy flavor that lets the sweet caramel topping take center stage. With an electric pressure cooker's gentle steam action, it is easier than ever to re-create this restaurant dish at home. The trickiest part, by far, is making the caramel topping. Resist the urge to stir the caramel, which can cause it to crystallize, and watch it very carefully. Caramel can go from perfectly cooked to burnt in a matter of seconds. (If you do burn the caramel, not to worry. Start over with a clean pot.)

1. Place 1 cup of the sugar and ¼ cup water in a small saucepan and stir just once to combine. Cook over medium-high heat, without stirring—an occasional swirl of the pan is okay—until the mixture turns a golden amber color and smells like caramel, 6 to 8 minutes.

2. Working quickly, divide the caramel evenly among six 6-ounce ramekins or custard cups, swirling each ramekin after adding the caramel to coat the bottom evenly. Set aside.

3. Combine the milk, vanilla bean, and orange zest (if using) in a medium saucepan. Slowly bring to a simmer over medium-low heat, stirring frequently.

4. Meanwhile, in a large bowl, whisk together the eggs, egg yolks, remaining ½ cup sugar, and a pinch of salt until pale yellow in color.

5. When the milk is just at a simmer, remove it from the heat. While whisking continuously, gradually and slowly pour the warm milk mixture into the egg mixture to temper the eggs. (Do not rush this step or add too much milk at one time or you will scramble the eggs.)

6. Place a fine-mesh strainer or piece of cheesecloth over a pitcher or large measuring cup with a spout. Strain the custard into the pitcher to remove the orange zest and any bits of cooked egg.

7. Divide the custard evenly among the ramekins, pouring it on top of the caramel. Cover each ramekin with foil.

8. Place the trivet in the inner pot of your electric pressure cooker and pour in 1½ cups water. Arrange three ramekins on top of the trivet and carefully stack the remaining three ramekins on top of the first three. (If you have an additional rack, use it for stacking the ramekins.) Close the lid and make sure the pressure release valve is closed. Select the Pressure Cook function and set the cooking time to 9 minutes at low pressure.

9. When the cooking program is complete, allow the pressure to release naturally for 15 minutes, then manually release the remaining pressure and remove the lid. Carefully remove the ramekins and place them on a wire rack. Allow the custards to cool to room temperature, then cover and refrigerate for at least 4 hours or preferably overnight.

10. To serve, remove the cover and run a thin knife around the inside of each ramekin. Place a dessert plate over the top of one ramekin, then flip the ramekin and plate together and gently lift away the ramekin, leaving the crème caramel on the plate. Repeat with the remaining ramekins and separate plates. Serve immediately. Crème caramel will keep in the refrigerator, covered, for up to 3 days.

Butterscotch Budino with Salted Caramel Sauce

SERVES 4

BUDINO

2 cups heavy cream

½ cup dark brown sugar, lightly packed

½ vanilla bean, split lengthwise (optional)

Fine sea salt

5 large egg yolks

1 teaspoon pure vanilla extract

SALTED CARAMEL SAUCE

¾ cup heavy cream

½ cup granulated sugar

1 tablespoon corn syrup

4 tablespoons (½ stick) unsalted butter

2 teaspoons pure vanilla extract

1 teaspoon fine sea salt

Flaky sea salt, for garnish

Whipped cream or crème fraîche, for garnish

One last lovely little custard recipe. Few people had heard of budino before it appeared on the menu of Chef Nancy Silverton's casual eatery Pizzeria Mozza in Los Angeles. But Mozza's butterscotch budino, which is served with a salted caramel topping and a pine nut rosemary cookie on the side, quickly became one of the city's most iconic desserts. Copycat versions have popped up all over the country. *Budino*—the Italian word for "pudding"—is typically cooked on the stovetop and thickened with cornstarch, but for this version, I eschew cornstarch and steam the puddings in the electric pressure cooker like a pot de crème. Naturally I keep the salted caramel topping, which is incredibly decadent. *Photo on page 177.*

1. Make the budino: Combine the cream, ¼ cup of the brown sugar, the vanilla bean (if using), and the salt in a small saucepan. Slowly bring to a simmer over medium-low heat, stirring frequently.

2. Meanwhile, in a large bowl, whisk the egg yolks with the remaining ¼ cup brown sugar and vanilla extract until lightened in color and frothy.

3. When the cream mixture is just at a simmer, remove it from the heat. While whisking continuously, gradually and slowly pour the warm cream mixture into the egg yolks to temper the eggs. (Do not rush this step or add too much cream at one time or you will scramble the eggs.)

4. Place a fine-mesh strainer or piece of cheesecloth over a pitcher or large measuring cup with a spout. Strain the custard into the pitcher to remove the vanilla bean and any bits of cooked egg.

5. Divide the custard evenly among four 8-ounce ramekins or glass jars, leaving room at the top for the caramel sauce. Cover each ramekin with foil.

6. Place the trivet in the inner pot of your electric pressure cooker and pour in 1½ cups water. Arrange the ramekins on top of the trivet. Close the lid and make sure the pressure release valve is closed. Select the Pressure Cook function and set the cooking time to 6 minutes at low pressure.

7. When the cooking program is complete, allow the pressure to release naturally for 5 minutes, then manually release the remaining pressure and remove the lid. Carefully remove the ramekins and place them on a wire rack. Remove the foil coverings and allow the budinos to cool to room temperature, then cover and refrigerate for at least 3 hours or overnight.

8. Meanwhile, make the caramel sauce: Bring the cream to a boil in a small saucepan over high heat, then turn the heat down to low to keep the cream at a simmer.

9. Combine the granulated sugar, corn syrup, and ¼ cup water in a large, heavy-bottomed saucepan. (A large pan is necessary because the mixture will bubble up when you add the cream.) Stir once just to combine, then do not stir again. Bring the mixture to a boil over high heat, occasionally brushing down the sides of the pot with a pastry brush dipped in water to dissolve any sugar crystals, until it turns golden brown and smells like caramel, 4 to 5 minutes. Turn down the heat to medium and, while stirring, slowly pour in the cream. The mixture will bubble furiously.

10. Remove the pot from the heat and stir in the butter until it is melted and the mixture is completely smooth. Then stir in the vanilla and salt. Set aside to cool. (This can be done up to 2 weeks in advance; cover and refrigerate until needed. Allow to come to room temperature or reheat prior to serving.)

11. Just prior to serving, top each budino with about 2 tablespoons of the caramel sauce and a sprinkle of flaky sea salt. (You will have caramel sauce left over.) Garnish with a dollop of whipped cream or crème fraîche, if desired, and serve.

NOTE: For an especially adorable presentation, use pretty 8-ounce glass jars, such as those made by Weck, to steam and serve the budinos.

7

AIR FRYER RECIPES

Baba Ghanoush

**MAKES ABOUT
2 CUPS**

2 medium eggplants,
peeled and cut into
1- to 1½-inch cubes

3 tablespoons extra-
virgin olive oil, plus
more for drizzling

2 teaspoons kosher
salt, plus more for
seasoning

2 garlic cloves, peeled

1 tablespoon tahini

Juice of 1 lemon, plus
more for seasoning

1 teaspoon ground
cumin

½ teaspoon freshly
ground black pepper

¼ teaspoon smoked
paprika

Chopped fresh flat-leaf
parsley, for garnish

Whole Wheat Pita
(page 58), pita chips,
or raw vegetable
crudités, for serving

Baba ghanoush, a smoky spread made with roasted eggplant, is one of the classic starters or mezze in Middle Eastern restaurants. It's related to the French *caviar d'aubergine*, but turns toward the Levant with the addition of tahini. Typically, to make baba ghanoush, you begin by roasting whole eggplants until blackened and soft, which can take as long as an hour in the oven. By cutting the eggplant into cubes and roasting the cubes in the air fryer until lightly charred, we can achieve that same smoky flavor in a fraction of the time. Serve with pita, or create a mezze spread with hummus (page 41), Matbucha (page 45), and Pumpkin Chershi (page 48). *Photo on page 184.*

1. Preheat the air fryer to 400°F for 3 minutes.

2. Toss the eggplant with 2 tablespoons of the olive oil and the salt. Working in batches as necessary, arrange the eggplant in a single layer in the air fryer basket.

3. Cook the eggplant until it is browned and charred in parts, 10 to 15 minutes, depending on the size of the cubes. Remove the cooked eggplant to a bowl. Repeat with the remaining eggplant.

4. Combine the cooked eggplant, remaining 1 tablespoon olive oil, the garlic, tahini, lemon juice, cumin, pepper, and smoked paprika in a food processor and pulse several times, until the mixture is smooth, but still has some texture.

5. Transfer the eggplant mixture to an airtight container and refrigerate for several hours to allow the flavors to develop.

6. Taste and adjust the seasoning, adding additional salt or lemon juice as necessary. Spread the baba ghanoush on a platter or in a shallow bowl. Drizzle the top with additional olive oil and garnish with parsley. Serve with pita bread, pita chips, or crudités.

Muhammara (Syrian Red Pepper & Walnut Dip)

SERVES 4 TO 6 AS AN APPETIZER

---

3 red bell peppers

¾ cup fresh bread crumbs

1 cup walnuts, lightly toasted

2 garlic cloves

Juice of 1 lemon, plus more for seasoning

2 tablespoons pomegranate molasses, plus more for drizzling

2 tablespoons extra-virgin olive oil

1 tablespoon Aleppo pepper

1 teaspoon ground cumin

1 teaspoon ground sumac

1 teaspoon kosher salt, plus more for seasoning

1 or 2 pinches of sugar

¼ cup chopped fresh flat-leaf parsley, for garnish

Whole Wheat Pita (page 58) or vegetable crudités, for serving (optional)

Muhammara is a roasted red pepper and walnut spread of Syrian origin. Throughout the Middle East and Turkey, you see it served as a dip with pita or flatbread, spread onto sandwiches, or garnishing grilled meat and fish. Some muhammara recipes call for jarred roasted red peppers, but roasting fresh peppers is so easy in the air fryer and they add an authentic smoky note to the dip.

Pomegranate molasses, a common Middle Eastern ingredient, is simply pomegranate juice that has been reduced to a thick sauce. It resembles nothing so much as balsamic vinegar, which is an acceptable substitute. But you should be able to find the real thing at grocery stores with a good selection of international ingredients, or you can make it yourself by cooking down bottled pomegranate juice until syrupy. *Photo on page 185.*

1. If your air fryer has a deep basket, you can roast the bell peppers whole. Simply brush the outside of the peppers with oil and place them in the air fryer basket. Roast the peppers at 400°F, turning several times, until blackened on all sides, 25 to 30 minutes. (You may not be able to fit all three peppers at the same time, so work in batches if needed.)

2. If you have a toaster oven–style air fryer, you will likely not be able fit a whole pepper in the basket. Instead, cut the peppers into three or four pieces, removing the core and seeds. Brush the outside of the peppers with oil and arrange the pieces skin-side up in a single layer in the basket. Roast at 400°F until the skin is charred, about 15 minutes.

3. Place the cooked peppers in a bowl and cover with a clean towel. Allow the peppers to steam for 10 minutes. When cool enough to handle, remove the peppers from the bowl and peel off the skin. Remove the stems and seeds, if you started with whole peppers. (This may be done in advance.)

4. Combine the roasted bell peppers, bread crumbs, walnuts, garlic, lemon juice, pomegranate molasses, olive oil, spices, salt, and sugar in a food processor. Pulse until you achieve a smooth but chunky texture. Taste and adjust the seasoning, adding more salt, sugar, or lemon juice as desired.

5. Drizzle with additional pomegranate molasses and garnish with parsley. Serve with pita bread or crudités.

Fried Potatoes with Smoked Paprika Aioli

**SERVES 4 AS A
SIDE DISH OR
STARTER**

**SMOKED PAPRIKA
AIOLI**
1 large egg

1 tablespoon minced
garlic

1 tablespoon freshly
squeezed lemon juice

1 teaspoon Dijon
mustard

1 teaspoon smoked
paprika

½ teaspoon kosher salt

½ cup extra-virgin olive
oil

½ cup neutral oil,
such as vegetable,
grapeseed or canola
oil

FRIED POTATOES
1½ pounds waxy
potatoes, such as
Red Bliss, cut into
1-inch pieces

2 tablespoons extra-
virgin olive oil

1 teaspoon kosher salt

½ teaspoon smoked
paprika

Crispy fried potatoes drizzled with garlicky mayonnaise is a simple yet beloved Spanish small plate. Walk into any bar in Spain at *la hora de aperitivo*, or the tapas hour, and you will see groups of friends, especially young people, sharing a dish of these addictive fried potatoes—in part because they are usually one of the least expensive tapas on the menu!

The air fryer turns out incredible, crispy-on-the-outside, soft-on-the-inside potatoes with just a few tablespoons of oil, making these potatoes far less indulgent than most bar snacks. The smoked paprika on the potatoes gives them an appealing golden color. If you have never made mayonnaise from scratch before, I encourage you to give it a try. A food processor or blender makes it easy to achieve a perfectly emulsified aioli with very little effort.

1. Make the smoked paprika aioli: Place the egg, garlic, lemon juice, mustard, smoked paprika, salt, and 2 tablespoons of the olive oil in a food processor and blend until smooth. With the motor running, slowly pour in the remaining 6 tablespoons olive oil followed by the neutral oil in a thin, steady stream. Keep blending until the mixture emulsifies and becomes thick like mayonnaise. Refrigerate until needed. (This may be done in advance. Aioli will keep in the refrigerator for up to 1 week.)

2. Make the potatoes: Toss the potatoes with the olive oil, salt, and smoked paprika in a large bowl. Preheat the air fryer to 400°F for 3 minutes.

3. Arrange the potatoes in a single layer in the air fryer basket, working in batches if necessary, to avoid overcrowding the basket. Cook the potatoes until browned and crispy on the outside and tender on the inside, 18 to 20 minutes, shaking the basket and tossing the potatoes halfway through cooking.

4. Transfer the potatoes to a platter. Serve with the smoked paprika aioli on the side for dipping or drizzle the aioli over the potatoes.

Halloumi with Roasted Grapes & Mint

SERVES 2 TO 4

1 bunch red or black grapes, or a combination

Oil for spraying

12 ounces halloumi, cut into ½-inch-thick slices

2 tablespoons extra-virgin olive oil, plus more for drizzling

1 tablespoon pomegranate molasses

1 tablespoon packed chopped fresh mint

Flaky sea salt and freshly ground black pepper

Firm, squeaky halloumi is the cheese of choice for cooking and grilling around the eastern Mediterranean because of how well it holds its shape. This dish, which would be a perfect first course for a romantic date night, is inspired by one served at the beloved West Village restaurant Jack's Wife Freda. Rather than grill or pan-fry the halloumi, as is typical, I cook both the halloumi and the grapes in the air fryer for just ten minutes. The halloumi becomes golden brown and slightly gooey and the heat intensifies the grapes' natural sweetness. Serve this super-easy yet elegant dish with crusty bread as part of a mezze spread or place the whole thing over a bed of greens for a special light lunch.

1. Cut several sprigs of grapes off the bunch and place them in the basket of the air fryer. Spray the grapes and basket with oil. Roast the grapes at 360°F until they are wrinkled, browned, and some have popped open, about 10 minutes. Arrange the grapes around the sides of a serving platter.

2. Measure out 1 additional cup of fresh grapes and cut them in half.

3. Brush the halloumi slices on both sides with the olive oil. Spray the basket with oil. Arrange the halloumi and the halved grapes in the air fryer basket.

4. Cook the halloumi and grapes at 360°F until the cheese is browned on both sides, about 10 minutes, turning the slices and tossing the grapes once, halfway through cooking.

5. Arrange the halloumi in the center of the platter, overlapping the slices slightly. Spoon the halved grapes on top of the halloumi. Drizzle with the pomegranate molasses and any remaining olive oil. Sprinkle the mint over the cheese and grapes and season with salt and pepper. (Halloumi is salty so go light on additional salt.) Serve warm.

NOTE: While this dish is delicious with regular supermarket grapes, it is really special with unusual varieties of grapes, such as Moon Drops, muscat, or Concord, which may be available at your local farmers' market, depending on the season.

Fattoush with Fried Halloumi

SERVES 4 AS A
MAIN COURSE,
OR 6 AS A FIRST
COURSE

SALAD

3 pita breads,
   homemade (page 58)
   or store-bought,
   preferably day-old

¼ cup extra-virgin
   olive oil

½ teaspoon kosher salt

8 ounces halloumi,
   cut into strips

1 English (hothouse)
   cucumber, halved
   and sliced

3 Roma (plum) or on-
   the-vine tomatoes,
   cut into wedges and
   halved

4 large or 5 small
   radishes, sliced

3 scallions, white and
   light green parts
   only, sliced

1 cup chopped fresh
   flat-leaf parsley

1 cup packed fresh
   mint leaves, cut into
   ribbons

DRESSING

Juice of 2 lemons

1 teaspoon ground
   sumac

Pinch of sugar

¼ cup extra-virgin olive
   oil

Kosher salt and freshly
   ground black pepper

Fattoush is a bread salad of Lebanese origin that you see throughout the Middle East. Like fatteh (see page 117), fattoush originated as a way to use up day-old pita breads. Traditionally, the stale pita is deep-fried until crisp and then combined with chopped seasonal vegetables and lots of herbs. Here, we use the air fryer to toast the pita to perfection with just a light coating of olive oil—much easier than deep-frying! Air-frying the pita until firm and crisp will keep it from becoming soggy when coated with the tangy lemon and sumac dressing.

To turn fattoush into a salad substantial enough for a meal, I add halloumi, a squeaky, firm Middle Eastern cheese that does not melt when grilled or fried. The halloumi, too, is cooked in the air fryer, which is both less messy and lighter than pan-frying it.

1. Brush the outside of the pitas with 2 tablespoons of the olive oil and sprinkle with the salt. Cut the pitas in half through the middle, and then cut each half into six or eight wedges.

2. Working in batches to avoid crowding, arrange one-third to half of the pitas in the basket of the air fryer. Toast the pitas at 350°F until golden brown and crisp, 6 to 8 minutes, turning once halfway through. Repeat with the remaining pitas. Set aside.

3. Brush the halloumi with the remaining 2 tablespoons olive oil and arrange in a single layer in the basket of the air fryer. Fry the halloumi at 350°F until the exterior is browned and crispy, 8 to 10 minutes, turning once halfway through.

4. In a large bowl, combine the cucumber, tomatoes, radishes, scallions, parsley, and mint.

5. To make the dressing, whisk together the lemon juice, sumac, and sugar in a small bowl. While whisking, slowly pour in the olive oil and continue whisking until emulsified. Pour the dressing over the vegetables and herbs in the bowl. Toss to combine.

6. Add the pita and the halloumi to the salad. Taste and season well with salt and pepper, keeping in mind that the halloumi is already quite salty. Serve immediately.

Moroccan Roasted Carrots with Labneh, Dukkah & Mint

**SERVES 4 AS A
SIDE DISH**

CARROTS

2 bunches carrots with
the tops on (around
1¼ to 1½ pounds
carrots), peeled

2 tablespoons extra-
virgin olive oil

1 tablespoon honey

½ teaspoon kosher salt

½ teaspoon ground
cumin

¼ teaspoon ground
cinnamon

¼ teaspoon Aleppo
pepper

Zest of 1 orange

DRESSING

2 tablespoons freshly
squeezed orange
juice

1 tablespoon freshly
squeezed lime juice

2 teaspoons harissa or
a smaller amount of a
different hot sauce

1 teaspoon honey

Kosher salt

¼ cup extra-virgin
olive oil

FOR SERVING

1 cup Labneh (page 52)
or Quick Labneh
(recipe opposite)

2 tablespoons chopped
fresh mint

1 tablespoon Dukkah
(page 81)

We spend so much time eating carrots raw that we forget how sweet and irresistible they are when roasted. While it can take as long as forty or fifty minutes to roast carrots in the oven, the high heat and fast-moving air of the air fryer roasts carrots to caramelized perfection in just ten minutes. Arranged on a bed of labneh and topped with mint and crunchy dukkah, these roasted carrots seasoned with earthy Moroccan flavors are a showstopping side dish that is equally delicious warm or at room temperature. Pair them with Mujadara (page 106) for a satisfying and flavorful meatless meal. For a particularly eye-catching presentation, seek out rainbow carrots in hues of purple, yellow, and white in addition to regular orange carrots.

1. Cut the carrots in half lengthwise and then cut each half into spears. Place the carrots in a large bowl. Whisk together the olive oil and honey and pour the mixture over the carrots. Sprinkle the carrots with the salt, spices, and orange zest and toss them until the carrots are evenly coated.

2. Preheat the air fryer to 360°F for 3 minutes.

3. Working in batches so as not to crowd the basket, arrange half or a third of the carrots in a single layer in the air fryer basket. Roast the carrots until fork-tender and browned, about 10 minutes, tossing once halfway through cooking. Transfer the cooked carrots to a plate and repeat with the remaining carrots.

4. While the carrots are cooking, prepare the dressing. Whisk together the orange and lime juices, harissa, honey, and a pinch of salt. Whisk in the olive oil in a steady stream. Set aside.

5. To serve, spread the labneh on a platter. Arrange the roasted carrots on top of the labneh and pour the dressing over the carrots. Garnish with the mint and dukkah. Serve warm or at room temperature.

Quick Labneh

**MAKES ABOUT
1²/₃ CUPS**

1 (17.6 ounce) container
full-fat plain yogurt
(about 2¼ cups
yogurt)

¼ cup sour cream

1½ teaspoons kosher
salt

Juice of half a lemon

While everyone should try making labneh from scratch in their pressure cooker at least once, sometimes you want labneh to garnish a dish—or just to eat out of hand—and don't have a day (or two) to wait. In those instances, you can make really thick and tasty labneh by straining store-bought yogurt for just a day or overnight.

Combine the yogurt, sour cream, salt, and lemon juice in a medium bowl and stir to combine. Place a large, fine-mesh strainer over a deep bowl and line the strainer with a paper towel, coffee filter, or several layers of cheesecloth. Ladle the yogurt mixture into the strainer. Allow the yogurt to drain for 4 to 8 hours until it is the consistency of cream cheese. Transfer the labneh to a clean container and refrigerate for up to 3 weeks until needed.

Cauliflower Steaks with Green Tahini Sauce & Dukkah

SERVES 2 AS A MAIN COURSE, OR 4 AS A SIDE DISH

GREEN TAHINI SAUCE

¾ cup tahini

⅓ cup freshly squeezed lemon juice

2 or 3 garlic cloves, coarsely chopped

½ teaspoon kosher salt

½ to ¾ cup cold water

1 cup packed fresh cilantro or fresh flat-leaf parsley, or a combination

CAULIFLOWER STEAKS

2 heads cauliflower

½ cup all-purpose flour

2 large eggs

2 cups panko bread crumbs

1 teaspoon ground cumin

1 teaspoon ground cinnamon

1 teaspoon ground sumac

1 teaspoon kosher salt

1 teaspoon freshly ground black pepper

Oil for spraying

2 tablespoons Dukkah (page 81)

1 lemon, cut into wedges

Cutting a head of cauliflower into thick slices or "steaks," rather than the more typical florets, makes it much easier to coat with a crispy breading and fry in the air fryer. These cauliflower steaks also make an elegant presentation that feels like a fitting centerpiece for a vegetarian meal, especially with the addition of tahini sauce and a sprinkle of dukkah. Because you can only get two, or at most three, steaks from one head of cauliflower, you will likely have a lot of leftover florets; save those to roast or turn into cauliflower rice.

Green tahini sauce is just tahini sauce enhanced with lots of fresh green herbs like parsley and cilantro. A blender, preferably a high-speed one, works better than a food processor for making a smooth, green sauce without little flecks of herbs.

1. Make the green tahini sauce: Place the tahini, lemon juice, garlic, and salt in a blender and pulse a few times until the mixture forms a paste. With the motor running, slowly pour in ½ cup cold water and blend until the sauce is lighter in color and fluffy, 1 to 2 minutes. If the mixture is still quite thick, which will depend on the consistency of your tahini, add the remaining cold water in the same manner. Add the herbs and process until the mixture is completely smooth and a light green color. Refrigerate until needed. (This may be done up to 2 weeks in advance.)

2. Make the cauliflower steaks: Remove the leaves and trim the cauliflower stems, leaving the cores intact. Stand the cauliflower up on a cutting board. Using a large knife, slice off the rounded sides of the cauliflower leaving the middle section still attached to the core. Slice this middle section into 2 or maybe 3 (depending on the size of the cauliflower) "steaks," 1 to 1½ inches thick.

3. Place the flour in a shallow dish or pie plate. Beat the eggs with 2 tablespoons water in a large, shallow bowl. In a separate shallow dish, combine the panko, cumin, cinnamon, sumac, salt, and pepper. Dredge two of the cauliflower steaks in the flour, then dip them in the beaten egg, and finally dredge in the panko mixture, coating both sides well. Transfer to a plate.

4. Preheat the air fryer to 375°F for 3 minutes. Spray both sides of the breaded cauliflower steaks with oil and place in the air fryer basket. Cook for 15 to 17 minutes, flipping the steaks once halfway through, until the cauliflower is fork-tender and the breading is browned and crispy. Repeat with the remaining steaks.

5. Drizzle the green tahini sauce over the steaks—you will likely have sauce left over—and sprinkle them with dukkah. Serve warm with lemon wedges.

Arancini di Riso (Sicilian Rice Fritters)

MAKES 18 ARANCINI

3 tablespoons unsalted butter

2 tablespoons extra-virgin olive oil

2 shallots, minced

Kosher salt

1½ cups Arborio rice or other short-grain Italian rice

¼ cup white wine

3¼ cups Chicken Broth (page 72), warm or at room temperature

½ cup grated Parmigiano-Reggiano or Grana Padano cheese

Zest of 1 lemon

3 large eggs

Freshly ground black pepper

3 ounces fresh mozzarella

¼ cup fresh or frozen peas

½ cup all-purpose flour

1½ cups panko bread crumbs

Oil, for spraying

Arrabiata Sauce (page 206), for serving

Near where I live in Chicago there is a restaurant called Forno Rosso that bakes authentic, Neapolitan-style pizza in a 900-pound, wood-burning oven that was imported from Italy. There is not much on the menu at Forno Rosso other than pizza, but among the handful of appetizers is arancini, a fritter made from risotto that my children adore almost more than the pizza. So, imagine my delight when I figured out that I could make arancini that are *almost* as good as those at Forno Rosso at home using the air fryer. My version is stuffed with mozzarella and peas and served with a spicy tomato sauce. Arancini, which means "little oranges" in Italian, was invented as a way to make use of the previous night's uneaten risotto. So while I give you instructions here for making the risotto in an electric pressure cooker—which is far easier than cooking it on the stove—you can also try this recipe with leftover risotto.

1. Make the risotto: Put 2 tablespoons of the butter and the olive oil in the inner pot of your electric pressure cooker. Select the Sauté function and set the heat level to "Less." When the butter has melted and the oil is shimmering, after about 2 minutes, add the shallots and sauté until softened, about 3 minutes. Season with a pinch of salt.

2. Add the rice and stir to coat the grains with the fat. Toast the rice until fragrant, about 3 minutes. Add the wine and simmer until the liquid has been absorbed, about 1 minute. Press Cancel to turn off the Sauté function.

3. Add the broth and stir to combine. Close the lid and make sure the pressure release valve is closed. Select the Pressure Cook function and set the cooking time to 6 minutes at high pressure. When the cooking program is complete, release the pressure manually and remove the lid.

4. Add the grated cheese and stir briskly until the rice has absorbed the remaining liquid. Add the lemon zest, 1 egg, salt, and pepper to taste. Stir to combine.

5. Spread the risotto out on a sheet pan, cover, and chill in the refrigerator for at least 1 hour and up to overnight.

6. Make the arancini: Line a baking sheet with parchment paper. Form the chilled risotto into fifteen 2-inch balls. Flatten each ball into a disc and put a ½-inch piece of mozzarella and 5 or 6 peas in the center. Close the risotto around the filling and roll into a ball.

7. Place the formed balls onto the prepared baking sheet and chill until firm, at least 15 minutes and up to overnight.

8. Beat the remaining 2 eggs with 2 tablespoons water in a large, shallow bowl. Place the flour on a small plate and spread the panko on a separate plate.

9. Roll one of the rice balls in the flour, shaking off any excess, then coat with the egg mixture. Dredge the ball in the panko and place the breaded rice ball on a lined baking sheet. Repeat with the remaining balls.

10. Spray the rice balls with oil and, working in batches, place 6 balls in a single layer in the air fryer basket. Cook at 400°F for 12 to 15 minutes, turning once halfway through, until browned and cooked through. Repeat with the remaining balls.

11. Serve the arancini right away with arrabiata sauce.

Herby Green Falafel

**MAKES 12 FALAFEL
OR 4 FALAFEL
SANDWICHES**

8 ounces dried
chickpeas

1 cup tightly packed
fresh flat-leaf parsley
or cilantro leaves, or
a combination

3 garlic cloves, peeled

3 scallions, white and
light green parts
only, sliced

1 teaspoon kosher salt

1½ teaspoons ground
cumin

1½ teaspoons ground
coriander

½ teaspoon cayenne
pepper (optional)

½ teaspoon baking
powder

Juice of ½ lemon

Oil for spraying

**TO SERVE
(OPTIONAL)**
Tahini Sauce (page 121)
or Green Tahini Sauce
(page 193)

Mango Amba (page
208)

4 Whole Wheat Pita
breads (page 58)

Smooth and Creamy
Hummus (page 41)

Israeli Salad (page 207)

By now, most of us are familiar with falafel, the deep-fried chickpea fritter that, when tucked inside warm pita and eaten on the go, is the Middle East's version of fast food. Because it is full of protein from the chickpeas, falafel is a favorite with vegetarians. It is surprisingly easy to make at home when you can air-fry the fritters instead of deep-frying them. The key to making falafel from scratch is starting with dried chickpeas, not canned. The dried chickpeas are then soaked overnight to soften them just enough to mince into a batter. Garlic, scallions, lots of green herbs, and some warm Middle Eastern spices add flavor. Falafel can be a bit dry on its own, so serve it with your favorite Middle Eastern condiments, such as Tahini Sauce (page 121), Mango Amba (page 208), hummus (page 41), and a fresh Israeli salad (see page 207) or tangy pickles.

1. Place the chickpeas in large bowl and cover with 10 cups of cold water. Let soak overnight, up to 24 hours, and drain. (Alternatively, to speed up this process, combine the chickpeas and 10 cups water in a large saucepan. Bring to a boil over high heat and boil for 2 minutes. Remove from the heat, cover, and allow to sit for at least 1 hour. Drain.)

2. Combine the chickpeas, herbs, garlic, scallions, salt, spices, baking powder, and lemon juice in a food processor. Pulse, scraping down sides as necessary, until the chickpeas are finely minced, but not pureed, and the mixture resembles small grains of couscous, 30 seconds to 1 minute. (When you gather a small amount of the mixture in your hand and squeeze, it should hold together.) Refrigerate the mixture for at least 1 hour and up to overnight.

3. Measure out 3 tablespoons of the chickpea mixture and form it into a tight ball or oval with your hands. Repeat until you have used all the mixture. You should be able to form at least 12 balls. Chill the formed patties for at least 15 minutes.

4. Spray the basket of the air fryer with oil. Place half of the falafel patties in the basket and spray the tops with oil. Cook at 400°F until the tops are browned and crisp, about 8 minutes. Flip the falafel and spray the second side with oil. Cook until the second side is browned, 5 to 7 additional minutes. Remove the cooked falafel and repeat with the remaining patties.

5. Serve with tahini sauce, green tahini sauce, or mango amba. Or to make a falafel sandwich, cut open the top of the pita bread to reveal a pocket. Spread the inside of the pita with 3 to 4 tablespoons of hummus. Tuck 2 or 3 falafel inside the pita. Add several tablespoons of Israeli salad. Drizzle the sandwich with tahini sauce, mango amba, or both.

Chicken Shawarma

SERVES 4

8 boneless, skinless chicken thighs, totaling around 1½ to 2 pounds

1 yellow onion, sliced

1 teaspoon ground cumin

1 teaspoon ground coriander

½ teaspoon ground turmeric

½ teaspoon paprika

½ teaspoon garlic powder

¼ teaspoon ground cinnamon

1 teaspoon kosher salt

1 tablespoon honey

2 tablespoons freshly squeezed lemon juice

3 tablespoons extra-virgin olive oil plus more, for spraying

FOR SERVING (OPTIONAL)
Whole Wheat Pita (page 58) or 8 rounds store-bought pita

Tahini Sauce (page 121) or Green Tahini Sauce (page 193)

Israeli Salad (page 207)

In the Middle East, shawarma refers to seasoned meat, such as lamb, turkey, or chicken, that is slow-roasted on a tall spit. When you order shawarma at a restaurant, the waiter shaves off slices from the meat on the spit and piles it high on a fluffy round of pita. While we cannot exactly re-create the delight of that big rotating piece of meat at home, we can approximate the flavors and juicy, tender meat of shawarma by marinating slices of dark meat chicken with warm, earthy spices and lemon juice and cooking them quickly in the air fryer. The chicken is delicious on its own or served over a bed of Rice with Vermicelli (page 101). But for the full shawarma experience, serve it with Whole Wheat Pita (page 58), a drizzle of Tahini Sauce (page 121), and a crunchy Israeli salad (page 207). Use the pitas as a wrap for the chicken or cut the pitas open and stuff the chicken and salad right in the pocket.

1. Cut each chicken thigh across the grain into 3 or 4 pieces and place them in a glass baking dish along with the onion.

2. In a small bowl, whisk together the spices, salt, honey, and lemon juice. While whisking, slowly pour in the oil in a steady stream. Pour the marinade over the chicken and toss the chicken to coat. Cover and refrigerate for at least 3 hours and up to overnight.

3. Preheat the air fryer to 360°F for 3 minutes. Spray the basket of the air fryer with oil. Use a slotted spoon to remove the chicken and the onion from the marinade, leaving the liquid behind. Working in batches as necessary to not crowd the basket, arrange the chicken and onion in a single layer in the air fryer basket. Cook until the chicken is browned and the internal temperature reaches at least 160°F, 7 to 8 minutes. Transfer the first batch of chicken to a serving platter. Repeat with the remaining chicken.

4. Serve the chicken and onion warm with pita bread, tahini sauce, and Israeli salad, if desired.

Chicken Piccata

SERVES 4

CHICKEN

½ cup all-purpose flour

1 teaspoon kosher salt

½ teaspoon freshly
ground black pepper

2 large eggs

1¾ cup panko bread
crumbs

4 thin-cut boneless,
skinless chicken
breast fillets
(1½ to 2 pounds
total)

1 lemon, halved

Oil, for spraying

SAUCE

½ cup white wine

½ cup Chicken Broth
(page 72)

1 tablespoon unsalted
butter, at room
temperature

1 tablespoon all-purpose
flour

2 tablespoons capers,
with their brine

Kosher salt and freshly
ground black pepper

Chopped fresh flat-leaf
parsley, for garnish

Chicken piccata is a delightfully simple dish of pan-fried chicken breasts in a piquant lemon and caper sauce. Cooking the chicken in the air fryer, instead of on the stove, creates a lighter and less messy version of the dish without losing any flavor. The all-important sauce comes together quickly on the stove and is thickened with a flour-butter paste known as a *beurre manie*. That's the only butter in the whole recipe! Enjoy this chicken piccata over rice or pasta with a fresh green salad on the side for a simple yet elegant family dinner.

1. Whisk together the flour, salt, and pepper on a large plate. Beat the eggs with 2 tablespoons water in a large, shallow bowl. Place the panko in a separate shallow bowl or pie plate.

2. Dredge one of the chicken breasts in the flour, shaking off any excess, then dip it in the egg wash. Dredge in the panko, making sure to coat the chicken breast completely. Shake off any excess crumbs and place on a plate. Repeat with the remaining chicken breasts.

3. Spray the basket of the air fryer with oil. Place as many of the battered chicken breasts in the basket as will fit without crowding and spray the tops of the chicken with oil. Cook the chicken at 360°F until the top side is browned, about 6 minutes.

4. Flip the chicken and spray the second side with oil. Cut four slices from one half of the lemon and place a slice on top of each chicken breast. Cook until the second side is browned and crispy and the internal temperature reaches 160°F, about 6 minutes. Transfer the chicken to a plate and keep warm. If necessary, repeat the cooking process with any remaining chicken.

5. To make the sauce, combine the wine, broth, and the juice from the remaining lemon half in a small saucepan and bring to a boil. Turn the heat down to low.

6. Mash together the butter and flour in a small bowl until the flour is completely coated in butter. (This is the beurre manie.) Whisk the butter-flour mixture into the sauce and simmer until thickened, 1 to 2 minutes. Add the capers and season with salt and pepper.

7. To serve, arrange the chicken breasts with their lemon slices on a rimmed platter and spoon the piccata sauce over the chicken. Garnish with parsley and serve immediately.

Italian Sausage with Fennel & Grapes

SERVES 4

2 bulbs fennel

1 red onion, halved and sliced

1 cup red grapes

2 tablespoons extra-virgin olive oil

½ teaspoon kosher salt

¼ teaspoon red pepper flakes

Oil, for spraying

8 Italian sausages, sweet or hot, pricked all over with a fork

1 navel orange

1 tablespoon red wine vinegar

1 tablespoon chopped fresh rosemary, for garnish

This Italian-inspired recipe is similar to a sheet pan dinner, but one that you cook in the air fryer. Fennel, red onion, and grapes are roasted in the air fryer along with the sausages, and even though you will need to cook the recipe in two batches, it still takes less than thirty minutes. The combination of sausage, fennel, and grapes may seem unusual, but it is classic Tuscan fare, especially for the fall months.

In the recipe, I give you instructions for supreming an orange. This is a technique that removes the membrane from citrus fruit so it can be served in slices. The process is a bit fussy, but the result is beautiful segments of fruit with no membranes attached, which look really elegant in the final dish. Once you have mastered this technique, you can use it for salads and desserts featuring both oranges and grapefruits and impress your friends and family.

1. Trim the stalks and bottoms of the fennel bulbs, reserving a small amount of the fronds for garnish. Cut the bulbs in half lengthwise through the core, then place the bulbs cut-side down and slice thinly.

2. Place the fennel, red onion, and grapes in a large bowl and drizzle with the olive oil. Add the salt and red pepper flakes and toss the vegetables to coat them with the oil.

3. Preheat the air fryer to 400°F for 3 minutes. Spray the basket with oil to prevent sticking. Working in two batches, so as not to crowd the air fryer basket, arrange half of the vegetable mixture in a single layer. Top with four of the sausages. Cook for 10 to 12 minutes, until the sausages are browned on the outside and cooked to an internal temperature of 160°F and the vegetables are softened and caramelized. Transfer the cooked sausages and vegetables to a plate. Repeat with the second batch of vegetables and sausages.

4. Meanwhile, supreme the orange. Trim the top and bottom of the orange to reveal the beginnings of the fruit beneath the peel. Set the fruit on one end, and cut the skin from its flesh, beginning at the top and following the curve down. Working carefully, cut away all the peel and pith from the orange. Cut out each section of the orange by inserting the blade of your knife between the flesh and the membrane on both sides. (Insert your knife as close to that membrane as possible and make a slice parallel to it, right to the center of the orange. Find the membrane on the other side of that orange section and make another slice down to the center of the orange.) You should be left with a tender, juicy orange segment. Place the orange segments in a small bowl. When you have removed all the segments, squeeze the remaining membranes over the bowl to extract any remaining juice. Add the vinegar to the orange segments.

5. To serve, arrange the fennel, onion, and grapes on a serving platter and top with the sausages. Arrange the orange segments on the platter and drizzle the orange juice and vinegar mixture over everything. Garnish with the rosemary and reserved fennel fronds. Serve immediately.

Lamb & Bulgur Kofta

SERVES 4

¼ cup fine bulgur wheat

¼ cup boiling water

1 pound ground lamb

½ onion, grated

¼ cup packed chopped fresh herbs, such as flat-leaf parsley, cilantro, mint, or a combination

1 teaspoon kosher salt

1 teaspoon ground cumin

½ teaspoon paprika

¼ teaspoon ground allspice

¼ teaspoon ground cinnamon

Oil, for spraying

FOR SERVING (OPTIONAL)
Cucumber Tzatziki (page 56)

Tahini Sauce (page 121) or Green Tahini Sauce (page 193)

Grilled kofta (or kefta) kebabs are one of the signature foods of the Middle East and eastern Mediterranean. When it is not convenient to grill, the air fryer is my appliance of choice for cooking these lamb kofta—they take just ten minutes! Serve them alongside Rice with Vermicelli (page 101) or Whole Wheat Pita (page 58) and your favorite condiments. When making a mixture with raw meat, it is hard to know whether you have seasoned the meat enough because no one wants to (or should!) taste raw meat. One trick I have learned is to take a small morsel of the raw mixture and microwave it just until cooked. I can then taste that small piece without any food safety concerns and decide if my mixture needs more salt or spices.

1. Mix the bulgur with the boiling water in a heatproof bowl. Let stand for 7 minutes.

2. To form the kofta, combine ½ cup of the cooked bulgur with the lamb, onion, herbs, salt, and spices in a medium bowl and mix thoroughly with your hands.

3. With damp hands, form the lamb mixture into 8 equal, tightly packed oval patties. Place the patties on a plate, cover, and refrigerate for at least 30 minutes and up to overnight.

4. When you are ready to cook the kofta, preheat the air fryer to 400°F for 3 minutes. Spray the basket with oil to prevent the patties from sticking. Working in two batches, so as not to overcrowd the air fryer basket, arrange half of the patties in a single layer. Cook until the kofta are browned and the internal temperature reaches 145°F, about 10 minutes, turning once halfway through cooking. Repeat with the second batch of patties.

5. Place the cooked kofta on a paper towel–lined plate to absorb any excess oil. Serve warm with tzatziki, tahini sauce, or green tahini sauce.

NOTE: For a gluten-free version of this recipe, substitute ½ cup cooked quinoa for the bulgur.

Polenta Fries with Arrabiata Sauce

**SERVES 4 TO 6 AS
A SIDE DISH**

POLENTA

4 tablespoons (½ stick)
unsalted butter, plus
more for greasing

1 cup polenta, yellow
corn grits (not
instant), or coarse
stone-ground
cornmeal

1 teaspoon kosher
salt, plus more for
seasoning

½ cup grated
Parmigiano-Reggiano
or Pecorino Romano
cheese, plus more for
serving

Freshly ground black
pepper

Oil for spraying

ARRABIATA SAUCE

2 tablespoons extra-
virgin olive oil

6 garlic cloves, minced

1 to 2 teaspoons red
pepper flakes

1 teaspoon kosher salt

1 (28-ounce) can
crushed tomatoes

2 teaspoons sugar

When warm, polenta is smooth and creamy, like porridge, which makes it a wonderful base for hearty stews and braises. Once chilled, however, polenta becomes firm and set so that you can cut it into slices, or other shapes, and cook those pieces in entirely new ways. Here, we cut polenta into thick, french fry–size batons and cook it in the air fryer until we have crispy-on-the-outside, creamy-on-the-inside polenta "fries." I like to serve these polenta fries with a spicy tomato sauce known as *arrabiata*, which means "angry" in Italian. This is a fun dish for a party or just to liven up a weeknight dinner. While I give you instructions here for cooking the polenta in your electric pressure cooker, this recipe also works well with leftover polenta that is firm enough to slice.

1. Add 2 tablespoons of the butter to the inner pot of your electric pressure cooker. Select the Sauté function and set the heat level to "Less." When the butter has melted, after about 2 minutes, add the polenta and stir to coat the grains with the butter. Toast the polenta for 1 minute.

2. Press Cancel to turn off the Sauté function. Add 3¾ cups water and the salt to the polenta and stir to combine. Close the lid and make sure the pressure release valve is closed. Select the Pressure Cook function and set the cooking time to 10 minutes at high pressure.

3. When the cooking program is complete, allow the pressure to release naturally for at least 15 minutes, then manually release the remaining pressure and remove the lid. Stir the polenta thoroughly with a spatula, scraping up anything stuck to the bottom of the pot. (Typically, the top layer of the polenta will be thin and more liquid while the bottom layer will be thick and may even stick to the bottom. Continue to stir until all the polenta is a similar, thick consistency.)

4. Cut the remaining 2 tablespoons of butter into pieces and add it to the polenta, stirring until the butter is melted. Stir in the cheese. Taste and adjust the seasoning, adding the pepper and more salt if needed.

5. Grease an 9 x 9-inch baking dish. Spread the polenta in an even layer in the baking dish. Cover and refrigerate until chilled and very firm, at least 4 hours and preferably overnight.

6. Meanwhile, make the arrabbiata sauce: Heat the olive oil in a medium saucepan over low heat. Add the garlic, red pepper flakes, and salt. Sauté until fragrant, about 2 minutes. Add the tomatoes and sugar and stir to combine. Turn the heat to high and bring to a boil. Reduce the heat and simmer until thickened, 20 to 25 minutes. Remove from the heat and set aside.

7. Once the polenta is firm, remove it from the baking dish and cut into "fries" that are around 1 inch thick and 4 inches long. Working in batches as necessary, arrange the fries in a single layer in the basket of the air fryer and spray with oil. Cook at 350°F until browned and crispy on the outside but still soft on the inside, 12 to 15 minutes, turning once halfway through cooking. Repeat with the remaining polenta.

8. Serve the polenta fries warm with the arrabbiata sauce.

Sabich (Fried Eggplant, Hard-Boiled Eggs & Hummus in Pita) with Israeli Salad

MAKES 4 SANDWICHES

ISRAELI SALAD

1 English (hothouse) cucumber, finely diced

2 plum or on-the-vine tomatoes, finely diced

½ red onion, finely diced

1 cup fresh flat-leaf parsley, chopped

Zest and juice of 1 lemon

3 tablespoons extra-virgin olive oil

¾ teaspoon kosher salt, plus more for sprinkling

Freshly ground black pepper

SANDWICHES

4 large eggs

1 medium eggplant, preferably Italian, cut into ½-inch-thick slices

Olive oil

4 Whole Wheat Pitas (page 58) or store-bought, warmed

1 cup hummus, homemade (page 41) or store-bought

Mango Amba (page 208)

Tahini Sauce (page 121) or Green Tahini Sauce (page 193)

Sliced pickles and shredded cabbage, for topping (optional)

Forget about falafel: sabich is *the* iconic Israeli street food. There are conflicting stories of who invented sabich and why, but the important thing to know is that a sabich sandwich is an entire meal stuffed into a messy, dripping pita. At a Tel Aviv sabich stand, you can craft your perfect sandwich from an array of possible fillings, but the essential elements are fried eggplant, hard-boiled eggs, hummus, a chopped salad, and a drizzle of funky mango amba.

This recipe for sabich has many elements, most of which you can make from scratch using other recipes in this book. Or you can streamline the process and use store-bought pita, hummus, and amba sauce—your sabich will still taste delicious. The air fryer is the real secret to making fantastic sabich at home because deep-fried eggplant often ends up greasy. Here, just a light coating of oil is all that is needed for crisp, meaty slices of fried eggplant.

1. To make the Israeli salad, combine the cucumber, tomato, onion, and parsley in a large bowl. Add the zest and juice of the lemon and the olive oil and toss to combine. Season with the salt and pepper. If not using right away, cover and refrigerate until needed, for up to 1 hour.

2. To cook the eggs, place the trivet in the inner pot of the electric pressure cooker and pour in 1 cup water. Arrange the eggs on the trivet. Close the lid and make sure the pressure release valve is closed. Select the Pressure Cook function and set the cooking time to 7 minutes at low pressure. While the eggs are cooking, fill a medium bowl with ice and cold water.

3. When the cooking program is complete, release the pressure manually and immediately move the eggs to the ice water. Once the eggs are cool enough to handle, drain and peel them. Slice the eggs and set them aside until needed.

4. To cook the eggplant, lightly brush both sides of the eggplant slices with olive oil. Preheat the air fryer to 400°F. Arrange as many slices of eggplant as will comfortably fit in a single layer in the air fryer basket. Cook until the slices are brown and crisp, 10 to 12 minutes, flipping once halfway through cooking. Transfer the cooked eggplant to a paper towel–lined plate and sprinkle immediately with salt. Repeat the process with the remaining eggplant.

5. To assemble the sandwiches, cut the pitas at the top and open the inside to form a pocket. Spread 3 to 4 tablespoons of hummus on the inside of each pita. Fill each pita with several slices of fried eggplant and one of the hard-boiled eggs. Add several tablespoons of Israeli salad to each pita and drizzle with the amba and tahini sauce. Add any additional toppings as desired. Serve immediately.

NOTE: Hard-boiling eggs in a pressure cooker is a revelation! It does not necessarily take less time than hard-boiling eggs on the stove, but eggs cooked under pressure are much easier to peel. I like to pressure cook a dozen eggs at the beginning of the week and keep them in the refrigerator for easy snacking.

Mango Amba

**MAKES ABOUT
1 QUART**

- 4 large unripe or green mangoes
- 1 tablespoon kosher salt, plus more for seasoning
- 3 tablespoons vegetable oil
- 2 teaspoons yellow mustard seeds
- 5 garlic cloves, minced
- 2 serrano chiles or other hot green chiles, seeded and minced
- 1 tablespoon fenugreek
- 1 teaspoon ground turmeric
- Pinch of cayenne pepper
- ¼ cup brown sugar, lightly packed
- ¼ cup apple cider vinegar, plus more as needed
- Juice of 1 lime

Amba is a spicy, sweet-tart sauce made from pickled unripe mangos. It is immensely popular in Israel, but it hails originally from Iraq. Most of the once-thriving Jewish community in Iraq migrated to Israel in the 1950s, bringing their unique cuisine with them. Some of those dishes, like amba, have become enshrined in Israel's culinary melting pot. In Israel, amba is usually served with falafel, shawarma, and grilled meats. And it is an indispensable part of sabich. You may be able to find bottled amba at Middle Eastern grocery stores or even Trader Joe's, but if not, it is easy to make at home using an electric pressure cooker to soften the firm, unripe mango in record time. This recipe makes a large quantity of amba, but it will keep for weeks in the refrigerator.

1. Peel the mangoes and cut the flesh away from the pits. Chop the fruit and toss it with the salt in a large bowl. Cover and refrigerate overnight.

2. Pour the oil into the inner pot of your electric pressure cooker. Select the Sauté function and set the heat level to "Normal." When the oil is shimmering, after about 2 minutes, add the mustard seeds. When the seeds start to pop, after about a minute, add the garlic and chiles and sauté until softened, about 2 minutes. Press Cancel to turn off the Sauté function.

3. Place the mangoes in the inner pot of the pressure cooker and add the fenugreek, turmeric, cayenne, and brown sugar. Stir to combine. Add ½ cup water. Close the lid and make sure the pressure release valve is closed. Select the Pressure Cook function and set the cooking time to 3 minutes at high pressure.

4. When the cooking program is complete, release the pressure manually and remove the lid.

5. Stir the amba, making sure to scrape up any browned bits stuck to the bottom of the pot. Add the vinegar and lime juice and stir to combine.

6. Purée the sauce directly in the inner pot using an immersion blender. Alternatively, transfer the sauce to a blender and purée until smooth.

7. Taste and adjust the seasoning, adding additional salt or vinegar as needed. Keep in the refrigerator in an airtight container for up to one month.

Caramelized Peaches with Labneh, Honey & Almonds

SERVES 4

2 peaches, preferably freestone

1 tablespoon unsalted butter, melted

2 teaspoons brown sugar

1 teaspoon ground cinnamon

4 tablespoons Labneh (page 52), Quick Labneh (page 191), or plain Greek yogurt

1 tablespoon honey

¼ cup slivered almonds

2 sprigs fresh thyme

Sweet summer peaches with just a hint of caramelization are a perfect match with tangy Labneh (page 52) or Greek yogurt. Add some classic Mediterranean flavors like honey, almonds, and thyme and you have a quick, not-too-sweet weeknight dessert that could just as easily be a special breakfast during that heady time of year when peaches are at their peak. Try this method of caramelization in the air fryer with other stone fruits, like nectarines or apricots, as well.

1. Cut the peaches in half and remove the pits. Brush the peach halves with the melted butter, and sprinkle ½ teaspoon of brown sugar and ¼ teaspoon of cinnamon on each half.

2. Arrange the peaches in a single layer in the air fryer basket. Cook at 375°F for 8 to 10 minutes, until the peaches are soft and the tops are caramelized.

3. Transfer the peaches to a platter and top each with 1 tablespoon of the labneh. Drizzle with honey and sprinkle with the almonds.

4. Remove the leaves from the sprigs of thyme and sprinkle them over the peaches. Serve warm.

Churros with Chocolate Sauce

**MAKES 12 TO 14
CHURROS**

CHOCOLATE SAUCE

4 ounces semisweet or
    bittersweet chocolate
    (at least 60% cacao)
    finely chopped

½ cup heavy cream

¼ cup light corn syrup

½ teaspoon espresso
    powder (optional)

CHURROS

10 tablespoons
    (1¼ sticks) unsalted
    butter

½ cup whole milk

½ cup plus 1 tablespoon
    sugar

Fine sea salt

1 cup all-purpose flour

3 large eggs, beaten

Oil, for spraying

2 teaspoons ground
    cinnamon

Deep-fried churros are a popular street food in Spain, where they are often served alongside hot chocolate (for children) or coffee (for adults). While a sweet treat like churros might seem like classic dessert fare, in Spain, churros are served for breakfast or a midafternoon snack, not for dessert after a meal—much like doughnuts in America. The batter for the churros is made from choux pastry, the same batter that is used for éclairs and cream puffs. Choux pastry cooks especially well in the air fryer, and these air-fried churros emerge crispy on the outside and tender inside, with no oil. Roll the hot churros in some cinnamon sugar and serve them with a chocolate dipping sauce for an authentic taste of Spain.

1. Make the chocolate sauce: Place the chocolate in a heatproof bowl. Combine the cream and corn syrup in a small saucepan and bring to a simmer. Pour the warm cream mixture over the chocolate and stir until the chocolate is melted. Add the espresso powder (if using). Set aside.

2. Make the churros: Combine 8 tablespoons (1 stick) of the butter, ½ cup water, the milk, 1 tablespoon of sugar, and a pinch of salt in a medium saucepan and bring to a simmer over medium heat, stirring to melt the butter.

3. Add the flour, turn the heat down to low, and stir vigorously to form a dough ball. Cook, stirring, until the mixture looks dry and thick and smells toasty, about 3 minutes.

4. Transfer the dough to the bowl of a stand mixer, or a large mixing bowl, and allow it to cool for a few minutes. Using the paddle attachment for a stand mixer, or a handheld electric mixer, beat in the eggs a little bit at a time, making sure each addition is fully incorporated before adding the next. The mixture will look curdled at first but will begin to come together. Beat the mixture, stopping and scraping down the sides as necessary, until thick and completely smooth. Let the batter rest for 30 minutes.

5. Preheat the air fryer to 360°F.

6. Place the batter into a piping bag outfitted with a large star-shaped tip. Spray the basket of the air fryer with oil.

7. Working in batches, pipe churros that are 5 to 6 inches long and ¾ to 1 inch in diameter directly onto the air fryer basket. Use a knife or scissors to cut the batter when you reach the desired length. Do not crowd the basket.

8. Cook the churros for 12 to 14 minutes, turning once halfway through cooking, until the outside is firm and brown and the inside is soft, but cooked through. Repeat with the remaining batter.

9. While the churros are cooking, whisk together the remaining ½ cup sugar with the cinnamon. Melt the remaining 2 tablespoons of butter and place in a small dish.

10. Remove the cooked churros from the air fryer and immediately brush them with the melted butter and dredge in the cinnamon sugar.

11. Serve the churros warm with the chocolate sauce on the side for dipping.

Profiteroles with Ice Cream & Chocolate Sauce

MAKES 12 TO 14 PROFITEROLES

CHOUX PUFFS

8 tablespoons (1 stick) unsalted butter

2 teaspoons sugar

Fine sea salt

½ cup whole milk

1 cup all-purpose flour

3 large eggs, beaten

CHOCOLATE SAUCE

4 ounces semisweet or bittersweet chocolate (at least 60% cacao), finely chopped

2 tablespoons unsalted butter, at room temperature

1 cup heavy cream

¼ cup light corn syrup

Pinch of espresso powder (optional)

Oil, for spraying

1 pint vanilla, chocolate, or coffee ice cream, for serving

Profiteroles seem like elegant French restaurant fare, but they are really just dressed-up ice cream sundaes. They also happen to make an ideal dessert for entertaining because they look impressive but, in reality, are quite simple to prepare—and much of that preparation can be done in advance. Just assemble the profiteroles right before serving and watch your guests exclaim with delight. As with Churros (page 211), choux pastry is the base for the profiterole shells. You start by cooking the batter on the stove and then, off the stove, beat in the eggs. You will notice that there is no leavening agent in this recipe: the eggs themselves cause the dough to puff up when baked in the heat of the air fryer. Once you master choux pastry, you will find any number of uses for it.

1. Combine the butter, sugar, a pinch of salt, the milk, and ½ cup water in a medium saucepan and bring to a simmer over medium heat. Add the flour, turn the heat down to low, and cook, stirring vigorously, until the mixture forms a ball of dough. Cook, stirring, until the dough looks dry and thick and smells toasty, about 3 minutes.

2. Transfer the dough to the bowl of a stand mixer fitted with the paddle attachment (or use a large bowl and a handheld mixer) and allow it to cool for a few minutes. Beat in the eggs a little bit at a time, making sure each addition is fully incorporated before adding the next. The mixture will look curdled at first but will begin to come together. Beat the mixture, stopping and scraping down the sides as necessary, until thick and completely smooth. Let the batter rest for 30 minutes.

3. Meanwhile, make the chocolate sauce: Place the chopped chocolate and butter in a heatproof bowl. Combine the cream and corn syrup in a small saucepan and bring to a simmer over medium heat. Remove from the heat and pour the cream mixture over the chocolate and butter in the bowl. Stir until the chocolate and butter have melted and the sauce is smooth. Stir in the espresso powder (if using). Set aside.

4. Preheat the air fryer to 360°F.

5. Place the choux batter in a piping bag outfitted with a large round tip, such as Wilton 1A. Spray the basket of the air fryer with oil. Working in two batches, pipe round puffs of dough approximately 2 inches wide and 1 inch tall directly onto the basket of the air fryer. Use a knife or scissor to cut the dough when you have achieved the desired size. With a damp finger, press down on the swirl at the top of each puff to make it more round.

6. Cook the choux puffs for 18 to 20 minutes, until the outside of the puffs is golden brown and crisp and the inside is fully cooked and airy. Carefully remove the puffs from the air fryer basket using a thin spatula. (The puffs will stick, even if you spray the basket with oil, so be patient and careful in detaching them.) Spray the basket again and repeat with the remaining batter. (The choux puffs may be made 1 day ahead and stored in an airtight container at room temperature.)

7. To serve, halve the choux puffs horizontally and place a scoop of ice cream in the bottom half of each one. Cover the ice cream with the top of the puff and spoon chocolate sauce over the whole thing. Serve immediately.

Metric Charts

The recipes that appear in this cookbook use the standard US method for measuring liquid and dry or solid ingredients (teaspoons, tablespoons, and cups). The information on these pages is provided to help cooks outside the United States successfully use these recipes. All equivalents are approximate.

Metric Equivalents for Different Types of Ingredients

A standard cup measure of a dry or solid ingredient will vary in weight depending on the type of ingredient. A standard cup of liquid is the same volume for any type of liquid. Use the following chart when converting standard cup measures to grams (weight) or milliliters (volume).

STANDARD CUP	FINE POWDER (ex. flour)	GRAIN (ex. rice)	GRANULAR (ex. sugar)	LIQUID SOLIDS (ex. butter)	LIQUID (ex. milk)
1	140 g	150 g	190 g	200 g	240 ml
¾	105 g	113 g	143 g	150 g	180 ml
⅔	93 g	100 g	125 g	133 g	160 ml
½	70 g	75 g	95 g	100 g	120 ml
⅓	47 g	50 g	63 g	67 g	80 ml
¼	35 g	38 g	48 g	50 g	60 ml
⅛	18 g	19 g	24 g	25 g	30 ml

Useful Equivalents for Dry Ingredients by Weight

(To convert ounces to grams, multiply the number of ounces by 30.)

OZ	LB	G
1 oz	¹⁄₁₆ lb	30 g
4 oz	¼ lb	120 g
8 oz	½ lb	240 g
12 oz	¾ lb	360 g
16 oz	1 lb	480 g

Useful Equivalents for Length

(To convert inches to centimeters, multiply the number of inches by 2.5.)

IN	FT	YD	CM	M
1 in			2.5 cm	
6 in	½ ft		15 cm	
12 in	1 ft		30 cm	
36 in	3 ft	1 yd	90 cm	
40 in			100 cm	1 m

Useful Equivalents for Liquid Ingredients by Volume

TSP	TBSP	CUPS	FL OZ	ML	L
¼ tsp				1 ml	
½ tsp				2 ml	
1 tsp				5 ml	
3 tsp	1 Tbsp		½ fl oz	15 ml	
	2 Tbsp	⅛ cup	1 fl oz	30 ml	
	4 Tbsp	¼ cup	2 fl oz	60 ml	
	5⅓ Tbsp	⅓ cup	3 fl oz	80 ml	
	8 Tbsp	½ cup	4 fl oz	120 ml	
	10⅔ Tbsp	⅔ cup	5 fl oz	160 ml	
	12 Tbsp	¾ cup	6 fl oz	180 ml	
	16 Tbsp	1 cup	8 fl oz	240 ml	
	1 pt	2 cups	16 fl oz	480 ml	
	1 qt	4 cups	32 fl oz	960 ml	
			33 fl oz	1000 ml	1 L

Useful Equivalents for Cooking/Oven Temperatures

	FAHRENHEIT	CELSIUS	GAS MARK
FREEZE WATER	32°F	0°C	
ROOM TEMPERATURE	68°F	20°C	
BOIL WATER	212°F	100°C	
	325°F	160°C	3
	350°F	180°C	4
	375°F	190°C	5
	400°F	200°C	6
	425°F	220°C	7
	450°F	230°C	8
BROIL			Grill

Acknowledgments

I developed these recipes and wrote this book in 2020, which was a strange and unhappy time for our planet. If I had to spend most of the year at home, it was fortunate that I had such an engaging and fulfilling project to occupy my time. I would like to acknowledge and thank all the people who helped me bring *Instantly Mediterranean* to life—sometimes despite adverse circumstances.

Thanks first to my literary agent Clare Pelino, who continued to believe in this book through several iterations and, in the end, found the perfect home for it.

Indeed, working with the team at Tiller Press was a complete joy. Thanks to my editor Anja Schmidt who saw potential in my idea and steered it in an even better direction than I had initially envisioned. Anja, you were a dream to work with and I am sorry that you had to put in all those Oxford commas. I would also like to thank senior designer Matthew Ryan and art director Patrick Sullivan for making this book look so beautiful and expressing the feel of the recipes through the visuals.

Thanks to Ivy McFadden and Laura Jarrett for their close copyediting and proofreading eyes. And thank you to Laura Flavin and Lauren Ollerhead, Tiller's wonderful marketing and publicity team.

What a thrill to work once again with the talented photographer Leigh Olson. This is our third book together and I feel incredibly fortunate to have found such a wonderful and simpatico collaborator. My only regret is that, because of the pandemic, we could not physically be together for this shoot, as we have been in the past. In my absence, Eric Biermann stepped in to help produce these stunning images, for which I am very grateful.

Thanks to Rebecca Andexler for her assistance with recipe development and for coming up with the genius technique for making paella in an electric pressure cooker.

Many people volunteered to test the recipes in this book. *Instantly Mediterranean* is better for their input and I am exceedingly grateful to them. They include Allison Brody, Alma Klein, Amy Hansmann, Carrie Ryan, Danielle Fague, Emily Teel, Iris Saavedra, Janice Moskoff, Jasmine Sheth, Julie Chernoff, Karen Shopoff Rooff, Leslie Weiss, Rose McAvoy, Sarah Hodge, Stacey Ballis, and Suzanne D'Agostino.

As I developed the recipes, there were several friends who were always willing to taste dishes and give me candid and helpful feedback. Thanks to Janice and Jordan Moskoff, Rowena Abrahams and Brian Zavalkoff, Liz and VK Badrinath, and Eric and Caroline Older for your friendship and support during this crazy pandemic year and for happily accepting so much unsolicited food.

My husband, Elliot Regenstein, and my children, Zoë and Jamie, were at home with me while I wrote this book, which was both challenging and lots of fun. Zoë, thank you for being understanding when I used ingredients that you are allergic to and for always knowing when a dish needed more salt or a hit of acid. You have the best palate of anyone I know. Jamie, thanks for adding "if you are not too busy" at the end of every request you made while I was working. I love discussing the history of the Mediterranean with you and daydreaming about our next trip—Turkey? Or perhaps Tunisia? Elliot, thank you for supporting me in a million different ways and for always being my biggest cheerleader. Lastly, thanks to my mother, Gail Paster, for everything, including first taking me to the Mediterranean all those years ago.

Index

About the Author

Lawyer-turned-food-writer Emily Paster brings passion, a sharp intellect, and attention to detail to her modern global Jewish cuisine. A lifelong Francophile, Emily has traveled extensively around the Mediterranean, from Spain to Israel. Her time living in Paris with a North African Jewish family sparked her fascination with Jewish foodways around the globe. At home in Chicago, Emily's culinary and DIY adventures are inspired by the city's diverse neighborhoods, its international markets, and the bounty of Midwestern farms—whether she is feeding her family of four, hosting a Yom Kippur breakfast for twenty, or developing a new recipe for an assignment.

Emily's recipes and writing have appeared in such print and online outlets as *Midwest Living*, *Allrecipes* magazine, Food52, Eater Chicago, and more. She is the writer and photographer behind the website West of the Loop, which has been called "a family food blog to savor." Her previous books include *Food Swap: Specialty Recipes for Bartering, Sharing & Giving*, *The Joys of Jewish Preserving*, and *Epic Air Fryer*. *Instantly Mediterranean* is her fourth book.